European Legal Aspects of E-commerce

Europa Law Publishing, Groningen 2004

European Legal Aspects of E-commerce

Martien Schaub

Europa Law Publishing is a publishing company
specializing in European Union Law.
For further information please contact Europa Law
Publishing via email: info@europalawpublishing.com
or visit our website at: www.europalawpublishing.com.

Typeset in Scala and Scala Sans, Graphic design by
G2K Designers, Groningen/Amsterdam

NUR 828; ISBN 90-76871-37-x

British Library Cataloguing-in-Publication Data
A catalogue record for this book is available from the
British Library

Preface

Despite the bursting of the e-commerce bubble in the year 2000, e-commerce continues to grow. Simultaneously, be it at a somewhat different pace, the legislative framework affecting e-commerce is developing.

This book addresses European legal aspects of e-commerce. The point of departure is the E-commerce Directive. As this directive is a framework directive, it cannot be considered in isolation. Therefore, six related legal texts are discussed.

It should be noted that this book does not describe all possible European legal aspects that can be relevant for e-commerce. This book discusses a selection of legislative texts that are considered to be particularly relevant for e-commerce.

The aim is to describe what the legal texts mean for business organisations involved with e-commerce. Besides this practical aim this book also hopes to contribute to the continuous legal discussion on an area of law that is still in its infancy.

This book contains a considerable part of my doctoral thesis, which was defended October 2004. Besides the analyses of the European legal aspects, the thesis addresses the Dutch implementation of the European legal texts. Additionally, the thesis presents a legal tool, which serves to assist business organisations to gain insight in, and comply with, the legal norms.

This book reflects the law as it stands on July 2004.

Martien Schaub
August 2004

Contents

CHAPTER I

E-commerce, the Business Organisation and the Legislator

1 Introduction

The year 2000 is a memorable year in the history of e-commerce. The expectations around the new economy had been building up, resulting in high investments in internet start-ups and rising stock value of ICT-related businesses. Perhaps inevitably, in the year 2000, the bubble burst and this became the year of the so-called 'dot.com shake-out'.

The year 2000 was also the year the European Union issued its e-commerce directive. In fact legislators worldwide were deploying regulatory initiatives to address the new way of doing business. Different news reports informed about the need for the new economy to wake up to the legal risks they were facing.[1]

This book addresses the European legal aspects regarding e-commerce. The point of departure of this work is the E-commerce Directive. This directive aims to provide a clear legal framework favourable for business organisations and protecting the interests of consumers. Notwithstanding this admirable aim, the reactions to the E-commerce Directive were not entirely positive. It has been referred to as a legal minefield[2] and accused of causing more problems then it solves.[3]

The perspective chosen for this work is that of the business organisation. Companies cannot afford to ignore the legal framework in which they operate. Awareness of the legal framework is relevant with regard to avoiding legal problems but this also allows the company to benefit from facilitative tools and protection offered by that framework.

This work aims to map out the relatively new European legal framework related to e-commerce for business organisations involved with e-commerce.

This introductory Chapter presents the context of the topic. The purpose is to acquaint the reader with some basic concepts and provide some general background knowledge to position the topic addressed in this work. To begin with, a definition for e-commerce is given as well as a description of different forms of e-commerce that can be encountered (Section 2). Subsequently, some remarks on the development of e-commerce are made (Section 3), and the relation between e-commerce and the European legislator is shortly discussed (Section 4). The last Section of this Chapter provides an outline of the book (Section 5).

---

1 For example 'Alarm voor Europese internet bedrijven' Computable 26-1-2001.

2 Drijber (2001).

3 Apel & Grapperhaus (1999).

2 E-commerce

2.1 Defining e-commerce

E-commerce is a term that quickly became widely used. When encountering the term e-commerce in scientific and popular literature, one finds that it is not always clearly defined. Writers often assume that the term is generally known and understood. Nonetheless, there are differences with regard to the meaning that is ascribed to the term. Several institutions have defined e-commerce for a variety of purposes. To give an impression of how e-commerce can be defined, table 1 presents an overview of several definitions.

WHO	**Definition of E-commerce**
World Trade Organisation (WTO)	*The production, distribution, marketing, sale or delivery of goods and services by electronic means.*[4]
United Nations Commission on International Trade Law (UNCITRAL)[5]	*Any kind of information in the form of a data message used in the context of commercial activities.*[6]
Choi, Stahl and Whinston	*E-commerce refers to the use of electronic means and technologies to conduct commerce, including within business, business-to-business, and business-to-consumer interactions.*[7]
Lodder and Kaspersen	*Any business transaction concerning goods and services, including relating commercial activities, where participants are not at the same physical location and communicate through electronic means.*[8]
'Webopedia'[9]	*Conducting business on-line. This includes, for example, buying and selling products with digital cash and via Electronic Data Interchange (EDI).*

Table 1: Definitions of e-commerce

Some writers do not define the term but use descriptions of e-commerce, usually accompanied with a list of examples.[10] The common factor in the

4 WTO, *Work programme on electronic commerce*, Adopted by the General Council on 25-9-1998.

5 Information on the Commission and their Model Law on Electronic Commerce can be found on their website: <www.uncitral.org>.

6 Article 1 of the UNCITRAL Model Law on Electronic Commerce.

7 Choi, Stahl and Whinston (1997).

8 Lodder and Kaspersen (2002), p. 3.

9 Webopedia is an on-line dictionary for terms related to computer and internet technology and can be consulted at <www.pcwebopedia.com>.

10 For example: Timmers (1999), p. 4, Hoque (2000), p. 7-12.

encountered descriptions and definitions is that it has something to do with business and the use of electronic communication means or ICT.

Often, e-commerce is linked to the commercial use of internet.[11] Indeed, the internet revolution has boosted the development of what is called e-commerce. However, before the internet age, e-commerce already existed in the form of Electronic Data Interchange (EDI) between companies.[12]

Although the words are sometimes used interchangeably, a distinction can be made between e-commerce and e-business. Within this work, e-commerce is considered to be a subset of e-business. E-business refers to the support of all business processes throughout the organisation with the help of ICT, including for example automated stock control, the ordering system but also the work flow system and the computerised business administration.

E-business can be divided in internally and externally focused e-business.[13] The internal focus refers to the re-engineering or automation of business processes that are primarily internal to the organisation, for example Enterprise Resource Planning (ERP) systems and work flow software. The external focus refers to the use of ICT in the interaction with business partners and customers. This external focus can then be labelled e-commerce.

This still leaves room for a division in a narrow and a broad understanding of e-commerce. If it is understood broadly, it includes all interactions with the external environment of the company, including the electronic representation of the company on internet. A narrow understanding of e-commerce entails that it refers simply to the electronic conclusion of a contract (or an electronic transaction). This line of thought is depicted in table 2.

<table>
<tr><td rowspan="3">E-business:
Business activities and processes supported by ICT</td><td>Internal:
Focused on internal processes, such as automating the back office</td><td></td></tr>
<tr><td rowspan="2">External:
Focused on communication and interaction with business partners and customers (e-commerce)</td><td>Broad: concerned with all interactions with the external environment of the company</td></tr>
<tr><td>Narrow: solely concerned with the electronic transactions</td></tr>
</table>

Table 2: Categorisation of business activities supported by ICT

[11] For example: Lichtenstein (1998).

[12] On EDI see Section 2.2. below.

[13] Peppard (2000), p. 314.

Within this work, e-commerce is understood from the broad perspective. To sum up the following definition for e-commerce can be formulated:

The use of ICT in how the business organisation interfaces with business partners and (potential) customers.

This includes simple internet presence of a company by means of a website with general information on the company and its products without possibilities to interact (also referred to as passive websites).

The definition explicitly refers to the use of electronic communications methods by *business organisations*. This is meant to indicate that the definition refers to the use of electronic communication methods for business purposes. As a result, transactions between private persons or consumers (C2C) are not considered to fall within the notion of e-commerce as meant in this work. Although the private persons undoubtedly act economically in buying and selling to each other, it is not in the course of a business. For the same reason the relations government-to-consumer (G2C) and government-to-business (G2B) are not covered by the definition. This is generally referred to as e-government. This does not mean a governmental institute cannot be a trading partner or customer of a business organisation using electronic means.

It should be emphasised that ICT-related business is not necessarily e-commerce as meant in this work. For example the exploitation of domain names is internet related, it only becomes e-commerce if the offering and possibly selling of domain names takes place on-line.

2.2 E-commerce techniques

There are several techniques that can be used to put e-commerce to practice. Below, EDI, internet, m-commerce and electronic agents are shortly introduced.

EDI

Electronic Data Interchange (EDI) is the exchange of standardised messages between information systems, commonly using a closed (*i.e.* accessible to a limited number of parties) and secure network. The standardised messages allow processing without human intervention. The functioning of automated EDI relies on the use of common standards and protocols, enabling computers to process each others messages. To advance the use of common standards, international standards are being developed such as the UN/EDIFACT standards.[14]

[14] See United Nations Directories for Electronic Data Interchange for Administration, Commerce and Transport at <http://www.unece.org/trade/untdid/welcome.htm>.

EDI requires some substantive investments in hard and -software and well-defined agreements on how the communication is to take place.[15] Such agreements are called interchange agreements. The interchange agreement can arrange organisational issues, specify technical standards and settle legal issues. EDI can be very useful for companies that have a business relationship that involves repeated transactions of the same nature, such as repeated stock orders. EDI is often referred to as the 'old' e-commerce, as opposed to the 'new' internet based e-commerce.[16] EDI predates internet by approximately 20 years and still represents a substantial amount of today's e-commerce value.[17]

Internet

Internet, the network of networks, is a publicly and internationally available network of computers. The application of Hyper Text Markup Language (HTML) has led to a rapid growth of what is called the World Wide Web (WWW). HTML allows for user friendly presentation of information and also facilitates hyperlinks. Hyperlinks allow the user of the WWW, commonly referred to as a web surfer, to jump from one web page to another by clicking on the indicated spot on screen.

Internet has proven to be a superb medium for communication and information exchange. The structure of the network allows *ad hoc* business relations. As opposed to EDI, it has an open structure allowing, in principal, trading with an unlimited amount of trading partners. Internet has boosted e-commerce and is a prominent medium for e-commerce especially for small firms, for whom internet is an easy point of entry into the electronic business environment.[18]

M-commerce

The advent of mobile communication technologies has led to yet another buzzword: m-commerce. M-commerce is e-commerce using a mobile terminal, for example a mobile telephone or a Personal Digital Assistant (PDA), to communicate. The term is also used in the context of products and services related to mobile telephony. M-commerce has its own particular communication

---

[15] Van Esch (1999), p. 31 points out that it is only profitable to use EDI if certain data are exchanged between parties with sufficient regularity. The investments needed to implement EDI are not economically sound without that sufficient amount of exchange.

[16] The European Commission has made the distinction between traditional e-commerce and internet e-commerce in this respect. See Commission Communication COM (1997) 157, p. 3. About the relation between EDI and e-commerce: Van Esch (1999), p. 14.

[17] See the Eurostat report 'E-commerce and firm performance', issued 2-4-2004. Eurostat reports can be found on the website: <http://europa.eu.int/comm/eurostat>, using the websites search option allows easy location of research reports.

[18] See the Eurostat report 'E-commerce and firm performance', issued 2-4-2004.

infrastructure, equipment, technological applications, content, standards and services.[19]

Electronic agents

Electronic agents[20] are programs (or software tools) that are capable to perform tasks according to parameters (specifications) entered by the user. An agent can for example gather and structure information from networks, compare prices or perform some other task without the users immediate presence. Agents are particularly useful when large amounts of information need to be assessed.

Advanced electronic agents can perform tasks without human intervention. An intelligent agent refers to an electronic agent with the capacity to act autonomously, such as independently negotiate and conclude an electronic contract.[21]

The use of electronic agents has led to concerns about the legal status of autonomous agents and whether or not such devices have the legal capacity to perform legally binding acts.[22] This issue can be resolved by considering the agent as a tool used by a person or organisation with legal capacity. When an electronic agent concludes a contract, the agent is the means to transmit the intentions of its user.[23] The activities of the electronic agent are then attributed to this person or organisation.[24]

For effective use of agents standardisation of communication protocols is necessary. The standards facilitate the communication of the agent with its user, its electronic surroundings and other agents.

2.3 Enabling services

There is an important group of companies that supplies enabling and supportive goods and services in relation to e-commerce. In this category we find companies that supply software and hardware, but also consulting services, parties that provide trusted services, parties that enable electronic payment etc.

---

19 On mobile e-commerce see Tsalgatidou & Pitoura (2001), Barnes (2002).

20 Also: software agents, intelligent agents, softbots, taskbots.

21 For a more extensive discussion of intelligent agents see Lodder & Voulon (2002). See on the use of agents in e-commerce: the special issue of *Electronic Commerce Research* 2001/1-2 of Kluwer Academic Publishers.

22 *Cf.* Kerr (2001), Voulon (2002).

23 Finocchiaro (2003), p. 22, Voulon (2004).

24 *Cf.* Prins & Gijrath (2000), p. 127-129. They argue that the most workable theory is to assume that the will to be bound by the acts of the agents is enclosed in the putting into use of the system. See also Kerr (2001).

Special attention can be paid to intermediary service providers, for example Internet Service Providers (ISPs) and Application Service Providers (ASPs).[25] Such service providers are an important link when companies take their business on-line. ISPs can offer a variety of services such as hosting and access services, e-mail accounts, but also content and advertising services.

ISPs have a special position; they can, to a certain extent, set the conditions for web use. They are often the party that is addressed when there are problems with regard to web use, for example related to illegal content or copyright infringements.

E-commerce needs another important group of service providers: Trusted Third Parties (TTPs). Suppliers of trusted services are important as internet facilitates *ad hoc* business relations with previously unknown partners across the world. TTPs can offer certification services that confirm the identity of electronic business partners or provide escrow[26] services to ensure the proper performance of the electronic contract.

2.4 Different types of e-commerce

Different types of e-commerce can be distinguished:

1) open vs. closed,
2) direct vs. indirect,
3) B2B vs. B2C,
4) traditional vs. innovative, and
5) pure players vs. click and mortar.

Ad 1) Open – closed e-commerce

Closed e-commerce has a limited set of participants as opposed to open e-commerce where the number of participants is (potentially) unlimited. An example of closed e-commerce is the 'old' form of e-commerce: Electronic Data Interchange (EDI). Controversially, the 'new' internet e-commerce is based on the open structure of the internet with no limit to the possible partners.[27] The open structure plays an important role in enabling consumer directed e-commerce, as consumers can be easily reached using internet.

---

[25] Application Service Providers (ASPs) are third-party entities that manage and distribute software-based services and solutions to customers across a wide area network from a central data centre. ASPs are a way for companies to outsource some or almost all aspects of their information technology needs.

[26] A contract, deed, bond, or other written agreement deposited with a third person, by whom it is to be delivered to the grantee or beneficiary on the fulfilment of some condition.

[27] *Cf.* COM (1997) 157, indicating that in traditional e-commerce, 'the market is a club', and in internet e-commerce, 'the network is the market'.

Ad 2) Direct – indirect e-commerce

Another distinction that can be made is between direct and indirect e-commerce.[28] In case of indirect e-commerce, the contract is concluded electronically, but it is subsequently performed in the physical environment. Direct e-commerce means that the contract is concluded and performed electronically. Evidently, direct e-commerce cannot be applied if the ordered product or service cannot be delivered electronically. Direct e-commerce therefore only concerns services that can be delivered on-line or so-called digitised goods.

A digitised good or a soft product is a product that can be delivered in the form of bits and bites, such as music, software products, or text. In the physical world these products are connected to a physical carrier such as a CD or paper. Network technology allows the transfer of such products without their physical carrier. Digitised goods are often products connected with intellectual property rights.

Ad 3) B2B – B2C e-commerce

Business organisations that trade electronically with professional partners are involved in what is called business-to-business e-commerce (B2B). When companies direct their e-commerce activities at consumers[29] this is referred to as business-to-consumer e-commerce (B2C). The relations are quite different and subject to different laws. The consumer is generally considered as being the weaker party with less bargaining powers in face of a business organisation and thus in need of protection. As a result there is a wide set of consumer protection regulations that business organisations have to take into account when they are involved in B2C e-commerce.

It was already noted above that the consumer-to-consumer (C2C) relation is not considered e-commerce as meant in this work. However, it is interesting to note that internet has caused an immense growth in C2C trading. A well-known example of a company facilitating C2C transactions is eBay. eBay provides an electronic platform where people can make offers to either buy or sell and come to an agreement.[30]

Ad 4) Traditional – innovative e-commerce

Internet has allowed innovative forms of conducting business. Traditional business activities such as selling goods can be taken to the on-line environment where it becomes e-commerce. Such activities can be labelled as traditional e-commerce. Innovative e-commerce refers to utilisation of the possibilities offered by the electronic environment to explore new or innovative forms of

---

[28] See for example the e-commerce and development report 2001 of the UN in the executive summary at p. 39.

[29] 'Consumer' here refers to natural persons who do not act out of business or professional interests.

[30] See <www.ebay.com>.

business activities. In innovative e-commerce the electronic means are not solely used to communicate but they are also deployed to offer the customer a new product or service. Innovative e-commerce refers to business models that were difficult if not impossible to effectuate without the possibilities of electronic communication. One can think of information brokerage or buyer aggregation on internet. Some examples of such innovative business models are given in the next Section, where some e-commerce business models are highlighted.

Ad 5) Pure players – click and mortar e-commerce

'Click and mortar' e-commerce refers to business organisations that combine their on-line shops with traditional 'brick and mortar' shops (for example www.barnesandnoble.com). Pure players rely solely on virtual presence and do not have a physical shop (for example www.amazon.com). The pure player can become even more virtual, if it solely sells products or services that can be delivered electronically (direct e-commerce).

3 E-commerce and the business organisation

3.1 E-commerce business models

To gain more insight in what e-commerce is, this Section discusses some ways in which it is put to practical use by business organisations. To this end, several e-commerce business models are discussed.[31] The discussion does not intent to be exhaustive. Different elements from the here-mentioned models can be mixed so that numerous variations can be found. Each model can also have different gradations of complexity, varying from a simple electronic flyer to the interactive site with different options, functions, combination of services etc.

E-shops (selling)

E-shops or e-tailing is simply the traditional model of selling goods or services taken on-line, for example with the help of internet.[32] In this model there is normally one seller and there can be multiple buyers. It is possible for sellers to become a part of a web portal representing an on-line shopping mall. A portal is a website that offers a wide array of resources and services. A portal can be an internet starting point or a collection of on-line shops. Being included in a portal can enhance the sellers' visibility on the web.

---

[31] 'Business model' here means the method of doing business and making a profit. See Timmers (1998) for a more precise discussion of the term 'business model'.

[32] On internet retailing see Grewal, Iyer & Levy (2004).

Making optimum use of possibilities of internet technology the electronic shopkeeper can add functions and elements to his e-shop. One can think of: additional feedback or tips relating to the offered products, for example book reviews in a book-selling site, an e-mail service to notify customers about new offers, the construction of a personal shopping list which makes it easy to check on previous orders, an on-line track system to follow the ordered products, etc.

E-procurement (buying)

This model involves one buyer (or a limited amount of buyers) and various sellers. A powerful buyer can force his electronic procurement system on various suppliers. A group of buyers can team and negotiate lower prices for their joint purchases. This can be done in a closed setting with a fixed set of suppliers, or an open setting for example in a call for tender on the web. Different methods to implement e-procurement are available such as:[33]

- E-sourcing: searching for sellers, products or services.
- E-tendering: suppliers are requested to make a proposal concerning certain goods or services.
- E-reverse auctioning: the prospective buyer specifies the goods or the services that he wishes to purchase (possibly in combination with a maximum price). Sellers of the specified goods or services can respond to this by stating the price for which they can deliver the requested goods or services. The supplier with the lowest price 'wins' the reverse auction.

E-intermediary

The electronic intermediary uses electronic networks to bring other parties together. The service levels can vary from merely providing a platform, to the inclusion of more extensive services including information exchange, contract formation, payment facilitation, dispute resolution, trusted services or logistical services. Examples of electronic intermediaries are:

- E-markets: electronic platforms that bring buyers and sellers together. Characteristic for e-markets is that it involves multiple buyers and sellers. E-markets can be brand or branch-specific.
- E-auctions: electronic platforms that enable sellers to auction their products or items, (www.eBay.com) or enable reversed auctions where a buyer names his price to which sellers can respond.
- Buyer aggregation: uniting buyers, which enables individual buyers of the same product to group and thus get a lower price (www.letsbuyit.com).

[33] On various forms of e-procurement: Harink (2003). He also presents a method that serves to determine the suitability of one or more of the e-procurement forms for organisations.

Information Brokers

As noted above, internet has proved a sublime medium for information exchange. This has led to business models that rely on the provision of information. Most information brokers are involved in innovative e-commerce. Examples of information brokerage:

- price-comparing sites,
- route-planning systems,
- search engines and specialised search agents,
- subscription sites: offering (high value) information at a regular subscription fee.

E-advertising

Advertising models cover on-line activities that rely on advertisement incomes for profit. Advertising can easily be combined with all sorts of activities. Many of the above discussed information brokers rely on advertising incomes. Examples of sites that rely on e-advertising are:

- Websites that offer visitors something for free, or where visitors can earn points or reductions in return for watching electronic advertisements or play promotional games.
- Portals either specialised in a certain topic or of a general nature that generate traffic over the site, which makes it interesting for advertising purposes (yahoo.com, altavista.net).

3.2 Opportunities for business organisations

E-commerce has been attributed welfare increasing characteristics. Indeed e-commerce holds the promise of countless possibilities. All kinds of benefits can be realised through e-commerce: cost reductions, more efficiency, more profits by product innovations such as on-line services and marketing innovations leading to more customers and higher turnovers. Internet facilitates the bridging of physical barriers and low cost global marketing has become reality. Some go as far as stating that e-commerce has the potential to be one of the greatest economic developments of the 21st century.

However, early on it could be established that the actual spread of e-commerce is limited. Although there has been a considerable growth of e-commerce it only accounts for a small percentage of total trade.

As e-commerce and e-business became widely used buzzwords, some made the down to earth observation that e-business in the end is just business.[34] In other words a well thought-out strategy is needed to reap the benefits of e-commerce. Simply taking business on-line is not a guarantee that profits will rise. Many business organisations were confronted with this in the year

[34] Peppard (2000), at p. 315.

2000, the year of the so-called 'dot.com-shake-out'. Many internet start-ups proved unsuccessful and investors lost faith. Nonetheless, the use of electronic communication methods, and more in particular internet, for business purposes continues to grow. E-commerce development has certainly not come to a stand still.[35]

3.3 Barriers for e-commerce

Some barriers can be identified that might explain why e-commerce has not fully lived up to its early promises and might not yet have realised its full potential. This can be attributed to technical issues, organisational problems, lack of trust (including security risks) and last but not least to legal barriers.

Technical barriers

E-commerce is benefited, if a proper technical infrastructure is widely available, preferably at low costs. This includes availability of hardware components, networks, network services and access providers. There is also a need for technical standards that facilitate the electronic communication.

Organisational problems

The business organisation must be capable of handling the new way of doing business. Employees must be able to work with the systems and production and logistics might need adaptation. Another issue relevant here is that business organisations need to think about their e-commerce strategy. Simply building a company website is not enough to benefit from the possibilities offered by e-commerce.[36]

Lack of trust

Trust can be described as a mechanism that governs exchange relationships characterised by uncertainty, vulnerability and dependence.[37] Various researchers have identified trust as a critical success factor for e-commerce.[38] Lack of trust in e-commerce is related to factors such as the lack of personal contact, geographic dispersion of e-traders, the lack of being able to see or test the offered goods and (data) security issues.

---

[35] See for example the research report of Eurostat 'E-commerce in Europe', issued 20-8-2002. Reports of Eurostat can be found on the website: <http://europa.eu.int/comm/eurostat>, using the websites search option allows easy location of research reports.

[36] On this topic: Saanen, Verbraeck & Sol (1999), Boudestijn & Notenboom (2000).

[37] Jarvenpaa, Tractinsky & Vitale (2000).

[38] See for example Jarvenpaa, Tractinsky & Vitale (2000), Nöteberg, Christiaanse & Wallage (2000), Ba (2001), Noll (2002) and the there mentioned references.

Legal barriers

One of the main issues raised in relation to e-commerce and law is legal uncertainty. The bulk of the existing legal rules were written for the paper based business environment, which leads to uncertainty on how these rules should be applied in the electronic environment. For example: is an electronic document equal to a written document? Does an electronic signature have the same value as a handwritten signature? It is thought that a coherent legal framework taking into account the particularities of the electronic business environment, benefits e-commerce development.

4 E-commerce and the legislator

4.1 Problems posed to law

Law has both a facilitative as well as a normative function. It is facilitative in that it can ensure that electronic contracts are valid and electronic documents recognised. At the same time it is normative in that it puts constraints on the business organisation, for example by instating consumer protection laws. The previous Section mentioned that law, and more in particular legal uncertainty, constitutes a potential barrier to the development of e-commerce. Vice versa the electronic environment has created some issues for the law and its practitioners. Some of these issues are shortly discussed.[39]

Intellectual property

One of the most apparent issues combined with the rising use of internet is copyright infringement. The ease with which internet allows the spreading of any kind of content, including copyright protected materials, has alarmed many copyright holders.

The protection of intellectual property in an on-line environment especially in a cross-border setting has proven to be difficult.

A well-known example in relation to this is the *Napster* case. Napster allowed individuals to exchange music on-line. After several legal procedures, Napster was forced to cease its activities. This by no means meant the end of on-line music sharing. Copyright holders face ever-advancing programs, such as Kazaa, that allow sharing of copyright protected material.

Dematerialisation

From a legal point of view it is important to distinguish between goods and services, because in certain cases law has different rules for either goods or services. Technological developments have led to difficulties on this point. The

[39] On this topic: Endeshaw (1998).

advent of so-called digitised goods (also: soft products) entails a blurring distinction between the two.

Above, it was already explained that a digitised good is a product that in the off-line world is connected to a physical carrier, but in the on-line environment it can be transmitted without its physical carrier. This raises the question if the delivery of the digitised good is the delivery of a good or, because no tangibles change hands, the provision of a service. It seems unfair to treat the same product differently from a legal perspective depending on the manner in which it is delivered.

Another consequence of the dematerialisation of the electronic environment is the lack of paper. Many legal systems rely on (signed) paper documents for evidential purposes. Both paper and pen are lacking in the on-line environment. Law, inevitably, will have to adapt to these issues.

Internationalisation

The majority of legal rules is bound to geographic areas. Controversially, internet has an inherent international nature. As a result, it can be problematic to enforce territorial related laws to on-line situations. A well-known example of an international internet related conflict is the *Yahoo* case. On an American based Yahoo website nazi memorabilia were offered. French groups against discrimination objected to this. The offering of such items is against French law and therefore Yahoo was sued before a French court. The French judge found that Yahoo acted illegal according to French law and summoned that Yahoo should make sure the site was not accessible to the French.[40] An American judge ruled that French law was not applicable worldwide, indicating that French law could not limit the American highly valued freedom of speech.

Rapid technological developments

Law making is often a slow and rigid process. The technological developments of the latest decades have been described as 'technological turbulence'.[41] This is a problem when there is a need for the law to respond to social, technological and commercial customs in cyberspace. Even newly made laws risk being outdated within several years due to the rapid technological developments. To avoid this, lawmakers strive to formulate technology neutral legislation that is applicable irrelevant of the used technology. The downside is that this often leads to vague and open norms that do not offer a substantial amount of legal security.

---

40 After having ordered a technical inquiry to find out if this was indeed possible, the inquiry resulted in the conclusion that it was technical possible to block the majority of French visitors from the infringing sites of the American provider.

41 *Cf.* Van der Hof (2002), p. 275.

Another consequence of the slow process of law making, is the possibility that technical developments set the standard before any legal norms are installed. For example when a certain system or standard is widely spread and used this becomes *de facto* the norm, without any legal underpinning.

4.2 Regulatory initiatives with regard to e-commerce

It was soon recognised that the legislative framework, originally written for a paper-based environment, did not meet with the needs of the modern communication methods. Law- and policy makers from around the world have tried to find regulatory answers.

For example, the World Trade Organisation (WTO) adopted a work program on electronic commerce.[42] The purpose of this work programme was to examine trade related issues relating to global e-commerce. The programme involved the review of the existing WTO trade agreements (GATS, GATT and TRIPS)[43] to examine the treatment of e-commerce in these instruments.[44] Other international examples are the initiatives developed within the United Nations (UN). The United Nations Commission on International Trade Law (UNCITRAL) adopted a model law on electronic commerce in 1996. In 2001 the UNCITRAL adopted the model law on electronic signatures.[45] Besides these international initiatives national lawmakers worldwide have begun to adapt their legal systems to the electronic environment.

Relevant for this research are the regulatory initiatives of the European Union (EU). The regulative efforts of the EU with regard to e-commerce can be traced back to 1987 when the TEDIS programme encouraging the use of EDI was established.[46] A communication in 1997 titled *'A European Initiative in Electronic Commerce'*[47] underlined the need for European initiatives with regard to e-commerce and formulated several key elements that should be focused on:

---

42 Adopted by the general council on 25 September 1998.

43 General Agreement on Tariffs and Trade (concerning goods), General Agreement on Trade in Services: (concerning services) and the Trade Related aspects of Intellectual Property Rights.

44 Information on the WTO work programme can be found on their website: <www.wto.org>. Follow the links 'trade topics' and 'electronic commerce'.

45 Information on UNCITRAL as well as the adopted texts can be found on the website: <www.uncitral.org>.

46 Council Decision 87/499/EEC of 5 October 1987 introducing a communications network Community programme on trade electronic data interchange systems (TEDIS), OJ L 285, 8-10-1987, p. 35 and Council Decision 91/385/EEC of 22 July 1991 establishing the second phase of the Tedis programme (Trade electronic data interchange systems) OJ 1991 L 208, 30-07-1991, p. 226.

47 Communication to the European Parliament, the Council, the Economic and Social Committee and the Committee of the Regions of 15-04-1997, COM (1997) 157.

- access to infrastructure, technology and services,
- creating a favourable regulatory framework,
- promoting a favourable business environment, and
- work to a global consensus from a common European framework.

The Commission states in its initiative that the framework of legislation should be created with the application of four principles:

1) no regulation for regulation's sake,
2) based on single market freedoms,
3) taking account of business realities,
4) meet general interest objectives effectively and efficiently.

Since the 1997 communication several legislative instruments have been adopted that see to the creation of a favourable regulatory framework. Central in this framework is the E-commerce Directive, issued in June 2000.[48] Its aim is to establish a clear legal framework ensuring the prosperous development of e-commerce. However, due to the many references and exemptions, scope and content of the directive are not clear upon first sight.

Early publications on the directive were not altogether positive. Although it was recognised by some as a landmark directive[49] it has also been labelled 'a legal minefield'.[50] Many writers have established that the directive constitutes a political compromise that will be problematic to work with for both national lawmakers and legal practitioners.[51] Some go as far as stating that the directive creates more problems then it solves.[52] News reports claimed that the directive would have far reaching consequences for companies involved in on-line activities. Substantial amounts of money would be needed to adapt the ordering procedures to the stipulations of the directive.

What is more the E-commerce Directive did not come alone: various other texts affecting the electronic business environment were adopted. This has lead to the characterisation of European legislative framework as an avalanche of e-commerce legislation.[53] Other relevant laws are the Directive on Distant Selling, the Directive on Privacy, the Directives related to Electronic Communications Networks and Services and the Electronic Signatures Directive.[54]

---

48 Directive 2000/31/EC of the European Parliament and of the Council of 8 June 2000 on certain legal aspects of information society services, in particular electronic commerce, in the Internal Market ('Directive on Electronic Commerce'), OJ L 178, 17-07-2000, p. 1.

49 Pearce & Platten (2000).

50 Drijber (2001), p. 123.

51 Moerel (2000), Gijrath & Kolthek (2002).

52 Apel & Grapperhaus (1999).

53 Saxby (2000).

54 Directive 97/7/EC, Directive 95/46/EC, Directive 2002/19/EC, Directive 2002/20/EC, Directive 2002/21/EC, Directive 2002/22/EC, Directive 2002/58/EC and Directive 1999/93/EC.

Adding to this, the EU has tried to face the challenges to intellectual property rights by adopting a directive on certain aspects of copyright and related rights in the information society.[55] A directive protecting the rights of software developers was adopted as early as 1991, known as the software directive.[56] Various laws were issued to support electronic payments.[57] With regard to technical standards the EU has launched the European Electronic Signature Standardisation Initiative Conference 19 June 2001 (EESSI).[58] Furthermore, there are initiatives on the safe use of information systems.[59] Finally, there are steps being taken to implement the .eu-domain for the use of European companies.[60]

5 Outline

After having set the stage in this Chapter, the subsequent Chapters turn to the content of the European legal framework regarding e-commerce. It must be noted that not all laws that are possibly relevant for e-commerce are discussed in this book. A selection is made. The selection of laws that is addressed consists of:

- Directive 2000/31/EC,
- Directive 1999/93/EC,

---

55 Directive 2001/29/EC of the European Parliament and of the Council of 22 May 2001 on the harmonisation of certain aspects of copyright and related rights in the information society, OJ L 167, 22-6-2001, p. 10.

56 Council Directive 91/250/EEC of 14 May 1991 on the legal protection of computer programs, OJ L 122, 17-5-1991, p. 42.

57 For example: Council Framework Decision of 28 May 2001 combating fraud and counterfeiting of non-cash means of payments, OJ L 149, 2-6-2001, p. 1, Directive 2000/46/EC of the European Parliament and of the Council of 18 September 2000 on the taking up, pursuit of and prudential supervision of the business of electronic money institutions.

58 Information on this initiative can be found on <http://www.ict.etsi.fr/EESSI/EESSI-homepage.htm>.

59 For example: Proposal for a Council Framework Decision on attacks against information systems, COM (2002) 173 final. Decision No. 276/1999/EC of the European Parliament and of the Council, 15-1-1999, adopting a multi-annual Community action plan on promoting safer use of the Internet by combating illegal and harmful content on global networks. Decision No. 1151/2003 of the European Parliament and of the Council of 16 June 2003, amending Decision No. 276/1999/EC adopting a multi-annual action plan on promoting safer use of the internet by combating illegal and harmful content on global networks.

60 Regulation (EC) No. 733/2002 of the European Parliament and of the Council of 22 April 2002 on the implementation of the .eu Top Level Domain, OJ L 113, 30-4-2002, p. 1 and Regulation (EC) No. 874/2004 of 28 April 2004 laying down public policy rules concerning the implementation and functions of the .eu Top Level Domain and the principles governing registration, OJ L 162, 30-4-2004, p. 40.

· Directive 97/7/EC,
· Directive 95/46/EC,
· Directive 2002/58/EC,
· Regulation (EC) No. 44/2001, and
· the 1980 Rome Convention.

This selection of laws is considered to be particularly relevant for e-commerce.[61] Occasionally, reference will be made to other legislation, but other laws will not be considered in-depth.

The legal texts are discussed from the business perspective. This means it is sought to distil what they mean for business organisations. Additionally, suggestions are made as to how business organisations might comply with the rules.

With regard to these suggestions the present state of technology is determinative. This means a considerable amount of attention for e-commerce via internet. This is because internet (at present) is the most prominent medium for e-commerce.[62] In fact, the legislative framework is particularly relevant in the open environment of internet and for the *ad hoc* business relations that are facilitated by it. The framework is of less significance with regard to e-commerce via closed networks such as EDI, where prior agreements, the so-called interchange agreements, arrange the legal issues connected to the electronic communication process and the electronic transactions.

This book does not venture to look too far ahead and make assumptions in the sphere of future applications in e-commerce. All the same, as far as the legislative framework is not changed, future means used for electronic communication will have to take this legal framework into account. What is more, the European legislator has indicated that it strives to formulate the norms independent of the state of the art of the technology.

The discussion addresses both B2B and B2C relations. The text will indicate whether the discussed norms are applicable to B2B or B2C or both. The distinction between goods and services is of less relevance for the discussion, as the legal framework addresses both. However, on several points a distinction between the two is made. On these points the analyses will include an evaluation in how far this creates problems with regard to so-called soft products.[63]

Each of the following chapters addresses a law and is structured in the same manner. First an overview of the legislative instrument is given: the law is shortly presented, it is stated why it is considered particularly relevant for

[61] *Cf.* Smith (2002), Dickie (1999), Lodder & Kaspersen (2002), Trunk (2002), Hoeren (2002).

[62] For an easy to read introduction on internet for lawyers see Terrett & Monaghan (2000).

[63] Soft products are products that can be transported in a digital form, such as music, software and text. In the off-line environment these products are connected to a physical carrier (such as a CD), which makes them a tangible good. In the on-line world they can be transported without that carrier, hence making the qualification as a tangible good problematic.

e-commerce and its aims and scope of applicability are set out. Subsequently, the relevant rules are discussed in relation to events that occur in the e-commerce process. The final chapter contains several general findings and conclusions. Besides the practical aim of this book to explain the content of the legal texts, it is sought to make a contribution to the continuous discussion regarding legal aspects of e-commerce. To this end, some critical remarks are included in the discussion.

CHAPTER 2

The E-commerce Directive

1 General

Directive 2000/31/EC (the E-commerce Directive)[1] lies at the heart of the European legislative framework regarding e-commerce. The relevance of this directive for e-commerce is self-evident. Apart from the title, the directive does not use the term e-commerce; instead it uses the concept *information society services*. This concept covers all sorts of on-line commercial activities (see below Section 2) and coincides with the definition if e-commerce formulated in Chapter 1.

The aim of the E-commerce Directive is to establish a legal framework that ensures that information society services can fully benefit from the internal market. Additionally, the directive hopes to lay down a clear legal framework to enhance legal certainty and consumer confidence.[2] The directive tries to balance the interests of consumers and the interests of business organisations. This is a delicate undertaking, as these interests do not always coincide. Measures that protect consumers often form obstacles for business organisations. A compromise was struck because it was recognised that e-commerce can only flourish with a substantial amount of consumer confidence. Considering the conflict of interest and the complexity of some of the material,[3] the directive can be considered quite an achievement.[4] On the other hand the directive is a political compromise, and the quality and the achievements of the instrument have been questioned.[5]

The directive prescribes that the Member States have to remove any legal barriers that obstruct the development of electronic trade within the internal market. Additionally, several special rules for the on-line environment are introduced. It is stressed that the applicability of the E-commerce Directive does not affect the applicability of other (general) European rules. The adoption of this directive does therefore not free the electronic environment from the application of existing laws and regulations.

The E-commerce Directive introduces harmonized rules on the following issues:

- general information requirements for providers of information society services,
- on-line advertising (commercial communications),

1 Directive 2000/31/EC of the European Parliament and of the Council of 8 June 2000 on certain legal aspects of information society services, in particular electronic commerce, in the internal market.

2 Article 1 and recital 7 of Directive 2000/31/EC.

3 The liability of intermediary service providers was considered a very important and sensitive area by the Commission (see amended proposal COM (1999) 427, at p. 7), other problematic issues were the moment of contract formation and consumer protection.

4 Pearce & Platten (2000) refer to it as a 'landmark directive'.

5 As was done by Gijrath & Kolthek (2002), Drijber (2001), Apel & Grapperhaus (1999), Moerel (2000).

- electronic contracting and
- liability for intermediaries such as internet services providers (ISPs).

Furthermore, the directive contains provisions relating to codes of conduct, out-of-court dispute settlement, court actions and co-operation between Member States.

A key provision of the E-commerce Directive is the country of origin principle. In short this principle entails that cross-border e-commerce activities only have to comply with the laws of the country of establishment of the company. Other Member States cannot restrict the activities by applying their laws to a company in another Member State. This principle, which is discussed in detail in Section 3 below, is important with regard to achieving the level playing field for companies that are involved in cross border e-commerce within the EU. The country of origin principle can even be labelled essential for the development of pan-European e-commerce.

As was noted in the previous Chapter, Internet Service Providers (ISPs) play an important role in the exploitation of internet. The directive contains several rules that limit the liability of intermediaries with regard to information on their servers. Insofar as ISPs provide information society services as meant in the E-commerce Directive they have to comply with the rules of the directive. But the special characteristics of the legal position of ISPs as intermediaries, and more in particular if they can be held liable for the information they store and transmit, are not considered in this work.[6]

2 Scope of applicability

2.1 Information society services

The E-commerce Directive affects 'information society services'.[7] An information society service is:

---

[6] See on this topic: Van der Net (2003), Schellekens (2001), Julià-Barceló & Koelman (2000), Siemerink (2003a).

[7] This concept was introduced by Directive 98/34/EC (OJ L 204, 21-7-1998, p. 37) on the notification of technical standards and regulations as amended by Directive 98/48/EC (the Transparency Directive), OJ L 217, 5-8-1998, p. 18, and Directive 98/84/EC on the protection of services based on, or consisting of, conditional access, OJ L 320, 28-11-1998, p. 54.

'...any service normally provided for remuneration, at a distance, by means of electronic equipment for the processing (including digital compression) and storage of data, and at the individual request of a recipient of a service.' [8]

'Any service'

In the recitals of the directive it can be read that the concept information society services covers a wide range of economic activities which take place on-line and in particular the selling of goods on-line.[9] This is not restricted to services that lead to an on-line contract. It also includes enabling services such as transmission, access and hosting services.[10] The concept 'information society service provider' is somewhat confusing in the sense that a 'service provider' is commonly associated with ISPs providing hosting-services, access-services and services such as routing or caching of information (or combinations of those services). Indeed, the concept refers to such intermediaries but it also covers on-line sellers of goods or companies that exploit a search engine. The use of electronic mail or equivalent individual communications by natural persons acting outside their trade business or profession is not an information society service. On the other hand a company providing electronic mail services can be considered an information society service provider. The keyword in determining if a service falls within the definition is: on-line.[11] The E-commerce Directive only sees to the on-line aspect of business activities. The off-line delivery of on-line ordered goods is not an information society service.

'Provided for remuneration'

The definition speaks of services provided for remuneration. This element means that there needs to be a consideration for the service: someone has to pay for the electronic services. The recitals state the services need not be *directly* remunerated.[12] Services that are not directly paid for by the recipient such as on-line information, on-line advertisements and search tools are also considered to

---

8 Recital 17 of Directive 2000/31/EC. The Definition as cited in the recitals of the E-commerce Directive differs slightly from the definition as formulated in Directive 98/34/EC as amended by Directive 98/48/EC. The words 'by electronic means' in the latter have been replaced by 'by means of electronic equipment for the processing (including digital compression) and storage of data', it is assumed that both phrases intent to refer to the same: communication by electronic means.

9 Recital 18 of Directive 2000/31/EC, delivery of goods or delivery of services which take place off-line are specifically excluded from the concept information society services.

10 Recital 18 of Directive 2000/31/EC.

11 The word 'on-line' is repeatedly mentioned in the recitals 18 and 21 of Directive 2003/31/EC.

12 This is in line with the interpretation of the element 'normally provided for remuneration' in Article 50 (former Article 60) of the EC Treaty. The Court of Justice stated in Case 352/85 (*Bond van Adverteerders)* that it is not required that the service is paid for by those for whom it is performed.

be information society services, insofar as they constitute an economic activity.[13] The receiver or user of these services normally only pays for the communication costs. Income for the provider of such a free service can for example be generated by selling advertising space on the site. The element 'for remuneration' indicates that the E-commerce Directive targets commercial on-line activities thereby excluding on-line activities of governmental bodies, political parties, non-profit organisations etc.[14] Established case law of the European Court of Justice[15] confirms that 'services provided for remuneration' refers to economic[16] or gainful[17] activities.

'At a distance'

At a distance means that the service should be provided without the parties being simultaneously present.[18] Services not provided at a distance are: medical examinations or treatments using electronic equipment where the patient is physically present; the consultation of electronic catalogues in a shop while the customer is present; plane ticket reservation at a travel agency in the physical presence of the customer by means of a network of computers and electronic games made available in a video arcade where the customer is physically present.[19] These examples have in common that the on-line service was used in an off-line setting: the customer is present when the seller or provider of the service uses the on-line facilities. If someone goes to a travel agent and the agent makes an on-line booking for a charter seat at an airline company in the presence of the customer the travel agent does not provide an information society service to this customer. In this setting, the airline company provides an information society service to the travel agent. The use of ICT to provide a service to a customer does therefore not necessarily mean that the service is an information society service as meant by the E-commerce Directive.

'By means of electronic equipment'

The element 'by means of electronic equipment' or 'by electronic means' signifies that the service should be sent initially and received at its destination

---

13 Recital 18 of Directive 2000/31/EC.

14 This is supported by recital 18 stating that information society services span a wide range of *economic* activities, as well as activities that do not result in on-line contracts in so far as they represent an *economic* activity.

15 In cases relating to the former Article 60 (the present Article 50) of the EC Treaty on the definition of services provided for remuneration.

16 Case C-51/96 *Deliège* [2000] ECR I-2549, Case C-158/96 *Kohll* [1998] ECR I-1931, Case C-275/92 *Schindler* [1994] ECR I-1039, Case C-159/90 *Grogan* [1991] ECR I-4685.

17 Case C-109/92 *Wirth* [1993] ECR I-6447.

18 Article 1(2) of Directive 98/34/EC as amended by Directive 98/48/EC.

19 See Annex V of Directive 98/48/EC amending Directive 98/34/EC.

by means of electronic equipment for the processing (including digital compression) and storage of data, and entirely transmitted, conveyed and received by wire, by radio, by optical means or by other electromagnetic means.[20]

This does not cover automatic cash or ticket dispensing machines and devices that provide access to road networks and car parks.[21] Equally excluded is the off-line distribution of CD-ROMs or software on diskettes, as well as voice telephony services, telefax/telex services,[22] telephone or telefax consultation of a doctor or a lawyer, and direct marketing using telephone or telefax.

'By electronic means' refers to the technique used to provide the service or transfer the data. The last sentence of recital 17 indicates that 'data processing and storage' are essential in determining whether the service is provided 'by electronic means'. At the time of the negotiation of the E-commerce Directive the commercial use of internet was taking flight. Indeed reading the directive one gets the strong impression that the directive was written for internet.

'At the individual request of a recipient'

The element 'at the individual request of a recipient' can cause some confusion and the relevance of this element has been questioned.[23] The element is to exclude services provided by transmitting data without individual demand for simultaneous reception by an unlimited number of individual receivers (point to multi-point transmission).[24] This means that television broadcasting, radio broadcasting and teletext are not covered by the definition.

What causes the confusion is that an abundance of information communicated to the user of internet is not particularly presented 'at an individual request'. For example electronic advertisements (or: commercial communications, addressed by the E-commerce Directive in Articles 6 and 7) are more then often provided without an individual request.[25] On the other hand, surfing the web can be considered as a search for information. All information found is then information at an individual request.[26] In this respect, the difference between *push* and *pull technology* can be considered relevant. Where the push technology transmits the information irrespective if anyone is tuned in (TV and radio), the pull technology only transmits the information after a request. The

---

[20] Article 1(2) of Directive 98/34/EC as amended by Directive 98/48/EC.

[21] See Annex V of Directive 98/48/EC as amended by Directive 98/48/EC. Note that commercial offers communicated via such machines therefore do not have to comply with the obligations of the E-commerce Directive.

[22] Even if these services increasingly take place digitally, *i.e.* including data processing and storage.

[23] As was done by Grosheide (2000), at p. 11/12, Foss & Bygrave (2000), at p. 116.

[24] See Annex V of Directive 98/48/EC as amended by Directive 98/48/EC.

[25] However, it has been argued that commercial communications do not have to fall within the definition of information society services, see Moerel (2002), p. 13-14.

[26] Lodder (2002) feels that visiting a website is invariably a service delivered on demand because the visitor has either typed in an URL or followed a link (p. 72).

WWW is a pull technology: a browser needs to request the web page before it is send to the receiving PC and can be viewed by the user. Nonetheless internet allows the use of both pull and push technology rendering the technical background less relevant for the determination whether or not an on-line service falls within the scope of the directive. Moreover, for non-technicians, turning on the TV and choosing a channel is not very different from turning on the PC and typing in an URL. The distinctive value of this element is not altogether clear. If its sole purpose is to exclude broadcasting services from the scope of the definition it might have been easier simply to state this instead of using this element.

Conclusion

It can be concluded that information society shortly means on-line commercial activities. This coincides with the definition formulated in Chapter 1: the use of ICT in how the business organisation interfaces with business partners and (potential) customers.

Critical remark

The concept 'information society service' and its definition have a forced feel to them. The problem appears to be that the European legislator has attempted to include a variety of topics that are difficult to cover by one single definition: commercial communications, on-line contracting, on-line service provision and the position of ISPs.

The facilitative services provided by ISPs have a central position in the provision of information society services. Their central role, as well as the problems related to this, justifies the consideration of their position in the E-commerce Directive, but a separate definition for these intermediaries might have been more practical.

Broadcasting services are excluded from the scope of the definition. This is supported by the recitals that state that television broadcasting in the meaning of Directive 89/552/EEC (the TV Directive) is not an information society service because it is not provided at an individual request. The question then comes up how web-radio and web-television are to be understood. It is possible to listen to radio shows via internet. Equally, television shows (or parts of it) can be viewed on internet. This requires data processing and storage and the services can be provided at an individual request as the recipient requests that the services are delivered electronically on his PC. If the web television or web radio is also provided for remuneration such activities can be considered information society services to which the E-commerce Directive is applicable.[27] On the other hand broadcasting activities are explicitly excluded from the applicability of the directive. What rules are to apply to these activities? It is likely that the E-commerce

27 *Cf.* Moerel (2002) at p. 12.

Directive should be observed in addition to the rules that exist for broadcasting services.

C2C

Internet also facilitates trading between two parties that do not act for professional or business purposes, so-called consumer-to-consumer (C2C) trading. For example the auction site <www.ebay.com> allows for everyone to sell on-line. The question can be raised whether a consumer that sells on-line should be considered an information society service provider as meant by the E-commerce Directive.[28] The only element that might prove problematic with regard to this is the element 'for remuneration'. It was indicated above that this refers to economic or gainful activities. It can be argued that consumers act economically in that they strive for optimum satisfaction of their needs.[29] Adding to this, the directive does not contain an indication that this type of trading is explicitly excluded from its scope, such as was done for the use of e-mail by consumers to conclude contracts amongst each other and contractual relationships between employers and employees.[30]

Nevertheless, in my view, a consumer selling on the web should not be considered an information society service provider. The obligations of the directive are clearly directed at business organisations. For example, the general information requirements state that a trade registration number and a VAT identification number should be provided.

This is an issue that might be open to debate, but I will not further explore this topic. The discussion in how far C2C electronic trading falls within the ambit of the definition of information society services is not relevant within this work, which focuses on the consequences of the legal framework for business organisations.

Geographical applicability

The E-commerce Directive is directed at the Member States of the EU. Recital 58 of the directive explicitly mentions that the directive should not apply to services supplied by service providers established in a third country.

---

[28] Schmidt & Franken (2003) are of the opinion (at p. 120) that C2C trading belongs to the domain of e-commerce as it generates and distributes economic value.

[29] See on consumer behaviour Brack (1981), Chapter II.

[30] See recital 18 (at the end) of Directive 2000/31/EC.

2.2 Exemptions

Article 1 of the E-commerce Directive enumerates a list of topics that are excluded from its scope of applicability. The following issues are excluded:

a) taxation,
b) protection of personal data,
c) cartel law issues,
d) activities of notaries (or equivalent professions) directly connected with the exercise of public authority,
e) the representation of a client before courts,
f) gambling, including lotteries and betting, involving the wagering of money,
g) measures taken to promote cultural and linguistic diversity and to ensure the defence of pluralism.

There are other European laws that cover taxation, protection of personal data and cartel law issues. The remaining topics are left to the discretion of Member State law. With regard to most of these issues the Member States are far from political agreement to regulate them on a European level, because strong domestic interests are involved.

Considering activities of notaries directly connected with the exercise of public authority, it can be argued that such activities do not constitute 'commercial activities' and on that ground alone would not fall within the scope of the E-commerce Directive. As for the representation of a client before courts, this seems to be intended for situations where the representative of the client does not appear in person before the court but uses electronic communication to appear 'virtually' before the court. The situation seems somewhat futuristic; nonetheless the drafters of the directive wanted to make clear that the directive was not intended for such activities.

With regard to gambling activities it is relevant to note the decision of the European Court of Justice concerning the criminal proceedings against *Gambelli and others.*[31] In this decision the Court of Justice considered if national restrictions on gambling activities are compatible with European law. The Court held that such restrictions constitute a restriction to the freedom of establishment and the freedom to provide services. However, the national restrictions might be justified by virtue of moral, religious, cultural factors, and the morally

[31] Case C-243/01, *Criminal proceedings against Piergiogio Gambelli and Others.* Cases of the European Court of Justice can be accessed at the website of the Court: <http://curia.eu.int>.

and financially harmful consequences of gambling for the individual and society.[32]

Gambelli; Case C-243/01, criminal proceedings against Piergiogio Gambelli and Others

Gambelli and a number of others exploited data transmission centres in Italy allowing people to bet on sports events via a bookmaker in England. The bets were collected in Italy and communicated to the English bookmaker by internet. Betting activities in Italy may only be exploited by the state or companies authorised by the state. Gambelli and others were sued before a criminal court for having organised illegal bets in Italy. In a preliminary ruling the Italian court asked the European Court of Justice (ECJ) if the Italian restrictive legislation on betting is contrary to principles of freedom of establishment and freedom to provide services (Articles 43 and 49 EC). The ECJ found that the Italian rules constitute a restriction on the freedom of establishment and the freedom to provide services. However, the ECJ also held that restrictions on gaming and betting could be justified under the Articles 45 and 46 EC. To this end, the restrictions must be justified by imperative requirement in the general interest, suitable in order to achieve their objective and proportionate.

In previous cases the Court already established that moral, religious, cultural factors, and the morally and financially harmful consequences for the individual and society could serve to justify national restrictions. The national court is to determine whether the national restrictions satisfy the conditions and if the restrictions are proportionate.

An important consideration for the Italian Court to question legality of the national restrictions was the fact that the Italian State itself promoted betting activities in order to raise tax-incomes. The ECJ commented on this. It stated that in as far authorities encourage betting to the financial benefit of the public purse, they cannot at the same time invoke public order concerns to reduce other opportunities for betting. In other words: the national finances cannot be used as a justification for limiting on-line gambling activities.

---

32 Paragraph 63 of the judgment concerning *Gambelli*, with references to the judgments in Case C-275/92 *Schindler* [1994] ECR I-1039, Case C-124/97 *Läärä* [1999] ECR I-6067 and Case C-67/98 *Zenatti* [1999] ECR I-7289.

3 The country of origin principle

3.1 General

To aid the cross border development of e-commerce, the E-commerce Directive contains the country of origin principle:

'Each Member State shall ensure that the information society services provided by a service provider established on its territory comply with the national provisions applicable in the Member State in question which fall within the coordinated field.'[33]

And:

'Member States may not, for reasons falling within the coordinated field, restrict the freedom to provide information society services from another Member State.'[34]

This is also referred to as the 'internal market clause' or 'home state control'. The country of origin principle entails that an information service provider is supervised by its home state while providing services throughout the EU, without extra requirements being imposed by other Member States. This entails that Member States have to apply 'mutual recognition' with regard to each others' legislation.

The country of origin principle has given rise to much debate in literature.[35] Especially its relation to the rules of private international law has been questioned (see below Section 3.9). Before elaborating on this, the scope of the country of origin principle is discussed.

3.2 Coordinated field

To be able to determine the scope of the country of origin principle, the concept 'coordinated field' is decisive. As can be read in cited passages above, the country of origin principle relates to provisions that fall within the 'coordinated field'. The definition of coordinated field reads:

'requirements laid down in Member States' legal systems applicable to information society service providers or information society services, regardless of whether they are of a general nature or specifically designed for them.'[36]

---

[33] Article 3(1) of Directive 2000/31/EC.

[34] Article 3(2) of Directive 2000/31/EC.

[35] See for example: Moerel (2000), Van Haersolte-Van Hof (2000), Drijber (2001), Mankowski (2001), Van der Hof (2002), p. 155-157, Spindler (2002).

[36] Article 2(h) of Directive 2000/31/EC.

This covers:
- requirements concerning the taking up of the activity of an information society service provider, such as qualifications, authorisation or notification,
- requirements concerning the pursuit of the activity of an information society service provider, such as requirements concerning the behaviour, quality or content of the service including those applicable to advertising and contract, or requirements concerning the liability.[37]

Explicitly not covered are:
- requirements applicable to goods as such,
- requirements applicable to the delivery of goods,
- requirements applicable to services not provided by electronic means.[38]

The recitals of the E-commerce Directive underline that the coordinated field covers requirements relating to on-line activities such as on-line information, on-line advertising, on-line shopping and on-line contracting. However these rules need not be specifically written for the on-line environment, which is indicated by the last sentence in the definition: *'...regardless of whether they are of a general nature or specifically designed for them'*. As a result, all rules that somehow affect commercial on-line activities fall within the coordinated field.

The coordinated field explicitly does not concern Member States' legal requirements relating to goods such as safety standards, labelling obligations, liability for goods, or Member States' requirements relating to the delivery or the transport of goods, including the distribution of medical products. Neither does it cover the exercise of rights of pre-emption by public authorities concerning certain goods such as works of art.[39]

Put shortly, the coordinated field includes rules that apply to the on-line selling of goods and services but it does not include the rules that apply to the physical delivery of those goods and services. As a consequence, a Member State of destination cannot prevent on-line selling or advertising of goods, but it can apply its rules if those goods are subsequently transported and delivered within its borders.

Negative harmonisation

Unfortunately, the definition, the examples and the clarification added by the recitals still leave some room for confusion as to the exact scope of the concept coordinated field.[40]

---

[37] Article 2(i) of Directive 2000/31/EC.

[38] Article 2(ii) of Directive 2000/31/EC.

[39] Recital 21 of Directive 2000/31/EC.

[40] See also Van den Oosterkamp (1999), p. 150.

A broad interpretation of the concept seems to be intended. During the law-making process the wordings of the provision originally being *'which fall within this directive's coordinated field'*[41] were altered to *'fall within the coordinated field'*.[42] The disappearance of the words *'this directive's'* indicates that the coordinated field concerns not only the subjects addressed by the E-commerce Directive but all regulations affecting the information service provider irrespective of whether they are harmonised by the E-commerce Directive or not. The coordinated field covers both public (including criminal law) and private law.[43] As a result, it does not matter whether the Member States choose to regulate matters using public or private law instruments.

As a consequence of the broad extent of the concept coordinated field, and therewith the country of origin principle, the area of law that has to be mutually recognised by the Member States is much broader than the area of law, which is harmonised by the E-commerce Directive.[44] This effect is referred to as 'negative harmonisation': the level playing field to advance the internal market is reached by declaring national rules inapplicable instead of by introducing harmonised European standards.

This broad extent of the coordinated field has been criticised.[45] One of the main objectives is that the consequential negative harmonisation can lead to the feared 'race to the bottom'. This means that companies can be inclined to establish themselves in the Member State with the least restrictive legislation. Another objective is that mutual recognition will not always be accepted if there are no common standards introduced on a European level.[46] Member States with high standards will not be inclined to allow incoming services that are below their acceptable standards. Nonetheless, this appears to be the intention of the directive.[47]

The discussion in the following Sections will show that the principle does not have such a far-reaching affect as it appears to have upon first sight.

---

41 Commission proposal COM (1998) 586 final and the amended proposal COM (1999) 427 final.

42 Common Position (EC) No. 22/2000 of 28 February 2000, OJ C 128, 8-5-2000, p. 32, as well as in the final text of Directive 2000/31/EC.

43 In this manner: Drijber (2001), p. 128-129, Spindler (2002), p. 639, Apel & Grapperhaus (1999), p. 1251. Different: Van der Hof (2002), p. 156.

44 Apel & Grapperhaus (1999) at p. 1251 point out that the concept 'coordinated field' is odd as it also covers non-coordinated rules.

45 Drijber (2001), p. 127, Moerel (2000), p. 206, Van den Oosterkamp (1999), p. 150. The narrow formulated coordinated field in previous drafts of the directive was questioned as well because it was understood to be too narrow, see Dickie (1999), p. 23.

46 See Drexl (2002).

47 See amongst others Moerel (2000), p. 206.

3.3 Exemptions

To begin with, the following subject areas are exempted from the applicability of the country of origin principle:[48]

- Copyright, neighbouring rights, rights referred to in Directive 87/54/EEC and Directive 96/9/EC as well as industrial property rights;
- The emission of electronic money by institutions in respect of which Member States have applied one of the derogations provided for in Article 8(1) of Directive 2000/46/EC on electronic money institutions;
- Article 44(2) of Directive 85/611/EEC: undertakings for collective investment in transferable securities (UCITS) must comply with the provisions governing advertising in the Member State where the products are marketed.
- Article 30 and title IV of Directive 92/49/EEC, title IV of Directive 92/96/EEC, Articles 7 and 8 of Directive 88/357/EEC and Article 4 of Directive 90/619/EEC: all these provisions concern the activities of insurance business;
- The freedom of parties to choose the applicable law to their contract;
- Contractual obligations concerning consumer contracts;
- Formal validity requirements concerning the transferring of rights in real estate (if subject to mandatory requirements of the Member State where the real estate is situated);
- Permissibility of unsolicited commercial communications.

With regard to these issues, the Member States are allowed to take measures against information society services originating in other Member States. With regard to electronic contracting, the exceptions concerning the freedom to choose the applicable law and the contractual obligation concerning consumer contracts are particularly relevant. Concerning unsolicited commercial communications it can be noted that Directive 2002/58/EC on privacy in the electronic communications sector determines that it is not allowed to send commercial e-mails to natural persons without their prior consent (see Chapter 5 below). As a consequence, the permissibility of unsolicited commercial communications to natural persons is now harmonised. The exemption with regard to unsolicited commercial communications remains relevant with regard commercial messages to legal persons. Also excluded from the country of origin principle are the topics exempted from the scope of applicability in the E-commerce Directive (summed up above in Section 2). Additionally, incidental derogations are allowed based on the derogation procedure formulated by the E-commerce Directive.[49]

---

48 Article 3(3) of Directive 2000/31/EC.

49 Article 3(4) to 3(6) of Directive 2000/31/EC.

3.4 Derogation procedure

The derogation procedure allows country of destination measures against on-line commercial activities originating in another Member State if three conditions are met:[50]

1) The measures are necessary in the light of public policy,[51] public health, public security or the protection of consumers, including investors,
2) The measures are taken against a given information society service that prejudices the objectives referred to under the previous point or which presents a serious or grave risk of prejudice of those objectives (the measures must be necessary),
3) The measures must be proportionate.

Procedure

Before taking any measures against incoming on-line services a Member State must ask the Member State of origin to take measures against the avenged services. If this does not lead to a satisfactory outcome, the Member State may proceed to take measures against the incoming services. Both the home state of the services and the Commission must be notified.

In matters of urgency, Member States may derogate from this and take measures instantly. The country of origin of the service and the Commission then have to be notified within the shortest possible time indicating why urgent intervention was necessary.[52] What is considered to be 'urgent' is not specified, one can think of acute threats to public health or public security.

While the Member State takes its notified action against an incoming information society service, the Commission examines if the measures are compatible with Community law. If the Commission finds that the measures are incompatible with Community law the Member State is requested to cease the measures or refrain from taking them. The Commission explicitly cannot demand from the Member State of destination to refrain from its restrictive actions.[53] If the Member State disregards the Commissions' request, the Commission can use the competences laid down in the EC Treaty. This means

---

[50] Article 3(4) of Directive 2000/31/EC.

[51] Public policy refers in particular to the prevention, investigation, detection and prosecution of criminal offences, including the protection of minors and the fight against any incitement to hatred on grounds of race, sex, religion or nationality, and violations of human dignity concerning individual persons.

[52] Article 3(5) of Directive 2000/31/EC.

[53] An earlier draft of the E-commerce Directive granted the Commission this authority (see Commission proposal for a European Parliament and Council Directive on certain legal aspects of electronic commerce in the internal market, COM (98) 586 final), but this authority does not appear in the final version of the directive.

the Commission must deliver a reasoned opinion and if necessary bring the matter before the European Court of Justice.[54]

The derogation procedure means to instigate the Member States to follow a course of discussion before taking restrictive measures. If this does not lead to a solution, the derogation procedure cannot prevent the Member State from taking restrictive measures, it merely provides for transparency by the obligation to inform both the Commission and the Member State of origin. This can uncover the fields where community intervention by harmonised standards might be required.

Measures

It is not specified what is meant by 'measures' against on-line services. This can be understood as including attempts to uphold existing legislation against incoming services. In this manner, both existing and future restrictions fall within the derogation procedure.[55] In any event, the Commission must be notified of any new legislation that affects information society services according to Directive 98/34/EC (the Transparency Directive).[56]

The derogation procedure is 'without prejudice' to court proceedings.[57] This means court proceedings concerning on-line commercial activities need not to be postponed. However, it does not mean that court proceedings and their results are excluded from the country of origin principle. Court decisions can be seen as 'measures' against incoming information society services.[58] As a result, to enforce any judgments against incoming information society services the derogation procedure as described above must be observed.[59]

3.5 Country of establishment

As a result of the country of origin principle, concerning the on-line activities a company is in first instance subject to the laws of the Member State where it is established. An established information society service provider is defined as:

---

[54] Article 226 of the EC Treaty.

[55] *Cf.* Smith (2002), p. 275.

[56] Directive 98/34/EC of the European Parliament and of the Council of 22 June 1998 laying down a procedure for the provision of information in the field of technical standards and regulations OJ L 204, 21-7-1998, p. 37-48, as amended by Directive 98/48/EC, OJ L 217, 5-8-1998, p. 18-26.

[57] Article 3(4) b of Directive 2000/31/EC.

[58] *Cf.* Spindler (2002), p. 676.

[59] Recital 25 of Directive 2000/31/EC. This recital confirms that national courts, including civil courts dealing with private law disputes, can take measures to derogate from the freedom to provide information society services in conformity with conditions established in the directive.

'a service provider who effectively pursues an economic activity using a fixed establishment for an indefinite period. The presence and use of the technical means and technologies required to provide the service do not, in themselves, constitute an establishment of the provider.'[60]

This does not necessarily point to a single country. Multinationals often have several offices in different countries. If those offices can be considered a fixed establishment where an economic activity is pursued, this means the company has more then one country of establishment. If a company has multiple places of establishment it is important to determine from which place of establishment a given service is provided to be able to determine the country of origin of the service.

The presence of a local establishment does not necessarily mean that this local establishment delivers the services in the area. The local offices could for example be set up with the sole purpose to handle complaints or returns, while the actual service is supplied from the main establishment situated elsewhere. If it is difficult to determine from which establishment the service is provided, the country of origin is the place where the provider of the service has the centre of his activities, relating to the provided service. This means that the determination of the place of establishment in the case of multinationals, can depend on the structure of the organisation and the nature of the service delivered.

In relation to the country of establishment the recitals of the E-commerce Directive repeat the elements as found in the cited article:

- the actual pursuit of an economic activity,
- through a fixed establishment,
- for an indefinite period.[61]

Controversially, the recitals also state that the last requirement is also fulfilled where a company is constituted for a given period, *i.e.* for a definite period.

The mentioned elements may give rise to confusion. The element *'fixed establishments'* does not necessarily point to the same country as where the *'actual pursuit of an economic activity'* takes place. Internet facilitates having a virtual office that is accessible all over the world; this allows the pursuit of economic activities worldwide. However, it is also stressed in the recitals that the place of establishment is neither the place at which the supporting technology is located, nor the place where the companies' website is accessible.[62] It is very unlikely that a virtual shop or an electronic agent can be considered as an establishment in the meaning of the directive.

---

60 Article 2(c) of Directive 2000/31/EC.

61 Recital 19 of Directive 2000/31/EC.

62 Trunk (2002) at p. 37 (footnote 52) suggests that the mere technical presence is not enough but that a leased server with some personnel might suffice.

The element *'actual pursuit of an economic activity'* of the E-commerce Directive should not be confused with the element *'pursuing commercial or professional activities in the Member State of the consumer's domicile'* of Article 15 of Council Regulation 44/2001.[63] The wordings in the regulation intent to link the activities of a company to the country of the consumers' domicile triggering the jurisdiction of that country. Controversially, the wordings in the E-commerce Directive point to the country of origin of the services by determining where the company is established.

A reference point as to where the company is deemed to pursue its economic activities is for example where the company pays its (transaction) taxes.

Case law

The E-commerce Directive indicates that the place of establishment should be determined in conformity with the case law of the European Court of Justice.[64] The question where a business is established has been taken to the Court mainly with regard to tax issues.

In relation to Value Added Tax (VAT) the primary reference point is the place where the business is legally constituted.[65] Referring to a different Member State as the country of establishment is possible when this primary reference point leads to unreasonable outcomes or to a conflict between Member States.[66] The secondary reference point is the fixed establishment of the business. According to the Court, for an office to qualify as a fixed establishment there should be technical and human resources with a certain degree of permanence.[67]

A similar viewpoint is found in relation to the case law related to Article 5(5) of the Brussels Convention that deals with branches, agencies and other establishments of business organisations.[68] With regard to this article, the Court refers to the appearance of permanency, material signs and the presence of a management.[69] An independent commercial agent that transmits orders to the parent undertaking without being involved with their terms or their execution does not constitute an establishment of that company.[70]

---

63 About this article see Section 5.2 of Chapter 7 on jurisdiction in relation to consumer contracts.

64 Recital 19 of Directive 2000/31/EC.

65 Article 9(1) of the Sixth Council Directive 77/388/EEC of 17th May 1977 on the harmonisation of the laws of the Member States relating to turnover taxes, OJ L 145, 13-6-1977, p. 1.

66 See §17 of Case 168/84 *Berkholz* [1985] ECR 2251.

67 *Cf.* Case 168/84 *Berkholz* [1985] ECR 2251, Case C-190/95 *ARO Lease* [1997] ECR I-4383, Case C-390/96 *Lease Plan Luxembourg* [1998] ECR I-2553.

68 Article 5(5) of the Brussels Convention. The Brussels Convention was replaced by Council Regulation (EC) No. 44/2001, but Article 5(5) was unaltered, and therefore the case law related to this article remains valid.

69 Case 33/78, *Samofar SA* v. *Saar-Ferngas AG* [1978] ECR 2183.

70 Case 139/80, *Blankaert & Williams PVBA* v. *Luise Trost* [1981] ECR 819.

3.6 Country of origin principles in other secondary legislation

The E-commerce Directive is not new in the inclusion of an internal market clause.

However, it can be noted that the inclusion of country of origin principles in European legislation is usually combined with several basic community standards. This approach can be found in Directive 89/48/EEC[71] with regard to the recognition of diplomas, Directive 89/646/EEC[72] with regard to banking and a series of directives affecting the insurance industry.[73]

Similar principles have also been included in the Directive on Electronic Signatures and Directive 89/552/EEC[74] (the TV Directive), with the significant difference that these directives contain a restrictive interpretation of the concept coordinated field.[75] In these directives the extent of the country of origin principle is limited to the requirements as harmonised by these directives. The country of origin principle of the E-commerce Directive affects a much larger part of the legislation: namely all rules that affect the on-line activities, irrespective whether they are harmonised by the directive or not (save the mentioned exemptions).

3.7 Consequences of the country of origin principle

The internal market clause is far reaching in the sense that Member States are not allowed to apply their own legislation to information society services originating in a different Member State. Several authors have noted that this particularly affects the application of national advertising laws.[76]

As a result of the principle, a Member State is not allowed to forbid the selling of goods through internet by a company in another Member State that

---

71 Directive 89/48/EEC of 21 December 1988 on a general system for the recognition of higher-education diplomas awarded on completion of professional education and training of at least three years' duration, OJ L 19, 24-1-1989, p. 16.

72 Second Council Directive 89/646/EEC of 15 December 1989 on the coordination of laws, regulations and administrative provisions relating to the taking up and pursuit of the business of credit institutions and amending Directive 77/780/EEC OJ L 386 30-12-1989, p. 1 (the Second Banking Directive).

73 Directives 73/239/EEC, 88/357/EEC and 92/49/EEC. With regard to life insurance: Directives 79/267/EEC, 90/619/EEC and 92/96/EEC.

74 Council Directive 89/552/EEC of 3 October 1989 on the coordination of certain provisions laid down by law, regulation or administrative action in Member States concerning the pursuit of television broadcasting activities, OJ L 298 17-10-1989, p. 23-30.

75 In joined cases C-34/95, C-35/95 and C-36/95 *De Agostini* [1997] ECR I-3843, the European Court of Justice held that the country of origin in the TV Directive is only relevant with regard to areas coordinated by the directive.

76 As illustrated by Kabel (2002). p. 109-111 with regard to Dutch law and Hennig-Bodewig (2001) concerning German law. See also Moerel (2002), p. 17.

allows the selling of the goods. On the other hand the Member State is allowed to restrict shipment into or within its borders, because such measures would regard the product as such and not the information society service.[77] If the Member State wishes to take measures against the display of certain material on commercial websites, the derogation procedure must be observed. The derogation procedure does not give the Commission or the other Member States the power to prevent national restrictive measures. The procedure merely forces the Member State to be transparent about its intentions and discuss the matter with the Member State of origin. If it proceeds with its action, the matter can be taken before the European Court of Justice (either by the Commission or by the Member State of origin), which is then to decide if the measures can be upheld or not.

Advancing free trade in the single European market in this manner can be problematic where there are no common standards, especially with regard to controversial products or services (such as fireworks or soft drugs) and certain marketing techniques. Whether or not this results in a feared 'race to the bottom' remains to be seen. If so, efforts should be made to introduce more or higher common standards on a European level. A proper functioning of mutual recognition is benefited by a certain amount of harmonisation of material rules on a European level.[78] Concerning such common standards work is still in progress, for example the EU legislator is working on a regulation that is to introduce harmonisation concerning the rules on sales promotion.[79] This regulation includes a principle of mutual recognition with clear reference to primary EU legislation.[80]

In theory, the country of origin principle eliminates the problem – at least within Europe – that on-line activities will have to comply with a variety of national rules. A closer look at the scope of the principle shows that the offered relief is subject to several reservations. The mentioned exemptions to the principle are extensive. Important issues for the information society such as copyright and consumer contracts are explicitly excluded from the country of origin.

Position of the intermediary service provider

Besides companies that use the internet to offer their goods and services, the directive also applies to intermediary service providers such as providers of hosting services. Although the position of such intermediaries is not a subject of

77 Such a ban of course would have to be tested against the freedom of movement principles.

78 *Cf.* Spindler (2002), p. 638.

79 See Communication from the Commission on sales promotions in the Internal Market, including a proposal for a Regulation of the European Parliament and the Council concerning sales promotions in the Internal Market, Brussels, 2-10-2001, COM (2001) 546 final, an amended proposal was presented in October 2002: Amended proposal for a European Parliament and Council Regulation concerning sales promotions in the Internal Market, Brussels, 25-10-2002 COM (2002) 585.

this thesis, it is interesting to note a problem that might occur if the provider of the content is not established in the same country as its host provider.

This problem occurs when a company exploits on-line activities that are legal in his home state, but illegal in the home state of the hosting provider.[81] In this case two laws apply to the information society service: the law of the country of the company and (at least as far as liability for the content is concerned) the law of the country of the ISP.

3.8 The country of origin principle and primary European legislation

3.8.1 Mutual recognition

The country of origin principle in the E-commerce Directive is related to the principle of mutual recognition that comes forth from Articles 28, 43 and 49 of the EC Treaty.[82] These articles lay down the freedom of movement of goods and services and the freedom of establishment. The principle of mutual recognition was first formulated by the Court of Justice in the famous *Cassis de Dijon* case[83] and refined in subsequent case law.[84]

The principle entails that Member States cannot prohibit the sale on their territory of goods that are lawfully produced and marketed in another Member State. The *Cassis* case concerned the freedom of movement of goods, but the principle applies equally in the area of services and establishment.[85]

Mutual recognition assures the freedom of trade within the EU without extensive harmonisation being installed. The idea is that if certain interests are taken into account by the home state legislation of certain products and services, and the product or service is in conformity with that law, it is unnecessary as well as an obstruction to free trade if the legislation of the importing country (which protects the same interests) is also applied to these products and services.[86]

---

80 See the Commission Communication on sales promotions in the Internal Market, p. 22.

81 See Van der Net (2003), p. 56.

82 Former Articles 30, 52 and 59 of the EC Treaty. The numbering of both the EU Treaty and the EC Treaty was changed as a result of the Treaty of Amsterdam, which came into force on 1 May 1999.

83 Case 120/78 *Cassis de Dijon* ECR 179, 649.

84 See for a thorough discussion of this doctrine Weatherill & Beaumont (1999), p. 500-619.

85 Case C-76/90 *Säger* [1991] ECR I-4221, Case C-288/89 *Mediawet I (Collectieve Antennevoorziening Gouda)* [1991] ECR I-4007, Case C-55/94 *Gebhard* [1995] ECR I-4165, Case C-180/89 *Alpine Investments* [1995] ECR I-1141, Case C-33/74 *Van Binsbergen* [1974] ECR 1299.

86 About the functioning of the principle of Mutual recognition: First biennial report on the Application of the principle of mutual recognition in product and services markets SEC (1999) 1106 of 13 July 1999 and the Second biennial Report on the application of the principle of mutual recognition in the single market, Brussels, 23-7-2002, COM (2002) 419 Final.

This freedom of movement of goods, services and the freedom of establishment as laid down in the EC Treaty is not unlimited. Deviation from the principle of mutual recognition is allowed if necessary in the light of overriding requirements of general public importance, such as health protection, consumer protection or the protection of the environment, if they are suitable to reach the aim of the requirement and the aim cannot be reached in a less restrictive manner. Furthermore, it does not apply to so-called selling arrangements.[87] These limits are laid down in the EC Treaty[88] and further developed by case law of the Court of Justice.[89]

The application of the principle of mutual recognition as found in primary law also causes the previously mentioned 'negative harmonisation'. This method of advancing the single market by denying applicability of national law without positive European harmonisation has been questioned.[90] The main objection is that it risks failing to recognise where there is a need for community harmonisation to remove the national barriers instead of (or at least additional to) the abolition of national trade obstructions. The concept 'coordinated field' to define the extent of the principle of mutual recognition is not found in primary European law. Instead, the Court of Justice sketches the boundaries to the principle.[91]

The country of origin principle in the E-commerce Directive reflects the doctrine of mutual recognition as laid down in the EC Treaty and refined by case law of the Court of Justice.[92] Both serve the same objective: advancing the internal market by abolishing national barriers to trade.

From that perspective, the country of origin principle in the E-commerce Directive can be seen as a part of the strategy to advance the development of the

---

87 Joined Cases C-267 and C-268/91 *Keck and Mithouard* [1993] ECR I-6097.

88 Article 30 and Article 46 of the EC Treaty (former Articles 36 and 56 of the EC Treaty, also known as the rule of reason).

89 With regard to services amongst others: Case 352/85 *Bond van Adverteerders* [1988] ECR 2085, Case C-353/89 *Mediawet II* [1991] ECR I-4069, Case C-76/90 *Säger* [1991] ECR I-4221, Joined Cases C-34/95, C-35/95 and C-36/95 *De Agostini* [1997] ECR I-3843, Case C-410/96 *André Ambry* [1998] ECR I-7875. With regard to goods: Case 145/88 *Torfaen Borough Council v B&Q plc (Sunday trading)* [1989] ECR 765, Joined Cases C-267 and C-268/91 *Keck and Mithouard* [1993] ECR I-6097, Case 227/82 *Van Bennekom* [1983] ECR 3883, Case 69/88 *Krantz* [1990] ECR I-583.

90 Weatherill & Beaumont (1999), p. 599.

91 The boundaries are not altogether clear and indicated by incidental litigation before the Court. The most import case limiting the application of the principle of mutual recognition is the much criticized *Keck and Mithouard* case and subsequent cases.

92 *Cf.* Smith (2002), p. 270, Moerel (2000), p. 205. See also the Report on the proposal for a European Parliament and Council directive on certain legal aspects of electronic commerce in the Internal Market of the Committee on legal affairs and citizens' rights, 23 April 1999, A4-0248/99, p. 38.

application of the free movement doctrine. The need to intensify this strategy has been underlined by the Commission and the Court of Justice.[93] Commission research has indicated that the application of the principle of mutual recognition is subject to certain difficulties and does not operate satisfactorily, especially in the area of services.[94] The Commission also noted that one of the difficulties in attaining the single market for services is an absence of mutual recognition clauses in Member State rules.[95]

Although similar, the country of origin principle of the directive is not the same as the principle of mutual recognition of the primary legislation.[96] The principle of the directive seems to go further, mainly because there are fewer possibilities to derogate from it.[97] Notably the derogation concerning selling arrangements is not allowed with regard to the country of origin principle as formulated in the E-commerce Directive. On the other hand, as was noted above, there are many exemptions allowed to the country of origin principle of the E-commerce Directive. If there are any restrictions to the free movement to information society services that fall within these exemptions, the freedom of movement principles of primary European law can be invoked to evaluate if the restrictions are justified.

The derogations allowed to the country of origin resemble the derogations allowed to mutual recognition on the basis of the EC Treaty, more in particular Articles 30 and 46. It can be argued that the derogation procedure of the E-commerce Directive does not constitute a different or new test for national restrictions then the existing test under primary EU law:[98] if Member States wish to maintain possible trade barriers they must have a good reason that justifies their action against incoming services.[99]

93 Case C-184/96 *Commission v France ("foie gras")* [1998] ECR I-6197. The case concerned the restriction on the marketing of a product. As previous case law of the Court of Justice shows, the Court tends to adopt parallel decisions in the areas of free movement of goods and services, it can be expected that this statement will be extended to the marketing of services.

94 First biennial report on the application of the principle of mutual recognition in products and services markets, p. 3.

95 P. 20 of the First biennial report.

96 Mankowski (2001) at p. 172 underlines that the freedom of movement principles of the Treaty are not the same as the country of origin principle of the E-commerce Directive and that they should be kept strictly separated.

97 Apel & Grapperhaus (1999) illustrate the consequences of the principle with several cases decided according to primary EC law to show the possible different outcomes (p. 1253-1257). *Cf.* also Mankowski (2001), p. 171, Drijber (2001), p. 126, Kightlinger (2003) p. 743. They all conclude that the principle of the E-commerce Directive has further reaching consequences then primary EC law.

98 See Smith (2002), p. 274. Different: Van den Oosterkamp (1999), p. 147, Drijber (2001), p. 126.

99 See also Spindler (2002), p. 673.

However, due to the transparency requirements the application of the derogation procedure has further reaching consequences then the application of the derogations of the EC Treaty. The derogation procedure prescribes that Member States must first notify and discuss its intended trade restrictions. The Commission will then examine the compatibility of the intended action with community law, *i.e.* the EC Treaty and case law of the Court of Justice. Under the principle of mutual recognition this test will not be performed until someone is willing to challenge the national restrictive measures before a court, either by a party that feels prejudiced by the measures or by the Commission if it has knowledge of the measures.

3.8.2 The problem of reverse discrimination

Although there are similarities between the doctrine of mutual recognition and the country of origin principle, some renewal can be seen in the in the E-commerce Directive. The principle as laid down in the directive appears to surpass the doctrine as laid down in the EC Treaty and explained by the Court in *Alpine Investments*.[100] According to the Court in this judgment Member States have no responsibility to guarantee the protection of consumers of other Member States. As a result, a Member State is not allowed to uphold its more stringent legislation in relation to service providers established on their territory that direct their activities at residents of other Member States with less stringent measures.

Controversially, under the E-commerce Directive Member States have to uphold their legislation to information society service providers established on their territory to the benefit of all Europeans. Applying the country of origin principle thus results in a reverse discrimination of companies established in countries with strict legislation. These companies are at a disadvantage vis-à-vis their competitors established in states with more lenient laws. This can be seen as a barrier to interstate trade and therefore the disadvantaged companies should be able to revert to the principles of free movement in primary EC law.[101]

3.8.3 The country of origin principle and minimum harmonisation

Minimum harmonisation means that Member States are allowed to maintain more stringent rules in the relevant subject area.[102] Where there is minimum harmonisation, the question arises if a Member State can apply its more stringent rules to the goods and services from a different Member State with lower standards.

---

100 Case C-384/93 *Alpine Investments* [1995] ECR I-1141.

101 *Cf.* Apel & Grapperhaus (1999).

102 On minimum harmonisation see Temmink (1995), Rott (2003).

The country of origin principle entails that the more stringent measures cannot be upheld against service providers established in other Member States. If a Member State wishes to deviate from this (*i.e.* uphold the more stringent laws against incoming services) the derogation procedure will have to be followed. This is in line with the general doctrine of free movement: more stringent national rules that are allowed according to minimum harmonisation still have to be tested against Articles 28-30 of the EC Treaty.[103] In other words, the competence of Member States to maintain more stringent rules, even if this is allowed by minimum harmonisation, is limited by the free movement doctrine of the EC Treaty and the country of origin principle.

3.8.4 *DocMorris*

The European Court of Justice has addressed the issue of internet selling in relation to the free movement principles in the *DocMorris* case.[104] This case concerns the selling of medication (both prescriptive and non-prescriptive) via internet. The Court held that the upcoming use of internet as a cross border selling channel placed the consideration of the national restrictions on mail order selling in a different perspective.[105] The Court stated to this end, that internet is an important means of accessing a foreign market without having to open a physical store abroad. A prohibition on internet marketing constitutes a disadvantage to foreign sellers vis-à-vis national sellers. The national seller can still market the products in his physical establishment, but the foreign seller is left with little possibilities to market the products abroad.[106]

DocMorris; Case C-322/01 Deutscher Apothekerverband v. DocMorris Judgment of 11-12-2003

A German association of pharmacists opposed to the selling of medication by the Dutch company 'DocMorris' via internet, based on the German prohibition on mail order selling of medicinal products. The Dutch pharmacy is close to Germany and the on-line ordered medication can be picked up at the pharmacy or send by courier service.

The German court that was seized in this matter by the German association posed several preliminary questions, amongst others about Articles 28 and 30 EC.

The European Court of Justice held that the German prohibition on mail order selling of non-prescription medication constitutes a measure having equivalent

---

[103] See Temmink (1995), Rott (2003), p. 1110-1112 and the there mentioned references.

[104] Case C-322/01 *Deutscher Apothekerverband* v. *DocMorris* [2003] ECR.

[105] Paragraph 73 of *DocMorris.*

[106] Paragraph 74 of *DocMorris.*

effect as a quantitative restriction as meant by Article 28 EC. Although the prohibition is a selling arrangement (possibly falling outside the scope of Article 28 EC by virtue of the Courts' judgment in *Keck and Mithouard*), the Court held that the prohibition on mail order selling does not have in law and in fact the same consequences for products originating in other Member States.

Subsequently, the Court indicates that the use of internet for cross-border trade entails that the prohibition, and its consequences, should be viewed in a wider perspective. The Court finds that the prohibition causes more hindrance to pharmacists outside Germany. German pharmacists are merely denied an extra selling channel by the prohibition; they can still sell the medication from their physical establishments in Germany. Controversially, foreign pharmacist are denied access to the German market altogether, because internet is an important means to enter the German market without having to open a brick and mortar pharmacy in Germany. Hence, the prohibition puts foreign pharmacists at a disadvantage.

With regard to prescription medication, the Court states that a prohibition of mail order selling can be justified, because of the risk that these medications might be abused or used incorrectly.

3.9 The country of origin principle and private international law

The country of origin principle raises some questions when considered in relation to private international law.[107] The principle affects the applicability of Member State law to incoming services and therewith potentially interferes with the rules of private international law concerning applicable law.[108] Indeed, the country of origin principle has the look and feel of a special conflict rule determining the applicable law to on-line commercial activities within Europe.

Controversially, the E-commerce Directive explicitly states that it does not aim to add rules to the area covered by private international law.[109] Moreover, it is stressed in the recitals that the directive does not intent to interfere with the jurisdictional and applicable law issues.[110] Notwithstanding this aim, a number of legal authors have argued that the country of origin principle in fact constitutes a special conflict rule, or at least has the same consequences.[111]

---

[107] Moerel (2000), p. 208, Van den Oosterkamp (2000), p. 12, Drijber (2001), p. 130, Mankowski (2001), p. 138, Hoeren (2004), p. 174, Smith (2002), p. 276, Trunk (2002), p. 36-38.

[108] It can be noted that the principle does not affect the rules of jurisdiction that appoint the competent court. Van Haersholte-Van Hof (2000), p. 327, compare also recital 25 of Directive 2000/31/EC.

[109] Article 1(4) of Directive 2000/31/EC.

[110] Recital 23 of Directive 2000/31/EC.

[111] A fiery argument for this viewpoint is given by Mankowski (2001) and (2002). Spindler (2002) finds that the country of origin principle is a hidden conflict rule. Van den Oosterkamp (1999), p. 149 also concludes that the principle constitutes a conflict rule.

There is another viewpoint with more respect for the statement that the principle does not aim to add a rule of private international law. This viewpoint adheres a two-step approach. First, the rules of private international law are to determine the applicable law. Second, it must be determined if this law contains any obstacles to interstate trade. If so, the country of origin principle prevents the application of the rules that constitute the obstacle. According to this two-step approach the country of origin principle functions as a correction to the material law applicable to the information society service.[112]

Yet another viewpoint is that the coordinated field, and therewith the country of origin principle, also includes the national rules of private international law. The applicable law is then to be determined according to the rules of private international law of the home state of the company. Little support can be found for this viewpoint.

With regard to this issue the E-commerce Directive contradicts itself: on the one hand it states that the country of origin does not affect the rules of private international law and on the other hand it explicitly exempts a central rule of private international law (namely the freedom to choose the law applicable to the country) of the scope of applicability of the country of origin principle. Why would this exemption be necessary if the principle did not affect this rule in the first place?[113]

The E-commerce Directive further declares that: '*...provisions of the applicable law designated by rules of private international law must not restrict the freedom to provide information services as established in this Directive.*'[114] These wordings indicate that the E-commerce Directive does not allow the application of private international law when this restricts the freedom to provide information society services.[115]

Although literature is divided, most support can be found for the viewpoint that although the directive claims not to interfere with private international law, the country of origin sets aside the rules of private international law as far as information society services are concerned.[116]

---

112 Proponents of this two-step approach: Hennig-Bodewig (2001), Van der Hof (2002).

113 Van Haersholte-Van Hof (2000), p. 325 suggest that the exemptions mentioned in the Annex are an indicative non-limitative list.

114 Recital 23 of Directive 2000/31/EC. With regard to this statement, the rapporteur of the recommendation for second reading on the Council Common Position (document A5/2000/106/), comments that by this stipulation there can be no doubt as to the primacy of the Directive over Private International Law.

115 See also Van der Hof (2002), p. 155-157.

116 Kabel 2002 notes that Article 1(4) merely pays lip service to the private international law (p. 110), Mankowski 2001 finds that Article 1(4) is erroneous (*'unzutreffend'* p. 179). Implied: Moerel (2002). Different: Van Haersholte-Van Hof (2000).

The problem of on-line contracting

The country of origin principle explicitly does not affect the freedom of parties to choose the law applicable to their contracts.[117] However, the country of origin principle covers the pre-contractual phase. As can be read in the subsequent Sections, the E-commerce Directive contains various pre-contractual obligations for on-line sellers. If the law chosen is not the same as the law of the home state of the on-line seller, two sets of law apply to the relation between buyer and seller: the law of the country of establishment of the company applies to the pre-contractual phase and once the contract is concluded, the law chosen by the parties is applicable to the contract.

The same problem can occur with consumer contracts. The contractual obligations concerning consumer contracts are excluded from the country of origin principle.[118] The phrase 'obligations concerning consumer contracts' does not make clear whether or not this includes the pre-contractual phase. To prevent that different laws are applicable to the contractual B2C relation this phrase can be interpreted broadly, including the obligations in the pre-contractual phase.[119] The result is then that private international law determines the applicable law of both the pre-contractual and contractual phase. As a result, in most cases the law of the home state of the consumer will apply.[120]

In this context, the company must also be aware of special conflict rules in several consumer protection directives (scope rules). Such scope rules determine that a consumer cannot lose the protection afforded to him by a certain directive if the consumer contract has a close link with the EU even if the law of a non-Member State was chosen as applicable law.[121]

3.10 Conclusion

It can be concluded that although the country of origin principle looks promising upon first sight, it only offers partial relief with regard to the problem that on-line services run the risk of being subject to multiple legal systems. Although broadly formulated, there are several rules that do not fall within the reach of the concept 'coordinated field', for example rules that affect the off-line delivery of goods. Adding to this both the exemptions to the E-commerce Directive and the exemptions summed up in the Annex to the directive do not fall within the scope of the principle. Finally, derogations to the principle

[117] Article 3(3) and the Annex (5th indent) of Directive 2000/31/EC.

[118] Article 3(3) and the Annex (6th indent) of Directive 2000/31/EC.

[119] As will be shown the E-commerce Directive as well as the Distant Selling Directive contain several rules that affect the pre-contractual stage.

[120] See Section 4 of Chapter 8 on applicable law to consumer contracts.

[121] See Article 12(2) of Directive 97/7/EC, Article 6(2) of Directive 93/13/EC, Article 7(2) of Directive 1999/44/EC.

on an incidental base are allowed as long as Member States follow the derogation procedure.

4 General information duties

Companies engaging in on-line business activities are information society service providers as meant by the E-commerce Directive and should make accessible easily, directly and permanently the following information:[122]

a) name of the company,
b) the geographic address where the company is established,
c) details which allow for quick contact and direct and effective communication, including an electronic mail address,
d) the trade – or similar – register where the company is registered as well as its registration number,
e) if subject to an authorisation scheme, the particulars of the relevant supervisory authority,
f) concerning regulated professions: the professional body where the service is registered, the professional title and where it was granted, reference to the applicable professional rules and means of access to these rules,
g) if applicable, the VAT identification number,[123]
h) when referring to prices, these are to be indicated clear and unambiguously and indicate whether these include tax and delivery costs.

These general information duties are binding in both business-to-business (B2B) and business-to-consumer (B2C) relations. They are additional to other information requirements in Community legislation.

The general information duties are applicable to all sorts of on-line commercial activities including the electronic representation of the company on a website with no ordering procedure. Although such an electronic representation is not 'directly remunerated', it is an on-line commercial activity. The recitals underline that the directive is relevant for services that represent an economic activity.[124] Websites that provide 'free' information or free services such as on-line route planners or price comparing sites also have to comply with these general information duties.

These general information duties can help the customer to assess whether the company actually exists and where it is situated. The geographic address can

---

[122] Article 5 of Directive 2000/31/EC.

[123] As referred to in Article 22(1) of the sixth council Directive 77/388/EEC of 17 May 1977 on the harmonisation of the laws of the Member States relating to turnover taxes – Common system of value added tax: uniform basis of assessment OJ L 145, 13-6-1977, p. 1, last amended by Directive 1999/85/EC.

[124] Recital 18 of Directive 2000/31/EC.

serve to determine the place of establishment of the country of origin principle. It can also serve to determine the habitual residence in the meaning of the Rome Convention (See Chapter 8 below) and the place of domicile as meant by the Brussels regulation (Chapter 7 below).

The trade registration number can also help to verify this, especially if the trade registration office has an on-line database that allows to check the number. Why the client needs to be informed about the VAT identification number is unclear, perhaps this number can help to clarify the location of the service provision?

Easily, directly and permanently

The information must be easily, directly and permanently accessible. What exactly is meant by 'easily, directly and permanently' is not specified by the E-commerce Directive. In case of a company website, in my view, a clearly visible and recognisable hyperlink on the website of the company is sufficient.[125] For example a hyperlink available in the main menu of the website that is visible on all pages of the site. Having the general information available on all pages makes it easier for the visitor to detect the origin of a page if it is accessed through a deeplink. A clear way to structure a website is to have a horizontal or vertical menu that is visible on all pages of the site.

The title used for the link should indicate which information is accessed when the link is clicked, such as *'general information'*, or *'about us'*. A German court decision[126] held that the label *'backstage'* on a link providing access to the general information could give rise to confusion. What is more, after clicking the link the visitor using a 800x600 pixel resolution needed to scroll to the right to see the information. The presentation was held not to satisfy the requirements 'easily directly and permanently'.[127]

Languages

Websites can be available in different languages. If the company has multiple establishments, it is possible to match the address information with the chosen language, for example the Greek address of the subsidiary office in Greece on the Greek language version of the site. This might give rise to confusion for the client, as it creates the impression the company is wholly Greek based. It can therefore be advisable to have all the companies' addresses accessible to the client visiting the website or at least clearly indicate the companies' main

---

[125] *Cf.* Van Esch (2001a), p. 143.

[126] Hanseatisches Oberlandesgericht Hamburg, 20-11-2002 available on <www.jurpc.de> Web-Dok. 79/2003, Abs. 1-25.

[127] *'Leicht erkennbar, unmittelbar erreichbar und ständig'* as required by paragraph 6 of the German *Teledienstgesätz*. For more German decisions related to this topic see Hoeren (2004), p. 192.

establishment. Using multiple language versions has as a consequence that the company runs a higher risk of being subject to foreign laws and jurisdictions.

Quick contact

With regard to the obligation under (c) (details that allow quick contact and direct communication) e-mail is mentioned. The wordings of the E-commerce Directive[128] suggest that the listing of an e-mail address is obligatory. In my opinion, if the company has provided other contact details that allow effective communication an e-mail address is not strictly necessary.

For example, the site can be equipped with an on-line form that can be filled in and send on-line by the customer. This has the advantage that the client does not need to use an e-mail program.[129] This makes submitting any questions or remarks from a public PC, for example in an internet cafe, easier.

A feature that is sometimes found is a link, such as *'contact'* or *'mail us'*, that (when clicked) automatically opens the customer's e-mail program. This is not a practical feature when the customer wishes to use a different program or has an on-line account, such as a hotmail account.[130] In that case clicking the link will not always work properly. If this feature is used it is preferable to also spell out the e-mail address so that the customer is given the opportunity to use a different program or an on-line account to reach the company.

Critical remark

These general information requirements are quite extensive; for example no such requirements are made when contracts are concluded at a distance using more traditional media such as paper, telephone or fax. In such cases of distant contracting, equal risks might exist with regard to the identity and trustworthiness of the other party due to the lack of direct contact.[131]

---

[128] Article 5(1) sub c of Directive 2000/31/EC reads: "*the details of the service provider, including his electronic mail address, which allow him to be contacted rapidly and communicated with in a direct and effective manner.*"

[129] Although the client will probably still need an e-mail address to receive an answer.

[130] An on-line account can be used if the user has a browser and an internet connection, there is no need to install an e-mail software program.

[131] About the strictness of these information requirements: Stuurman (2002), p. 152.

5 E-advertising

5.1 Introduction

Advertising is subject to a multitude of rules, both general and specific. In general, advertising may not be misleading.[132] Adding to this, there are special rules aimed at products such as medication, cosmetics and tobacco.[133] There are also special rules targeting the media on which the commercial messages are spread. The TV Directive[134] contains special rules with regard to commercials on television. The E-commerce Directive now adds special rules for on-line advertising.

Such e-advertising comes in a multitude of appearances. On the WWW, surfers are confronted with banners, buttons, pop-ups (or pop-unders), objects moving over the screen either with or without moving images, sound, interactive possibilities or promotional games. E-advertising can also be communicated using e-mail and electronic messages to mobile phones. As technology advances, more possibilities for e-advertising arise.

The special characteristics and possibilities of e-advertising raise questions on how the rules written for the off-line world should apply in the on-line world. Should internet be considered close to printed media and treated as such? Or is it more related to television? Is internet the same as 'press' and is all information on internet publicly available? The discussion on these questions is far from being closed, which means there is some uncertainty with regard to the legal norms that apply to on-line advertising.[135] It goes beyond the aim of this work to delve into this discussion. This Section will discuss the norms as introduced for electronic advertising by the E-commerce Directive.

---

[132] Directive 84/450/EEC as amended by Directive 97/55/EC concerning misleading and comparative advertising.

[133] Council Directive 92/28/EEC of 31 March 1992 on the advertising of medicinal products for human use (OJ L 113, 30-4-1992), Council Directive 76/768/EEC of 27 July 1976 on the approximation of laws of the Member States relating to cosmetic products (OJ L 262 of 27-9-1976), Directive 2003/33/EC of the European Parliament and of the Council of 26 May 2003 on the approximation of the laws, regulations and administrative provisions of the Member States relating to the advertising and sponsorship of tobacco products (OJ L 152, 20-6-2003).

[134] Directive 89/552/EEC of 3 October 1989 on the co-ordination of certain provisions laid down by law, regulation or administrative action in Member States concerning the pursuit of television broadcasting activities, OJ L 298, 17-10-1989, p. 23.

[135] On this topic: Kabel (2002).

5.2 Commercial communications

The E-commerce Directive does not refer to e-advertising, but uses the term commercial communications. Commercial communication is defined as:

'...any form of communication designed to promote, directly or indirectly, the goods, services or image of a company, organisation or person pursuing a commercial, industrial or craft activity or exercising a regulated profession.' [136]

This definition is not completely consistent with the definition of 'information society services' especially with regard to the element 'at the individual request of a recipient'. Many electronic advertisements are considered a nuisance rather then requested.

Combining the two definitions it can be concluded that messages of a commercial nature that are communicated electronically fall within the scope of the rules concerning commercial communications.[137] This includes a company website.

The scope of the concept is narrowed down by two examples that do not 'in themselves' constitute commercial communications:[138]

- information allowing direct access to the commercial activities such in particular domain name or an e-mail address, and
- communications that present information in an independent manner, particularly when this is without financial considerations.

The first exemption ('information allowing direct access') points to hyperlinks or the mention of a WWW-address. Presumably this is meant to exempt cases where the information allowing direct access is placed solely for informational purposes, such as on-line catalogues without commercial interests, or hobbyists.

For example, a person that has cycling as a hobby maintains a website with information on cycling. The site possibly contains hyperlinks to companies that offer goods and services related to cycling. As long as these companies do not pay for these links, the hyperlinks are not commercial communications, but merely a reference allowing direct access.

The second indent points to independent reports on available products or services, for example by consumer organisations.

---

136 Article 2(f) of Directive 2000/31/EC.

137 Here it is assumed that commercial communications should also be information society services to fall within the scope of the obligations. The exemptions to the concept information society services (for example TV broadcasting, cash dispensing machines) are therefore equally exempted from the scope of the concept commercial communications.

138 Article 2(f) of Directive 2000/31/EC.

The wordings 'in themselves' indicate that it is not entirely unthinkable that the mentioned information can nevertheless constitute a commercial communication in the sense of the directive. This can be the case if the information was clearly placed for promotional reasons. For example if the company pays the owner of a website to place a sponsored link.[139] Such sponsored links can be found when using the search engine 'google'. After performing a search the results are listed on the screen of the user. On the right hand side of the screen several sponsored links are placed for companies who have paid to have their name connected to the search that was performed. Equally, when the hobbyist is paid to place hyperlinks, the links can become a commercial communication.

Discounts, promotional offers and promotional competitions are explicitly included.[140] Product information where the purpose is to provide background or user information, which is not placed for promotional purposes, is not a commercial communication (but might be considered an information society service). Again, this might be different if the information is placed as such that the information has a promotional character. For example if a website about obesity contains a link to product information about a prescription medicine against obesity, the strategically placed link can be characterised as publicly promoting the product.[141]

5.3 Transparency requirements

If an electronic message qualifies as a commercial communication, the following must be taken into account:[142]

a) the commercial communication must be clearly identifiable as such;
b) the natural or legal person on whose behalf the commercial communication is made shall be clearly identifiable;
c) promotional offers, such as discounts, premiums and gifts, where permitted, shall be clearly identifiable as such, and the conditions which are to be met to qualify for them shall be easily accessible and presented clearly and unambiguously;
d) promotional competitions or games, where permitted, shall be clearly identifiable as such, and the conditions for participation shall be easily accessible and presented clearly and unambiguously.

According to thc obligation under (a) the commercial nature of the messages must be clear. This means the information should not be likely to be confused with independent, informational messages.

---

[139] See also Kabel (2002), p. 96.

[140] Recital 29 of Directive 2000/31/EC.

[141] Pres. Rb. Utrecht, 15-2-2000, IER 2000, p. 172-177 (*Staat der Nederlanden/Roche*).

[142] Article 6 of Directive 2000/31/EC.

It can be noted that this conflicts somewhat with a marketing trend called sponsored content. Sponsored content means the commercial messages on a website are closely connected to the information on a website. It can be hard to tell where 'information' (editorial content) ends and 'marketing' (paid advertisement) begins. For example information on outdoor activities is combined with companies that offer outdoor travel arrangements or outdoor gear.

The rules on commercial communications are primarily relevant for the company on whose behalf the commercial message is communicated. This company is responsible for the design and the content of the commercial message, even if the actual design is outsourced to a marketing company. Nonetheless the rules can also be relevant for website owners who place commercial messages of others on their web pages. These owners or operators are responsible for the design of their own websites and should not design it as such that the commercial messages of others can be mistaken for a different type of content or with their own commercial messages.

Vague norms

The rules on commercial communications make use of vague or 'open' norms such as 'clearly identifiable' and 'clearly and unambiguously'. These open norms leave room to appreciate each particular commercial expression on its individual merits. Future court judgments will have to narrow the norms down and hand more specific criteria as to what is to be considered 'clearly and unambiguously'.[143]

People that regularly surf the web are confronted with a diversity of information. Most of the commercial messages can be recognised at first sight as being advertisements. However, such communications can also take a more concealed form such as, for example, a banner in the shape of a Microsoft error message. When the non-experienced surfer encounters such a banner, it could take a few clicks until he finds out that he is confronted with a commercial message.

An advantage of the use of open norms is that it allows for an assessment of the commercial communications in accordance with current public views, which are likely to differ over the course of time. The disadvantage to the use of open norms is that they do not create substantial legal security.

[143] Van Esch (2001a) at p. 147 suggests the use of the word 'advertisement' (reclame) above the commercial statements to indicate the nature of the message.

5.4 Mutual recognition of commercial communications

As a result of the country of origin principle, the Member States may not apply their national rules to commercial communications originating in other Member States. The national rules with regard to advertising differ on various points and can contain restrictions on certain marketing strategies. One can think of national rules with regard to the prohibition on selling at a loss, bans on premiums, maximum limits on discounts, restrictions on promotional games and restrictions on 'three for the price of two' promotional offers.

As there is still some considerable diversity between the national rules in this area, Member States might not be willing to accept mutual recognition. Harmonisation on a European level stating some common minimum standards would greatly enhance the mutual acceptance.

Regulatory initiatives relating to advertising

This need was recognised within the EU, or rather by the Directorate-General Internal Market, which issued a communication containing a proposal for a regulation on sales promotions.[144] An amended proposal was presented in October 2002.[145] The aim of this proposal is to eliminate the national restrictions on the use of sales promotions. According to the proposal Member States are not allowed to impose:

- a general prohibition on the use of commercial communication, (except if imposed by community law),
- a limitation on the value of a sales promotion,
- a prohibition on discounts preceding seasonal sales,
- a requirement to obtain prior authorisation, or any requirement having equivalent effect, for the use or commercial communication of a sales promotion.

The proposal does not affect rules with regard to selling at a loss. Selling at a loss does not necessarily cause misleading effects, but it can be considered a distortion of competition.

Additionally, the Directorate-General responsible for health and consumer protection is making efforts to realise a directive concerning unfair B2C

[144] Communication from the Commission on sales promotions in the Internal Market, Brussels, 2-10-2001 COM (2001) 546.

[145] Amended proposal for a European Parliament and Council Regulation concerning sales promotions in the Internal Market, Brussels, 25-10-2002 COM (2002) 585.

[146] Proposal for a directive of the European Parliament and of the Council concerning unfair business-to-consumer commercial practices in the internal market and amending directives 84/450/EEC, 97/7/EC and 98/27/EC of 18-6-2003, COM (2003) 356 final.

commercial practices.[146] This proposal is to ensure fair-trading by prohibiting unfair commercial practices, such as misleading and aggressive commercial practices. The proposal indicates when a commercial practice is unfair, misleading or aggressive. The proposal also contains an internal market clause stating that traders shall only have to comply with national provisions falling within the field approximated by the directive of the Member State in which they are established.[147] The proposal explicitly states that it is without prejudice to the rules determining the jurisdiction of the courts.[148]

With regard to the relation between the proposed directive on unfair B2C commercial practices and the proposed regulation on sales promotions, the directive can be seen as the general framework while the regulation contains more specific rules.[149] The proposal for a directive explicitly states that the information requirements in relation to advertising, commercial communication or marketing established by Community law shall be regarded as material, with explicit reference to the proposed regulation.[150] Furthermore, in case of a conflict between provisions of the directive and other Community rules governing specific aspects of unfair commercial practices, the latter are to prevail over the directive.[151]

Finally, it should be noted that if personal information is used to target the commercial messages, the rules of the Privacy Directive have to be taken into account.[152]

6 E-mail marketing

6.1 Introduction

E-mail was quickly recognised as a powerful marketing tool: cheap and with a broad reach. The costs of sending a single message to a large group of receivers are very low: the recipients and transporters of the messages bare most of the communications costs.

Unsolicited e-mail messages are generally known as spam. Spam refers to all kinds of unwanted e-mail messages often send in large amounts and often (but not necessarily) with a commercial nature. Extremely large amounts of spam can clog inboxes and paralyse mail servers.

---

[147] Article 4 of the proposal for a directive concerning unfair B2C commercial practices.

[148] Article 3(6) of the proposal for a Directive concerning unfair B2C commercial practices.

[149] De Vrey (2004), at p. 4. He discusses the proposed Directive on unfair B2C commercial practices and notes the somewhat unfortunate concurrence with the proposed regulation on sales promotions.

[150] Article 7(4) and 7(5) of the proposal for a Directive concerning unfair B2C commercial practices.

[151] Article 3(5) of the proposal for a Directive concerning unfair B2C commercial practices.

[152] See Chapter 4.

A great resentment has grown against spamming activities. Service providers complain of the network capacity that is taken up by these messages and it is a source of growing irritation for many receivers. There has been a call for legislative action against spammers for quite some time. On the other hand there were companies that opposed to the regulation of unsolicited messages, as this would seriously restrict possibilities of e-mail marketing. Indeed marketing as well as direct marketing are allowed, but it should not place unequal burdens on the receiving end or on the networks.

Although all unwanted commercial e-mails tend to be characterised as spam, it can be argued that it is possible to make a distinction between the rude and aggressive form of sending bulk e-mail that is spam and the more moderately and neatly send unsolicited e-mails.[153]

Opt-in and opt-out

In the debate on the legislative action needed to control spam, two legislative approaches can be distinguished: opt-in and opt-out. The opt-in approach entails that it is not allowed to send electronic messages without the permission of the recipient. Under such a regime, the company that wishes to send electronic mail will have to actively seek the permission of the recipients. The opt-out approach means that it is allowed to send electronic messages as long as the recipient has not opposed to this. Under this regime it is up to the recipients to indicate that they do not, or no longer, want to receive messages.[154]

There are two directives relevant in relation to this topic: the E-commerce Directive and the Directive on Privacy and Electronic Communications (discussed in Chapter 5 below).

6.2 General rules

The E-commerce Directive does not use the term 'spam'.[155] The directive addresses 'unsolicited commercial communications by electronic mail'. It can be noted that the word 'unsolicited' is opposite to the requirement that information society service should be 'at an individual request'. Nonetheless, because the directive specifically addresses these messages it can be assumed that unsolicited electronic commercial communications fall within the scope of the concept information society services.

As opposed to the Directive on Privacy and Electronic Communications, the E-commerce Directive does not define electronic mail. To achieve some coherence, it is preferable to apply the definition of the Directive on Privacy and Elec-

[153] Gauthronet & Drouhard (2001), at p. 98. They argue that all spam is unsolicited commercial communication, but not all unsolicited commercial communication is spam.

[154] For additional reading: Khong (2001), Schaub (2002), Lodder & Bergfeld (2002).

[155] The term 'spam' is (as of yet) not a legal term.

tronic Communications for the purpose of the rules in the E-commerce Directive. This entails that any type of message (text, voice, sound or image) send over a public communications network is considered to be e-mail.[156]

The rules of the E-commerce Directive do not address the lawfulness of unsolicited messages. The choice of installing either an opt-in or an opt-out regime is left to the Member States.[157] The E-commerce Directive merely states that if the sending unsolicited messages is allowed some general rules have to taken into account: [158]

- the unsolicited commercial messages should be identifiable clearly and unambiguously as such as soon as it is received by the recipient, and
- the senders of these messages must consult regularly and respect the opt-out registers in which natural persons have registered themselves.[159]

Strictly taken, the provisions do not prescribe the obligation to install opt-out registers, it states that if such registers exist, these must be respected. Apparently the drafters have assumed that such registers are or will be installed.

Two years after the adoption of the E-commerce Directive, the Directive on Privacy and Electronic Communications was adopted. This directive prescribes some additional rules for e-mail marketing and, more importantly, an opt-in regime for e-mail marketing to consumers. This entails that Member States no longer have the choice to install either an opt-in or an opt-out regime with regard to B2C e-mail marketing.[160]

As a result of the obligation to install an opt-in approach the obligation under the second indent (consult and respect opt-out registers of natural persons) has become superfluous. This provision speaks of opt-out registers in which natural persons have registered themselves. However, the recitals of the Directive on Privacy and Electronic Communications extend the scope of this provision. Recital 45 of this directive states that if Member States establish an opt-out register for communications to legal persons this provision is fully applicable.[161]

---

[156] Article 2(h) of Directive 2002/58/EC. See Section 3 of Chapter 5 for a discussion of this definition.

[157] The permissibility of unsolicited commercial communications by electronic mail is one of the issues exempted from the application of the country of origin principle in the Annex to the directive.

[158] Article 7 of Directive 2000/31/EC.

[159] Note that this obligation does not mention legal persons, therefore it does affect B2B e-mail marketing.

[160] This is further discussed in Chapter 5 on the Directive on Privacy and Electronic Communications.

[161] Recital 45 of Directive 2002/58/EC.

7 E-contracting

7.1 Introduction

E-contracting (or: on-line contracting) refers to concluding contracts at a distance with electronic means.[162] There are various manners to conclude an electronic contract. Before the commercial use of internet, a common method for e-contracting was Electronic Data Interchange (EDI). Prior agreements (interchange agreements) between the parties using EDI specify the technical, organisational and legal issues. Commonly EDI is used in a closed network structure with a limited amount of parties.[163]

At present internet is a popular means for electronic contracting. Internet allows multiple ways of coming to an agreement. A common manner to conclude a contract over internet is by filling in and sending an on-line ordering form.[164]

An advanced manner of electronic contracting is to use electronic agents for the conclusion of contracts. Electronic agents are software programs containing instructions of the user of the agent. The agent can for example be used to trace and select information. Advanced agents (also referred to as 'intelligent agents') can independently negotiate and conclude electronic contracts, according to the parameters set by the user of the agent.[165]

Electronic contracts can also be concluded via electronic marketplaces. An electronic marketplace is an on-line forum with a number of participants that use the forum to find business partners, exchange information and possibly come to an agreement. The electronic marketplace provides an infrastructure that companies can use to do business.

Another manner of on-line contracting is the on-line auction. eBay is an example of such an auction. Professional sellers but also non-professional sellers can perform on-line auctions.

On-line contracts are sometimes referred to as click-wrap agreements.[166] This is meant as an analogy to the off-line shrink-wrap contract. Shrink-wrap and the related click-wrap are forms of contracting that are generally used to establish licence agreements, such as binding software users to licence terms of the software producers. Breaking the transparent wrap (behind which the terms

---

[162] It is possible that contracting partners use ICT to conclude a contract while they are in each others' presence. This kind of e-contracting, which falls in the category e-business rather then e-commerce, is not considered within this thesis.

[163] See on legal issues related to EDI: Van Esch & Prins (1993), Stuurman & Wijnands (1998).

[164] *Cf.* Murray (2000).

[165] On the use of electronic agents to conclude contracts: Weitzenboeck (2001), Kerr (2001), Finocchiaro (2003).

[166] Murray (2000), Girot (2000) p. 309.

of the licence contract are visible) concludes the shrink-wrap contract. Electronic variants of this manner of contracting are the presenting of licence terms and an 'I agree'-button to the customer before the software can be installed. Without clicking the 'I agree'-button, the software cannot be installed.[167] Shrink-wrap and click-wrap methods are subject to discussion as they one-sidedly force the licence terms upon the end-user. Both the validity of the contract as the applicability of the terms has been subject to legal scrutiny.[168]

Legal issues

Most legal textbooks on contract formation teach that contracts are formed by offer and acceptance. Although this seems simple enough, problems can occur in an early stage when it needs to be determined when there is – legally speaking – an 'offer' and when this is can be considered accepted, resulting in a legally binding contract.

In certain cases, what appears to be an offer is actually an 'invitation to treat' or an 'invitation to make an offer' in reaction to which an offer can be made. In negotiation processes it can be hard to determine who exactly made the offer and who consequently accepted it.[169]

The existing rules with regard to contract formation equally apply to on-line contracting. In general, the modern legal systems adhere the principle of informality with regard to the conclusion of contracts.[170] This entails that there are no requirements as to the form in which the offer and acceptance are communicated and therefore all means, including electronic means, can be used.

However, there are several exceptions to this general principle. For some contracts the use of paper documents and handwritten signatures is required to conclude a valid contract. In such cases electronic contracting is not possible.

Although it is long accepted that contracts can be concluded using electronic means,[171] there can be uncertainties on how existing law should apply to new techniques.[172] For example when can the electronic acceptance be considered effective? With its E-commerce Directive, the European legislator strives to eliminate some of these issues.

---

167 On shrink-wrap and click-wrap: Gatt (2002).

168 Girot (2000) generally concludes that the click-wrap licence can be valid, but unfair terms or terms to the detriment of the end user are invalid (p. 300). Scheltema & Tjong Tjin Tai (2003) question the validity of the click-wrap contract altogether as the clicking of the 'I agree'-button (comparable to the opening of the package) is not an expression of the will to be bound to the licence terms but a necessary action to be able to use a lawfully purchased product.

169 Zweigert & Kötz (1998), p. 356-357.

170 Zweigert & Kötz (1998), p. 366.

171 See *i.a.*, Smith (2002) Chapter 10, Allen & Widdison (1996).

172 On this topic see Allen & Widdison (1996) and Kerr (2001) (in relation to electronic agents), Kuhn (1991) and Van Esch (1999) (in relation to EDI).

7.2 E-contracting must be possible

The E-commerce Directive prescribes that Member States are to make sure that their legal systems allow contracts to be concluded by electronic means.[173] This entails that Member States have to scan their legislation and remove or adapt any rules that hinder electronic contracting.[174] This does not mean that Member States may not adopt (or retain) certain requirements for the conclusion of contracts, but it should be possible to meet such requirements by electronic means.

The simple rule that electronic contracting should be possible can have far reaching consequences. All rules that affect electronic contracting in a discriminative manner vis-à-vis traditional contracting must be revised. Although the directive does not state any rules with regard to evidential issues, paper documents or handwritten signatures, the general rule entails that Member States must review their legal system on these points and where necessary adapt this to suit the electronic business environment.[175]

The E-commerce Directive allows several exemptions to this general rule. With regard to the following contracts Member States can determine that e-contracting is not allowed:[176]

a) contracts that create or transfer rights in real estate,
b) contracts requiring by law the involvement of courts, public authorities or professions exercising public authority,
c) contracts of suretyship granted and on collateral securities furnished by persons acting for purposes outside their trade, business or profession,
d) contracts governed by family law or by the law of succession.

Most Member States have chosen to exclude all or some of these contracts from the electronic environment.[177]

7.3 Information duties

In addition to the information duties discussed in previous Sections, there are special information requirements that need to be fulfilled before the conclusion of an electronic contract. Prior to the order being placed, the

---

173 Article 9(1) of Directive 2000/31/EC.

174 *Cf.* recital 34 of Directive 2000/31/EC.

175 *Cf.* Kaufman Winn & Haubold (2002), at p. 577 they argue that the modification and abolition of writing or signature requirements is perhaps the main element of Art. 9 of Directive 2000/31/EC.

176 Article 9(2) of Directive 2000/31/EC.

177 The national implementations can be monitored on the TRIS website: <http://europa.eu.int/comm/enterprise/tris/>.

e-vendor should inform his counterpart clearly, comprehensibly and unambiguously of (at least) the following:[178]

a) the different technical steps that need to be followed to conclude the contract,
b) whether or not the concluded contract will be filed and whether it will be accessible,
c) the technical means for identifying and correcting input errors prior to the placing of the order,
d) the languages offered for the conclusion of the contract.

With regard to these information duties concerning the conclusion of the electronic contract business partners are allowed to make other arrangements. In B2C relations it is not allowed to deviate from these rules. These duties do not apply to contracts concluded exclusively by electronic mail or by equivalent individual communications.[179]

Clearly, comprehensible and unambiguously

The information must be given clearly, comprehensibly and unambiguously, prior to the order being placed. What this means in practical terms is not specified by the E-commerce Directive. It can be assumed that this means the information should be easy to understand and not open to misinterpretations. The wordings leave room for appreciation of practical situations on a case-by-case base, taking the particular circumstances of each case into account.

To fulfil these information duties, the company can for example present a prominent and clearly labelled hyperlink to a separate page where all the relevant information with regard to the on-line contracting is summed up.

As people are likely to go straight to the 'order now!'-button, it is advisable to provide information on the ordering procedure during each step that the customer needs to take. For example a short statement declaring the consequences of clicking through to the next stage, such as: *'By clicking the "order now button" you conclude a contract'*, or *'by clicking the "review button" you can check all the information about your order and if necessary make corrections'.*

This diminishes the chance that people conclude a contract without being aware of it or a contract with a faulty content. Clarity is benefited if all the relevant information can be seen on the screen without having to scroll down the page. The consequences of clicking on buttons that affect the ordering procedure should be indicated before or at the same level of the relevant button.

---

[178] Article 10 of Directive 2000/31/EC.

[179] Article 10(4) of Directive 2000/31/EC. See Section 7.7 below for remarks on these exemptions.

An informative feature that can be used while the customer is in the ordering procedure is to indicate the amount of steps needed to conclude the contract and indicate at which stage the customer finds himself (for example *'step 3 of 5'*).

Input correction

The information under (c) obliges the company to inform the customer of the means of detection and correction of errors. As can be read in Section 7.6 below, the company is also obligated to have these means available. On a website this is commonly implemented by presenting a recapulative page before the final order is placed, where the customer can review his order and if necessary make changes.

7.4 Codes of conduct

Adding to these information duties concerning the conclusion of the contract, the company must indicate any relevant codes of conduct and how these can be consulted electronically.[180] A code of conduct is a self-regulatory instrument that states a set of rules or principles related to good business practices.[181] Codes of conduct often restate and complement the rules laid down by law.

The information duty on codes of conduct is mentioned in a separate section, indicating that there are different (less stringent) demands on the presentation of this information compared to the above information which must be presented clearly, comprehensible and unambiguously and prior to the placement of the order. The wordings allow that the information on the codes of conduct is provided after the placement of the order.

To avoid having information scattered over the website, the information on the codes of conduct can be included with the above information.

The adherence to a code of conduct is often indicated by a label, trustmark or a seal on the website of the company. The placement of such a label can be used as a marketing strategy: by showing the label, the company underlines that it can be considered a trustworthy contracting partner.

Business partners are allowed to make other arrangements with regard to the information on codes of conduct. In B2C relations it is not allowed to deviate from this rule. The obligation with regard to the codes of conduct does not apply to contracts concluded exclusively by electronic mail or equivalent electronic communications.[182]

---

[180] Article 10(2) of Directive 2000/31/EC.

[181] Lerouge (2001), at p. 200 defines a code of conduct as a set of norms elaborated by a professional organism and that, without having a direct binding power, has for purpose to organise and guide the attitude of companies.

[182] Aricle 10(4) of Directive 2000/31/EC. See Section 7.7 below for remarks on these exemptions.

Legal value of codes of conduct

The E-commerce Directive encourages the drawing up of codes of conduct, preferably restating and specifying the rules of the European Community.[183] This supports the communication of the rights and duties and can contribute to compliance.

Codes of conduct can be drawn up by trade organisations or consumer associations possibly connected with a dispute resolution body and a sanctioning system. It is also possible for individual business organisation to draw up their code of conduct or a best practice statement. If taken seriously by the companies and their clients codes of conduct and best practices statements contribute to transparency and trustworthiness of the business relation.[184] There is a considerable amount of codes of conduct available on a variety of topics.[185].

The value of codes of conduct can vary. Much depends on whether the organisation behind the code is solid and trustworthy. If codes are drawn up by branch organisations one should realise that companies that are not a member of the organisation are not bound by the code. The value of the code can be increased if some sort of sanctioning system can ensure compliance.

The legal value of codes of conduct, as well as how they relate to the standard terms, is not always obvious.[186] The code of conduct will not be a part of the electronic contract unless the rules of the code are included in the standard terms or if they are in some other manner accepted by the customer as part of the contract. If the code is part of the electronic contract, breach of the code is a failure to comply with the contract terms. If the code is not part of the contract it can serve to complement the contract or can be used as a guide to interpret the contract. Otherwise breach of the code might be considered an infringement of the customers' reasonable expectations or a form of misleading advertising.[187]

7.5 Contract terms

The contract terms and standard terms are to be made available in such a manner that allows the recipient to store and reproduce them. This rule is obligatory in both B2C and B2B relations.

---

183 Article 16 of Directive 2000/31/EC.

184 On self-regulation in relation to e-commerce: Wagemans (2002), Terryn (2003).

185 Endeshaw (2001) discusses several codes of conduct. To support reliable codes of conduct, the Commission announced the e-confidence initiative, see press release of 10 December 2001, IP/01/1780, for further information see <http://econfidence.jrc.it>.

186 *Cf.* Siemerink (2003b), she discusses the legal value of codes of conduct in relation to ISPs and their customers.

187 *Cf.* Terryn (2003).

It is not expressly stated at what point during the ordering procedure the terms must be available in this manner. This suggests that the terms can also be presented in this manner only after the conclusion of the contract.

The two most popular browsers (Internet Explorer and Netscape Navigator) allow the storage and printing of the content shown on screen. However, simply presenting the contract terms on the screen of the user is somewhat meagre. It is advisable to have the terms available in a downloadable and printer-friendly form, preferably with simple instructions and the statement that the client should save the information for later reference.

A point of attention is that standard terms of a company can change over the course of time. Commonly, the company will have its most recent version of the standard terms available on its website. To avoid confusion as to the content of contracts that were concluded before such a change, the date of the standard terms can be indicated as well as the date when they were last revised.

Possibly the standard terms contain information that must be presented in a certain manner. For example, if the terms contain a provision with regard to the competent court, the Brussels regulation becomes relevant. This regulation contains some stipulations with regard to the form for agreements with regard to jurisdiction. Such an agreement should be (a) in writing (electronic communications are considered equal to writing if a durable record is provided), or (b) in a form which accords with the practices which the parties have established for themselves, or (c) in a form which is in accordance with the usage of the trade in question.[188] Another directive that is relevant in this respect is the Directive on Distant Selling which contains several detailed information duties and how these should be presented. For example information on the Right of withdrawal must be provided written or in another durable medium.[189]

Disclaimers

Many websites contain disclaimers. A disclaimer is a statement on a website or in an e-mail address with which the company intents to limit its liability. The here-discussed legislation contains no references to disclaimers or other general statements with regard to the use of the website. As the use of disclaimers is becoming widespread in e-commerce a few words are dedicated to them here.

A disclaimer on a website can commonly be accessed through a hyperlink placed on the homepage, for example behind a link labelled *'legal notice'* or simply *'disclaimer'*. If the disclaimer renounces any rights relevant with regard to the electronically concluded contract, these provisions should be part of the standard terms and be presented as such.

Often, the disclaimer is presented as a unilateral statement and the binding nature of the provisions in the disclaimer upon the visitor of the website can be

---

[188] Article 23 of Regulation (EC) No. 44/2001, see Section 5.3 of Chapter 7.

[189] See Chapter 3 on information duties in relation to B2C contracting.

questioned. In relation to consumers, the provisions might be considered unfair in the light of Directive 1993/13/EC on unfair terms in consumer contracts. According to this directive unfair terms will not be binding upon the consumer.

The disclaimer or legal notice can also contain statements with regard to the use of the website, such as *'the owner of the site cannot be held responsible for any mistakes'* or *'the visitor may not use any information on the site without prior permission'*. In case a website is approached through a deep link, the visitor can easily miss the disclaimer. If the user of the website wishes such a disclaimer to be binding upon its visitor, the visitor should somehow agree with the applicability of the terms laid down in the disclaimer. If the visitor of a website did not have the chance to take proper notice of the disclaimer it cannot be held binding with regard to him. If any unexpected terms are incorporated in the general terms or the disclaimer, it is advisable to pay extra attention to the presentation of the terms.[190]

Although the legal status of disclaimers is not always manifest, it can certainly be advised to use them. They may play a role if it comes to a dispute. As the use of disclaimers becomes more and more widespread people are more likely to expect them and take notice of them.

7.6 Contract formation

7.6.1 General rules

When it comes to concluding the electronic contract the following rules must be taken into account:

- Prior to the placement of the order appropriate, effective and accessible technical means that allow the identification and correction of input errors must be available.
- The vendor has to acknowledge the receipt of the recipient's order without undue delay and by electronic means.
- The order and the acknowledgement of receipt are deemed to be received when the parties to whom they are addressed are able to access them.

With regard to B2B contracting, the contracting partners are allowed to make other arrangements. The first two indents do not apply to contracts concluded exclusively by the exchange of electronic mail or by equivalent individual communications.[191]

The acknowledgement of the receipt may take the form of the on-line provision of the ordered service.[192]

---

[190] See Smith (2002), p. 456.

[191] Article 11(3) of Directive 2000/31/EC. See Section 7.7 for remarks on these exemptions.

[192] Recital 34 of Directive 2000/31/EC.

Means to correct input errors

To allow for correction of input errors, the ordering procedure can be equipped with an extra step where the clients' input is restated on the screen (a recapulative page) with a confirmation button and a button that allows the customer to erase (parts of) the input and re-enter it.[193]

According to the pre-contractual information duties the customer must be informed of how he can correct his input. At the moment a recapulative page is shown to the customer with the instruction that he should review and (if necessary) correct the information, both the opportunity to correct as well as the information on it are given at the same time.

7.6.2 Moment of contract formation

The E-commerce Directive explicitly does not harmonise the moment of contract formation. Former versions of the directive included a rule that specified the moment of conclusion of an electronic contract. In fact, the section on electronic contracting in former drafts was headed: *'Moment at which the contract is concluded'.*[194] This would have entailed a far-reaching harmonisation of European contract law with regard to the formation of electronic contracts. However, the heading now reads: *'Placing of the order'*, leaving the moment of contract formation up to Member States' law.

This entails that the directive does not establish the legal status of the order and the acknowledgement.[195] The consequences of these communications with regard to the conclusion of the contract are to be determined according to the rules of Member State law.

National laws have different rules with regard to the conclusion of contracts.[196] Although often related, the national rules can lead to different outcomes. A display of goods on a website is generally considered to be an invitation to treat according to English law, where Dutch law is inclined to qualify such a display as a public offer. According to Dutch law ordering the product can then be qualified as an acceptance of the offer resulting in a legally binding contract. Controversially, English law qualifies the customers' order as an 'offer to buy', requiring an extra step before the contract is formed: the acceptance of the vendor of the customers' offer. To avoid confusion as to the moment of contract formation, clarification of the legal consequences of the electronic

---

[193] In this manner: Noorda (2000), Van Esch (2001b).

[194] Amended proposal for a European Parliament and Council Directive on certain legal aspects of electronic commerce in the internal market, COM (1999) 427, OJ C 30, 5 February 1999, p. 4.

[195] Grosheide (2000), remarks (at p. 20) that *'from a dogmatic point of view it is not clear what kind of legal instrument the placing of the order provision (i.e. art. 11) has introduced'.*

[196] On the differences between legal systems with regard to formal and material validity of contracts see Van der Hof (2002), p. 17-24.

messages should be included in the information that states which technical steps must be followed to conclude the contract (see Section 7.3 above on information duties).

Moment of receipt

To determine the moment of contract formation it is relevant to know when the message containing the order or the acknowledgement of the order has legal effect. National laws generally have rules that indicate when a message has effect to determine the moment that the person sending the message is bound to it. For example the English 'mailbox rule' states that an acceptance of an offer has effect from the moment it is send (dropped in the mailbox) irrespective if it ever reaches the offeror.[197] Another variation is the 'reception theory': the acceptance of an offer has affect from the moment the party to whom it is addressed has received the message. This means the message is effective the moment the addressee takes notice of the message or from the moment the sender can reasonably expect that the addressee has taken notice of the message.[198]

For the electronic business environment the E-commerce Directive determines that the order and the acknowledgement of the order are deemed to be received when the parties to whom they are addressed are able to access them (in B2B relation it is allowed to make other arrangements with regard to this).

This means the electronic messages have legal effect the moment the message arrives in the electronic mailbox of the addressee. The directive does not state what these legal effects are. As was already noted above, the legal qualification of the messages (for example whether or not the receipt of the order creates a legally binding contract) is to be determined according to Member State law.

Contract law neutral

The directive states that the business organisation should send an acknowledgement of the receipt but does not mention if this affects the conclusion of the electronic contract. The E-commerce Directive also states the moment of receipt of the electronic messages, but not the legal consequences. The E-commerce Directive equally does not state any rules regarding the validity of the contract. Due to this lack of harmonisation introduced with regard to contracting the E-commerce Directive can be labelled 'contract law neutral'.[199]

---

[197] Zweigert & Kötz (1998), p. 358-359.

[198] Hartkamp & Tillema (1995), p. 59, Asser/Hartkamp (2001), p. 142-143.

[199] See also Kaufman Winn & Haubold (2002), p. 574.

7.7 Miscellaneous

7.7.1 Agreeing otherwise in B2B relations

With regard to several of the above-discussed duties professional partners are allowed to make other arrangements. This concerns the pre-contractual information duties concerning the contract formation, the duty to inform the contracting partner on codes of conduct, the duty to allow for input correction, the acknowledgement of the receipt of the order and the moment the messages are deemed to be received. In short, this means business partners can conclude a contract on how they wish to conclude their electronic contracts.

When using EDI this is common practice. An interchange agreement regulates the details for the individual contracts (also: transactions) that will be concluded using the (closed) network.[200]

In the internet environment, the relations are often *ad hoc*. It is then unlikely that there are any previous arrangements between the contracting partners.[201] To arrange the contracting procedure via internet a company can one-sidedly state that it will only do business under certain conditions. The potential contracting partner can then either accept those arrangements and do business or find a different business partner. This comes down to an implied consent to the contracting procedure.[202] Another way to make prior arrangements with regard to contracting can be the participation in an electronic marketplace. If an electronic marketplace supports on-line contracting it will commonly prescribe the procedure that needs to be followed by the participants of the market to come to a contract.[203] Upon entering the electronic marketplace the participants agree to the procedures of the electronic market.

7.7.2 The position of an electronic marketplace

An electronic marketplace is a forum where business partners can search for potential business partners. Advanced electronic marketplaces also allow for negotiation and conclusions of on-line contracts. Most electronic marketplaces can be approached using open networks. The electronic market has an intermediary position in bringing the contracting partners together and providing the infrastructure for electronic contracting. In registering with an electronic marketplace the participants agree with the rules set by the market-place. This agreement can be called a participation agreement. This participa-

---

[200] On interchange agreements see Van Esch & Prins (2002), p. 43-59.

[201] Mitrakas (1997), p. 150.

[202] *Cf.* Van Esch & Prins (2002), p. 45.

[203] On B2B markets and some legal implications see Ouwehand (2000).

tion agreement can include arrangements that are found in the traditional interchange agreements governing EDI.

However, the participation agreement is different in that it is concluded with the marketplace and not with the (future) business partners. This construction can lead to misunderstandings as regards the position of the marketplace as an intermediary. It is advisable that the legal position of each of the parties are well defined in the participation agreement so that there can be no misunderstandings about the responsibilities of the marketplace with regard to the contracts concluded between the participating parties. [204]

7.7.3 Individual communication

If the electronic contract is concluded exclusively using the exchange of e-mails or equivalent individual communications the information duties concerning the conclusion of the contract, the codes of conduct, the obligation with regard to the means of input correction and the obligation to acknowledge the receipt of the order do not apply.[205]

The intention of these exceptions appears to be exclusion of electronic contracting where these duties would be unnecessary or awkward. The recitals mention that the exception of the use of individual communication should not lead to a deliberate bypassing of the information requirements.[206] The wordings 'or equivalent individual communication' appear to be added to avoid technology specific legislation. The wordings are unnecessary if e-mail is defined in a broad manner such as was done in Directive 2002/58/EC. It was already noted that it is preferable to apply this definition in the context of the E-commerce Directive.

The exemptions for individual communications expressly do not affect contracts concluded by e-mail where the initial offer was made on a website. In that case the contract was not concluded exclusively with the use of e-mail.

The inclusion of these exemption for individual communications, at a late stage in the legislative process,[207] can be seen as an indication of the legislators' intention to capture all sorts of electronic contracting within the ambit of the E-commerce Directive and at the same time realising that the rules might have unwanted consequences for certain types of electronic communicating.

---

[204] In relation to this topic see: Stuurman & Wijnands (1998), they discuss agreements involving multiple parties in relation to EDI.

[205] Note that the rule concerning the moment the messages are deemed to be received applies to this type of communicating.

[206] Recital 39 of Directive 2000/31/EC.

[207] The provision was not included in the early proposals. It appeared in the Common position adopted by the Council on 28 February 2000, OJ C 128 of 8-5-2000.

7.7.4 Automated contracting and the use of agents

Automatic contracting without human intervention is possible, for example with the use of EDI or advanced electronic software agents. The use of automated transaction systems and so-called intelligent agents could lead to legal issues.[208]

If use is made of automatic contracting such as software tools to conclude contracts without human intervention, the user of the tool should see to it that it is programmed as such that the obligations prescribed by the E-commerce Directive can be fulfilled. [209] This means the agent negotiating a contract should for example be programmed to send an acknowledgement of an order. The consequences of the functioning of the agent, including any illegal actions, can be attributed to the user(s) of the electronic agents.[210]

7.7.5 Overview

Reading the duties that follow from the E-commerce Directive concerning e-contracting a general model of e-contracting can be derived. This is depicted below in figure 1.

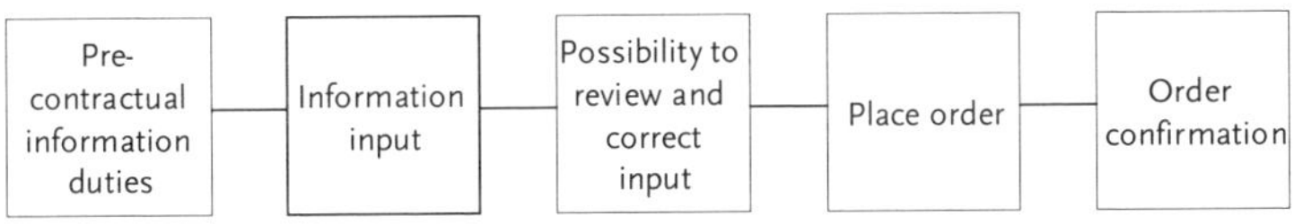

Figure 1: the contracting procedure as introduced by the E-commerce Directive

[208] *Cf.* Voulon (2002).

[209] See on this issue Lodder & Voulon (2002), p. 285.

[210] Allen & Widdison (1996), Van Esch (1999), p. 45-53 and Van Esch (2001b).

CHAPTER 3

The Distant Selling Directive

1 General

With regard to B2C contracts there are much more as well as more stringent rules that have to be taken into account by electronic vendors.[1] In the previous chapter it can be read that the E-commerce Directive does not allow deviation from the rules in B2C relations, while business partners – in some instances – are allowed to make other arrangements. Furthermore, all Member States have a body of mandatory consumer protection laws that need to be taken into account. According to the rules of private international law a consumer can often rely on the protective rules of its home state when involved in an international conflict (see Chapter 7 and 8 below for a discussion of several main rules of private international law). The country of origin principle of the E-commerce Directive does not offer relief here, because obligations concerning consumer contracts are explicitly excluded from the application of this principle.

Although large areas of consumer protection law are harmonised by the EU,[2] the measures often comprise minimum harmonisation, meaning that Member States are allowed to prescribe more stringent rules. Directive 97/7/EC[3] (the Distant Selling Directive) is such a minimum directive.[4]

The Distant Selling Directive covers contracts concerning goods or services concluded at a distance between a consumer and a supplier. This directive does not particularly target e-commerce; it sees to all kinds of techniques that allow distance contracting. Seen that electronic contracting as meant in this work is invariably contracting at a distance, the Distant Selling Directive is integrally applicable to B2C e-commerce.

At the time of drafting, there was no widespread use of electronic means to sell goods or services to consumers, but the drafters of the directive have shown awareness of the technical developments.[5] At present, the directive can be considered one of the core instruments regulating e-commerce.[6]

The Distant Selling Directive aims to protect the consumer that has no face-to-face contact with the vendor and – in case of goods – no opportunity to touch the goods that are sold. The directive prescribes a large amount of information duties to make sure the consumer has enough information to consider the distant contract. Adding to this, the consumer is awarded a period during which

1 *Cf.* Sander (2001).

2 De Cock Buning a.o. (2001).

3 Directive 97/7/EC of the European Parliament and of the Council of 20 May 1997 on the protection of consumers in respect of distance contracts, OJ L 144, 4-6-1997, p. 19.

4 Article 14 of Directive 97/7/EC, Straetmans (2000) at p. 321-322 discusses possible issues related to minimum harmonisation, for example how this relates to several other directives containing consumer protection rules.

5 See for example recitals 4, 6 and 7 of Directive 97/7/EC.

6 *Cf.* Dickie (1999), Salaün (1999).

he can withdraw from the contract. It was thought that consumers might enter into distant contracts too rashly and therefore they should be given the opportunity to change their mind. The Distant Selling Directive further addresses the performance of the distance contract, prohibits inertia selling and imposes the duty on the Member States to install appropriate measures to ensure redress in case of fraudulent use of payment cards.

The rights and obligations in the directive are of a binding nature. This means that the European consumer cannot waive the rights conferred on him by the national laws implemented as a result of this directive.[7] The Member States are to ensure that a choice of law does not interfere with these rights if the contract has a close relation with one or more Member States. This can affect choice of law clauses made by companies in contracts with consumers, even if the law of a non-Member State is chosen, the European consumer cannot lose the protection of the directive as long as the contract has a close connection with the EU.

2 Scope of applicability

2.1 Distant consumer contracts

The Distant Selling Directive is applicable to contracts concerning any goods or services concluded between a supplier and a consumer under an organised distance sales or service provision scheme run by the supplier, who, for the purpose of the contract, makes exclusive use of one or more means of distance communication up to and including the moment at which the contract is concluded.[8] Shortly, this means consumer contracts concluded without the parties being simultaneously present.[9]

Consumer

A consumer is a natural person acting outside his or her trade, business or profession.[10] Thus far, the European Court of Justice has upheld a narrow interpretation of the concept consumer as individuals acting for private (household) purposes.[11] Anyone acting out of reasons connected to professional purposes is

---

7 Article 12 of Directive 97/7/EC.

8 Article 2(1) of Directive 97/7/EC.

9 Recital 9 of Directive 97/7/EC.

10 Article 2(2) of Directive 97/7/EC. See also Article 2(e) of Directive 2000/31/EC, Article 2(b) of Directive 93/13/EC and Article 2 of Directive 85/577/EEC.

11 Case C-371/89 *Di Pinto* [1991] ECR I-1189 and Case C-45/96 *Dietzinger* [1998] ECR I-1199. A strict interpretation of the concept is also found in Case C-89/91 *Shearson* [1993] ECR I-139 and Case C-269/95 *Francesco Benincasa* v. *Dentalkit Srl* [1997] ECR I-3767 with regard to the 1968 Brussels Convention on Jurisdiction (now replaced by Regulation (EC) No. 44/2001).

excluded from the concept, even if their position is comparable to the position of a consumer.[12] A legal person cannot be considered a consumer,[13] not even if it is buying goods and services that are unrelated to the regular trade activities.

It should be noted that Member States possibly have different interpretations of the concept consumer; in some countries the concept can include legal entities and professionals.[14]

Organised distance sales or service provision scheme

The element organised distance sales or service provision scheme means to exclude sales on an occasional basis and outside a commercial structure from the scope of the directive.[15] This means that in case a consumer makes a telephone call to order a product from a shop-owner that normally sells his products from his physical shop this does not qualify as an 'organised distance sales or service provision scheme'. In such a situation, the shop-owner accepts the telephone order on an incidental basis, as where the Distant Selling Directive is meant for companies that systematically sell their products or services at a distance, for example by means of catalogue ordering by mail service or electronic ordering systems available via internet.

Questionable might be the situation where a company website has no electronic ordering procedure connected to it, but mentions contact information such as an e-mail address or a telephone number. Such a website is not necessarily an organised distance sales or service provision scheme. If the company systematically accepts orders via the contact information mentioned on the site, it is an organised distance sales scheme. If the website is solely meant for informational purposes and no orders (or only incidental distant orders are accepted) it is not an organised distant sales scheme. In such a situation it can be recommended to state clearly what the contact information is meant for: merely for information requests or also to place orders.

Means of distant communication

Up to and including the conclusion of the contract the seller must make exclusive use of means of distance communication. This refers to any means that, without the simultaneous physical presence of the supplier and the

---

12 Girot (2000), p. 75-78. Straetmans (2000), p. 315-316. For a treatise on the notion 'consumer' in community law see Mortelmans & Watson (1995).

13 Joined cases C-541/99 and C-542/99 (*Cape Snc-Idealservice*).

14 See Girot (2000), p. 78-88 on French, Dutch an English law and Hondius (2001), p. 461 citing an Italian case. See Van der Hof (2002) p. 25-34 on the concept 'consumer' in private international law in Europe and the United States.

15 *Cf.* recital 18 of Directive 2002/65/EC concerning distance marketing of consumer financial services. Directive 97/7/EG does not explain this notion.

consumer, may be used for the conclusion of a contract between those parties.[16] Annex 1 of the directive contains an indicative list of distant communication means. This open-ended list does not mention internet websites, but it mentions electronic mail. The definition is formulated in a technology neutral manner and it is without question that it covers internet websites with ordering procedures and any possible future electronic means that allow for distant selling.

2.2 Exemptions

The Distant Selling Directive does not apply to:[17]

- distant contracts relating to financial services,
- distant contracts concluded by means of automatic vending machines or automated commercial premises,
- distant contracts concluded with telecommunications operators through the use of public pay phones,
- distant contracts concluded for the construction and sale of immovable property or relating to other immovable property rights except for rental,[18]
- distant contracts concluded at an auction.

With regard to distant contracts concerning financial services the European legislator has adopted Directive 2002/65/EC[19] on the distance marketing of consumer financial services, which grants the consumer comparable rights as those granted by the Distant Selling Directive. Automatic vending machines refers (for example) to money distribution machines and ticket vending machines. As contracts related to immovable property are commonly associated with deeds drawn up and executed by notaries, this is thought to offer enough protection to the consumer.[20]

The exemption of distant contracts concluded at an auction is noteworthy. On internet the auction is a popular manner of vending. The highly successful auction site “eBay” is an illustration of this. eBay allows both incidental sellers and professional sellers to use the platform to sell their products. If it is not on an incidental bases, this can be seen as an organised distance sales scheme in the meaning of the directive. Nonetheless these contracts are explicitly excluded from the scope of the directive.

---

16 Article 2(4) of Directive 97/7/EC.

17 Article 3 of Directive 97/7/EC.

18 This is partly covered by Directive 94/47/EC of the European Parliament and the Council of 26 October 1994 on the protection of purchasers in respect of certain aspects of contracts relating to the purchase of the right to use immovable properties on a timeshare basis, OJ L 280 29-10-1994, p. 83 (the Timeshare Directive).

19 OJ L 271, 9-10-2002, p. 16.

20 Straetmans (2000), p. 316.

Additionally, for practical reasons,[21] several consumer contracts are excluded from the scope of some of the key provisions of the directive. This concerns:[22]

- contracts for the supply of foodstuffs, beverages or other goods intended for everyday consumption supplied to the home of the consumer, to his residence or to his workplace by regular roundsmen,
- contracts for the provisions of accommodation, transport, catering or leisure services, where the supplier undertakes, when the contract is concluded, to provide these services on a specific date or within a specific period.

The provisions concerning prior information, information confirmation, right of withdrawal and time limit set for the performance are not applicable with regard to these contracts. The contracts referred to in the first indent include for example delivery services of bakeries, the second indent covers for example hotel bookings and travel arrangements. This last exemption is unfortunate as hotel bookings and plane tickets are increasingly booked via internet. Nonetheless consumers booking on-line do not enjoy the protection of several key provisions of the Distant Selling Directive.

3 Pre-contractual information duties

Additional to the general information requirements and the pre-contractual information requirements summed up in the E-commerce Directive, the electronic vendor dealing with consumers has to comply with the information requirements of the Distant Selling Directive. Prior to the conclusion of the contract, the consumer has to be provided with the following information:

a) the identity of the supplier,
b) in case prior payments are requested: the suppliers' address,
c) the characteristics of the goods or services,
d) the price of the goods or services including all taxes,
e) delivery costs (where appropriate),
f) the arrangements for payment, delivery or performance,
g) the existence of the right of withdrawal (where appropriate),[23]
h) the cost of using the means of distance communication, if different from the basic rate,
i) the period for which the offer or the price remains valid,

---

[21] *Cf.* Straetmans (2000), p. 316.

[22] Article 3(2) of Directive 97/7/EC.

[23] If the consumer does not have this right he need not be informed of it. See Section 5 below on the right of withdrawal.

j) if the contract concerns the permanent or recurrent delivery of goods or services, the minimum duration of the contract.

This does not apply to: [24]

- contracts for the supply of foodstuffs, beverages or other goods intended for everyday consumption supplied to the home of the consumer, to his residence or to his workplace by regular roundsmen, and
- contracts for the provision of accommodation, transport, catering or leisure services, where the supplier undertakes, when the contract is concluded, to provide these services on a specific date or within a specific period.

There are several specifications as to how the pre-contractual information must be provided, namely:[25]

1) in good time before the conclusion of the contract,
2) the commercial purpose of the information must be clear,
3) in a clear and comprehensible manner,
4) in a way appropriate to the means of distant communication used,
5) with due regard to principles of good faith in commercial transactions,
6) with due regard to the principles governing the protection of those unable to give their consent, such as minors.

Seen these specifications, it is likely that more stringent demands will be placed on the presentation of these information duties of the Distant Selling Directive compared to the information duties of the E-commerce Directive, which (only) contains some general statements on the presentation of the information. The general information requirements of the E-commerce Directive have to be provided 'easily, directly and permanently', and the pre-contractual information duties of the E-commerce Directive are to be provided 'clearly, comprehensible and unambiguously'. In practice it might not be obvious how to distinct between these differentiations in how the information should be presented.

Whether or not a hyperlink would suffice for the presentation of the information duties of the Distant Selling Directive is debatable. This depends to a large extent on the design of the website and the ordering procedure.[26] If the information is not presented integrally during the ordering procedure, at least clearly labelled links should be provided, for example a link labelled 'delivery costs', 'information on the right of withdrawal'. The information or the hyperlinks

[24] Article 3(2) of Directive 97/7/EC, see on these exemptions Section 2 above.

[25] Article 4 of Directive 97/7/EC.

[26] Dickie (1999) feels that it would be fair to pay extra attention to the presentation of the information on the right of withdrawal as this is probably the most important provision of the directive and its value is diminished if consumers are not aware of it (p. 96).

to the information should be presented in such a manner during the ordering procedure that the consumer cannot overlook it. Although it cannot be assumed that consumers will read all the information presented to them, the information should be presented so that it is noticeable and likely to be read.

Name and address of the company are already provided to the consumer as a result of the general information duties of the E-commerce Directive. In my view it would be superfluous to provide this information a second time, as long as the presentation of the name and address meet are properly presented (taking into account the requirements of the Distant Selling Directive on this point).

Some of the information, for example the existence of the right of withdrawal is likely to be stated in the general terms of the company. A mere reference to the general terms where information on the right of withdrawal is stated is somewhat meagre and risks of being insufficient. In addition to this, it is preferable to place hyperlinks with relevant labels during the ordering procedure.

A German court formulated strict demands with regard to these information requirements.[27] It held that the consumer should inevitably come across the information. A link at the bottom of the pages of the website labelled 'contact', leading to the information was held to be insufficient.

OLG Karlsruhe 27-3-2002, accessable on <www.jurpc.de> under web-dok nr, 245/2002

A German website offers the possibility to participate in lottery games. On the left hand site of the site, a menu is available where the general conditions, including name of the company, can be accessed. Both at the top and at the bottom, of the pages of the site, several links are available, under which a link labelled 'contact'. The link gives access to an on-line form as well as name and address information and the names of the members of the board (under the heading ('impressum').

The German court held that the manner in which name and address of the company were presented on the site did not satisfy the requirements laid down in the 'Frenabsatzvertrag' (which implements the Directive 97/7/EC on distant selling in the German law).

This law requires that the information must be available in a clear and comprehensible manner. The court finds that the consumer who buys a lotto ticket via the site should inevitably come across this information. It held that both the link 'contact' and the heading 'impressum' were open to misinterpretation to the consumer.

Additionally, the court held that the company did not sufficiently supply information on the main characteristics of the service. This information was available in the standard terms. These terms were accessible via a hyperlink, but this was considered insufficient to satisfy the information requirements of the distant selling law.

[27] OLG Karlsruhe, 27-3-2002, 6 U 200/01, available on <www.jurpc.de>, Web-dok. 245/2002, abs. 1-23. On this case: Voulon & Lodder (2002).

4 Post-contractual information duties

4.1 Information confirmation

Most of the information that must be provided to the consumer according to the previous Section must be confirmed after the conclusion of the contract. The consumer should receive a written confirmation, or confirmation in another durable medium, of the information enumerated under (a) through (f). This should be provided in good time during the performance of the contract and at the latest at the time of delivery, except when the goods are delivered to third parties[28] or when the information has already been given to the consumer in such a form in an earlier stage.[29]

Additionally, *in any event* the following must be provided:[30]

1) written information on the conditions and procedures for exercising the right of withdrawal,[31]
2) the geographical address where the consumer can address his complaints,
3) information on after-sales services and guarantees,
4) how to cancel the contract, if it is of unspecified duration or of a duration exceeding one year.

The composition of the article indicates that the information duties under (1) to (4) do not have to be provided written or on a durable medium in good time during the performance of the contract. Except for the word 'written' with regard to the first requirement (information on how to exercise the right of withdrawal), there is no indication on how and when this information should be provided.

The paper link

The word 'written' mentioned under (1) has been interpreted by some Member States as an indication that the information has to be provided on paper and may not be provided on another durable medium. For example, the Dutch legislator explicitly excludes the possibility to provide this information on a durable medium.[32] The Explanatory Memorandum accompanying the Dutch implementation law[33] confirms that this information must indeed be provided in a paper form ('schriftelijk') and that this is in accordance of the wordings of the directive.

---

28 For example an electronic flower delivery service.

29 Article 5(1) of Directive 97/7/EC, first part of the article.

30 Article 5(1) of Directive 97/7/EC, second part of the article.

31 The consumer must also be informed when he may *not* exercise the right of withdrawal.

32 Article 7:46c lid 2 of the Dutch Civil Code.

33 *Kamerstukken II* 1999/2000, 26 861, nr. 3, p. 20.

A different viewpoint is found in English law (consumer protection regulations 2000) where it is stated that notice on the right to cancel is properly given if sent by hand delivery, post, fax or e-mail.[34]

If the information is stated in the standard terms of the company, the standard terms must be communicated in accordance with the rules of the Distant Selling Directive.

Not complying with the information requirements has consequences for the time period during which the consumer may exercise his right of withdrawal (discussed below).

Other concerns

The Distant Selling Directive leaves the matter of the used language for the contract to the Member States.[35] One has to keep in mind that according to Directive 1999/44/EC on the sale of consumer goods and associated guarantees[36] the Member States in which the goods are marketed may provide that the guarantee is drafted in one or more of the official languages of the Community. This directive also states that the guarantee shall be made available to the consumer on his request, in writing or featuring in another durable medium available and accessible to the consumer. [37] The supplied information must also comply with other relevant Community rules and in particular the rules stipulated in the Directive 84/450/EEC on misleading advertising.[38]

4.2 Exemptions

The post-contractual information duties are not applicable in case of services provided on only one occasion with the distant communication means and where the consumer pays for the costs of communication. This includes for example on-line traffic and route information, the use of an on-line catalogue, or some other form of free on-line information provision. However, the company is still obliged to state a geographic address where the consumer may address his complaints.

Also excluded are contracts for delivery by regular roundsmen of food and drinks or other everyday consumption products, and contracts for the provision of accommodation, transport, catering or leisure services, which are to be provided at a specific date or within a specific period.[39]

---

34 Simmons & Simmons (2001), p. 20.

35 Recital 8 of Directive 97/7/EC.

36 This directive aims to establish a minimum level of consumer protection relating to the non-conformity with the contract of goods sold to the consumer.

37 Article 6 of Directive 1999/44/EC.

38 Recital 11 of Directive 97/7/EC.

39 Article 3(2) of Directive 97/7/EC, discussed above in Section 2.

4.3 Durable medium

It was stated that (at least) the information under (a) through (f) must be provided in writing or in another durable medium. The wordings *or in another durable medium* indicate that *written* refers to the use of paper. A definition for the concept durable medium can be found in the Directive on the Distant Marketing of Financial Services:[40]

'Any instrument which enables the consumer to store information addressed personally to him in a way accessible for future reference for a period of time adequate for the purposes of the information and which allows the unchanged reproduction of the information stored.'[41]

According to the recitals of the directive on financial services durable mediums include in particular floppy disks, CD-ROMs, DVDs and the hard drive of the consumer's computer on which e-mail is stored. It is also stated that durable mediums do not include internet websites unless they fulfil the criteria contained in the definition of a durable medium.[42]

In practice, it is common to use e-mail to confirm the contract as well as the contract terms to the consumer. As the status of an e-mail message as a durable medium is questionable, it is advisable to include the statement that the client should save the information for later reference for example by printing or storing the information on the hard drive. The electronic vendor is then subjected to the cooperation of the consumer.

From literature it can be learned that several legal authors have argued that e-mail can be considered a durable medium,[43] while others argue that some additional measures are needed.[44] In any event, seen the common use of e-mail for this purpose as well as the possibilities offered by e-mail programmes to store e-mail messages it is a practical solution to accept e-mail as sufficient.

---

[40] Directive 2002/65/EC of the European Parliament and of the Council of 23 September 2002 concerning the distance marketing of consumer financial services and amending Council Directive 90/619/EEC and Directives 97/7/EC and 98/27/EC, OJ L 271, 9-10-2002, p. 16.

[41] Article 2(f) of Directive 2002/65/EC.

[42] Recital 20 of Directive 2002/65/EC. With regard to the concept durable medium in German law, the term durable (*dauerhaft*) is related to whether or not the data on the medium can be manipulated by the receiving end; see Hoeren (2004), p. 275.

[43] Loos (2001), p. 132, Olsen (2001), p. 157, Dickie (1999), p. 96, Linneman & Volgenant (2000), p. 22. They argue e-mail should be accepted as a durable medium because this can be stored on the hard drive of the consumer or printed.

[44] Sander & Bartels (1998), p. 410, they argue that strictly taken an e-mail message is not a durable medium, but seen the purpose, *i.e.* that the information should be available at a later point in time, an e-mail can be enough.

Simply confirming the information on screen is clearly insufficient.[45] To accommodate mobile commerce, sms-messages should be considered to fall within the scope of the concept e-mail.[46]

It would seem fair to place more (or less) stringent demands with regard to the quality of the durable medium used, depending on the nature of the contract. For example if the contract involves long term obligations or considerable amounts of money a paper letter confirming the contract and explaining the terms and conditions is in place.

The point of this provision is that the consumer should be able to check the information at a later stage. This can be used as a criterion to determine whether or not the information was given in a sufficient manner.

5 Right of withdrawal

5.1 Cooling-off period

An important right granted to the consumer by the Distant Selling Directive is the right of withdrawal.[47] This right entails that for a period of at least seven working days the consumer can withdraw from the contract without penalty and without giving any reason. This period is also referred to as the 'cooling off period'.[48] The underlying thought is that the consumer cannot actually touch the product or – as stated by the recitals – *'ascertain the nature of the service'*[49] when contracting at a distance.

The moment the seven-day period starts differs depending on whether the contract concerns goods or services. If the contract concerns goods, the time period for exercising the right starts on the day the consumer has received the goods. If the supplier has failed to provide the consumer with the information confirmation discussed the previous Section, the time period during which the right can be exercised will be three months. If the supplier provides the post-contractual information within this three-month period, the seven-day period begins from that moment.

The period for the exercise of the right of withdrawal in the case of services begins from the day of conclusion of the contract. Or, if the post-contractual information is supplied after the conclusion of the contract, from the day the consumer receives this confirmation, provided that the confirmation was

---

45 *Cf.* Van Esch en Bramer (2000), p. 286; see also Bramer (2000), p. 396.

46 Directive 2002/58/EC on privacy and electronic communications defines e-mail in this broad manner: including all types of electronic messaging, see below Section 3 of Chapter 5.

47 Article 6 of Directive 97/7/EC.

48 On cooling-off periods see Rekaiti & Van den Bergh (2000).

49 Recital 14 of Directive 97/7/EC.

supplied within three months after the conclusion of the contract. As was the case with contracts concerning goods, the time period is three months beginning from the day of conclusion of the contract, if the information confirmation is not supplied as required. When the supplier supplies the required information within this three-month period after all, this triggers the beginning of the 7-day period. The frame below gives an overview of these different time periods.

Overview of the different periods during which the right of withdrawal may be exercised

Goods

- 7 working days from the day of receipt of the goods provided that the post-contractual information duties are fulfilled
- 3 months from the day that the goods are received, when the post-contractual information duties are not fulfilled
- 7 working days from the moment the post-contractual duties are fulfilled within those three months.

Services

- 7 working days from the day of the conclusion of the contract provided that the post contractual information duties are fulfilled
- 7 working days from the day that the post-contractual information duties are fulfilled if the confirmation is provided after the conclusion of the contract (not exceeding three months)
- 3 months from the conclusion of the contract when the post-contractual information duties are not fulfilled
- 7 working days from the moment that the post-contractual information duties are fulfilled within those three months.

To indicate the beginning of the cooling-off period, the directive uses the wordings 'from the day'. These wordings raise the question whether the counting starts *on the day* of delivery (in case of goods) or contract conclusion (in case of services) or if the counting starts *on the day after.* The Dutch language version of the Distant Selling Directive uses the wordings *'op de dag'* ('on the day') which is a strong indication that the counting starts the same day as the receipt of the goods or the conclusion of the contract related to services.[50]

5.2 The exercise of the right of withdrawal

If the consumer chooses to exercise his right of withdrawal the supplier shall be obliged to reimburse the sums paid by the consumer free of charge. Such reimbursement must be carried out as soon as possible and in any case within 30 days. The only charge that may be made to the consumer is the

50 The French language version uses *'a compter du jour'* and the German version *'mit dem Tag.'*

direct cost of returning the goods.[51] These wordings indicate that the only financial risk for the consumer is the cost for returning the goods back to the company.

Direct cost of returning the goods refers to the postal charges for returning the good. These charges are commonly paid at the post office upon sending the goods. The 'charge' therefore does not necessarily refer to charges made by the company selling the goods. For the company this means all fees paid including the initial delivery costs must be reimbursed to the consumer. According to the above mentioned information duties the consumer has been informed about the existence of the right of withdrawal and how it can be exercised. The consumer must also be informed if he does not have this right.

5.3 Exemptions

With regard to the following situations, the consumer may not exercise the right of withdrawal:[52]

- with regard to services, if performance has begun, with the consumers' agreement, before the end of the seven working day period,
- if the price for the supply of goods or services is dependent on fluctuations in the financial market which cannot be controlled by the supplier,
- for the supply of goods made to the consumer's specifications or clearly personalised,
- for the supply of goods which, by reason of their nature, cannot be returned or are liable to deteriorate or expire rapidly,[53]
- for the supply of audio or video recordings or computer software which were unsealed by the consumer,[54]
- for the supply of newspapers, periodicals and magazines,
- for gaming and lottery services,
- contracts for the supply of foodstuffs, beverages, or other goods intended for everyday consumption supplied to the home of the consumer, to his residence or to his workplace by regular roundsmen,
- contracts for the provision of accommodation, transport, catering or leisure services, where the supplier undertakes, to provide these services on a specific date or within a specific period.

This does not preclude that the electronic vendor is allowed to offer his customers the right of withdrawal with regard to these contracts, for example as an extra service, even if he is not strictly obliged to do so.

---

51 Article 6(2) of Directive 97/7/EC.

52 Article 6(3) and Article 3(2) of Directive 97/7/EC.

53 It can be debated if digital goods (or: soft products) can fall within the ambit of this exemption.

54 Since no reference to either goods or services is made it can be assumed that this also covers breaking digital seals.

If the price of the goods or services is covered by credit granted either by the supplier or by a third party the credit agreement shall be cancelled without any penalty if the consumer exercises his right of withdrawal. The Member States shall determine the details regarding the cancellation of the credit agreement.[55]

The directive is silent with regard to the obligations of the consumer in relation to the exercise of his right of withdrawal. Besides the obligation to pay the cost of returning the good and the stipulation that audio and video recordings may not be unsealed, there is no stipulation on how fast the consumer should return the goods, nor if the goods should be in unopened packing or unused state.

5.4 Soft products

To determine the period during which the consumer can exercise his right of withdrawal in relation to soft products it is necessary to determine if such products are to be considered goods or services. If the soft products are considered goods, the period starts from the day of receipt and if they are services, the period starts from the day of the conclusion of the contract. The directive does not contain clues as to how this should be solved. In my view, an important characteristic of a good is its tangible nature. Soft products consist of bits and bites. Because no tangibles exchange hands, the delivery of bits and bites is the provision of a service. A consequence of this line of thought is, that if software is delivered on a CD by mail, it can be considered a good and if it is delivered electronically, it is a service. A judgment of the European Court of Justice is needed to resolve this.

Another problem with regard to soft products is the exercise of the right of withdrawal. Once they have been received on a computer system they can be deleted, but it is odd to speak of 'returning' the product in this respect. An example of a store that delivers digitally is the American based music store iTunes.[56] Visitors of the site can buy a song with a mouse click. The song is then delivered through the internet connection on the hard disc of the customer. The distant selling offers several possibilities to deny the customer the right of withdrawal in this setting. First, if the soft product is digitally sealed[57] breaking the digital seal means the right of withdrawal can no longer be invoked. It is also possible to consider the playing of the song as a form of breaking the seal and thereby forfeiting the right of withdrawal. Second, In the event that the soft products are qualified as a good, it can also be argued that these products 'by reason of their nature' cannot be returned. A third option is to argue that service

[55] Article 6(4) of Directive 97/7/EC.

[56] Available at <www.itunes.com>.

[57] This can be achieved with digital rights management techniques.

provision has begun with the consumers' consent, therewith forfeiting the right of withdrawal.

Sellers of digital products can make use of digital rights management techniques to limit the use of the digital product. A digital right management technique can consist of adding a code to the product that causes the product to become useless after a certain amount of time or a certain number of playing.[58]

5.5 Overview

Looking back at the contract model that was presented at the end of Chapter 2, it can be noted that the Distant Selling Directive adds several obligations to the contracting procedure. The model can be extended with these duties. Resulting in the overview below, which depicts the B2C electronic contracting procedure according to the E-commerce Directive and the Distant Selling Directive.

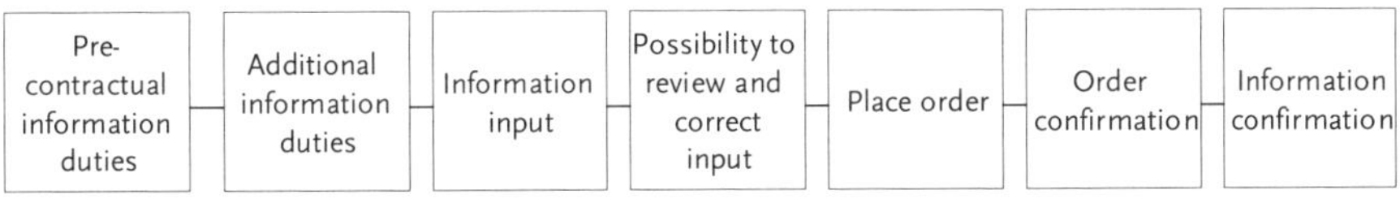

Figure 2: overview of the different steps for the conclusion of an electronic B2C contract

6 Additional rights

Besides the extensive information duties and the right of withdrawal the Distant Selling Directive grants the consumer rights relating to the performance, payment with cards and inertia selling. These rights do not in particular affect the electronic selling of goods and services to consumers, but are relevant for selling at a distance in general, including electronic selling.

Performance

Unless otherwise agreed, the contract must be performed within 30 days from the day following the day on which the consumer forwarded his order. If the ordered goods or services are unavailable, the consumer must be informed and if necessary refunded within 30 days. This is not applicable to:[59]

- contracts for the supply of foodstuffs, beverages, or other goods intended for everyday consumption supplied to the home of the consumer, to his residence or to his workplace by regular roundsmen,

[58] There are many interesting legal aspects with regard to digital rights management techniques, but the discussion of these goes beyond the scope of this research.

[59] Article 3(2) of Directive 97/7/EC.

- contracts for the provision of accommodation, transport, catering or leisure services, where the supplier undertakes, to provide these services on a specific date or within a specific period.

In case the goods or services are unavailable, and if allowed by Member State law, the consumer may be provided with goods or services of equivalent quality and price. The consumer should be informed about this possibility in a clear and comprehensible manner prior to the conclusion of the contract. In the event that the consumer exercises his right of withdrawal with regard to such goods of equivalent quality all costs (including the costs of returning the goods to the vendor) are to be borne by the vendor.[60]

This also applies to the mentioned exemptions. Only in case of outdoor leisure events, by way of exception and under specific circumstances the supplier can be freed from the obligation of informing the client of any unavailability of the service and refund any paid sums. This exception accommodates companies that organize activities that are dependable on weather conditions.[61]

Payment by card

In case of fraudulent use of payment cards, the Member States are to ensure that the consumer can request cancellation of the payment made in relation to the distant contract. Any sums paid should be returned to the consumer.[62] Depending on how this obligation is implemented by the Member States the risk of the fraudulent use could lie with the electronic vendor. If payments by card are accepted in relation to electronic contracts, the electronic vendor is advised to take security measures to avoid fraudulent use of the credit card information.[63]

Inertia selling

It is prohibited to supply goods or services to a consumer and request payment if the consumer did not order anything. In case a vendor provides any unsolicited goods or services, the consumer cannot be made to pay for anything. Not responding to the unwanted provision does not mean the consumer consents to a contract.[64]

---

60 Article 7 of Directive 97/7/EC.

61 Straetmans (2000) (at p. 320) mentions the cancellation of tennis matches due to rain at Wimbledon and hot air balloon trips in this context.

62 Article 8 of Directive 97/7/EC.

63 Reich (2001) feels that the protection against fraudulent use of the cards is not sufficient to protect the consumer in case of prepayment by credit cards. He argues (at p. 174) that if the consumer exercises his right of withdrawal after prepayment by card he can experience serious difficulties in getting his money back.

64 Article 9 of Directive 97/7/EC.

CHAPTER 4

The Privacy Directive

1 General

The advent of information technology, and in its wake e-commerce, have led to renewed possibilities with regard to collecting and using information about individuals for commercial purposes.[1] E-commerce activities are likely to involve the handling of personal information such as name, address, personal preferences and customer profiles. Often, the personal information is needed simply to perform the electronic contract, for example to deliver the electronically ordered goods or to give a personalised advice. Most e-commerce websites collect personal data when the customer is ready to order a product or service. The customer is then commonly presented with an on-line form that needs to be filled in.

Internet technology allows business organisations to track the online behaviour of customers and construct detailed profiles.[2] Such information can be used to design and target specific advertisements. Internet websites can offer free-coupons, games or prices in exchange for the personal information of the visitor. Sometimes a website requires the visitor to register before access to (parts of) the information on the site is granted. This means a visitor has to enter some personal information and obtain a password.[3]

Personal information and the therewith-connected privacy of European citizens are valued highly by the European legislator. The subject is addressed in Directive 95/46/EC[4] (the Privacy Directive).[5] The aim of the directive is to protect the fundamental rights and freedoms of natural persons, and in particular their right to privacy with respect to the processing of personal data as well as ensure the free flow of personal data between Member States.[6] The relevance

---

1 Prins & Schreuders (1998), at p. 436 feel that the possibilities of collecting information via internet entail that privacy and internet can hardly be reconciled.

2 The website of the CNIL, the French data protection authority, demonstrates what information can be traced while you are surfing and how this is done: on <www.cnil.fr> click the English flag for the English version and follow the link *'your traces'*.

3 Visitors can of course enter a fantasy name and false address information. It can be easy to assume a fake identity on internet. The legal consequences of assuming such a fake identity are not considered in this work.

4 Directive 95/46/EC of the European Parliament and of the Council of 24 October 1995 on the protection of individuals with regard to the processing of personal data and the free movement of such data, OJ L 281, 23-11-1995, p. 31.

5 On the Privacy Directive: Bergkamp & Dhont (2000), Dickie (1999), Lloyd (1996), Bainbridge (1996) (with a contribution on the background of the directive by N. Platten), in relation to EDI: Walden (1996).

6 Article 1 of Directive 95/46/EC.

of this directive for e-commerce has been underlined by the Working Party installed according to Article 29 of the Privacy Directive.[7]

The Privacy Directive enumerates a limited number of grounds on which personal data may be legally processed. Furthermore, the directive states the obligations of the data collector as well as the rights of the persons whose information is being handled. Furthermore, the Privacy Directive states general rules with regard to the lawfulness of processing of personal data. The Member States are to determine more precisely the conditions under which the processing is lawful.[8]

Less relevant for e-commerce activities are the rules with regard to special categories of data such as information relating to racial or ethnic origin, political opinions, religious or philosophical beliefs, trade-union membership and concerning health or sex life.[9] If an organisation handles such delicate information, strict rules have to be taken into account. The directive also has consequences for activities that are exploited by list brokers, such as the selling or hiring of address lists.[10]

To ensure that the personal data remain adequately safeguarded beyond the borders of the EU, the Privacy Directive states that the transfer of personal data to countries outside the EU can only be allowed if these countries provide for an adequate level of protection.[11] The following Sections focus on the rules of the Privacy Directive that are particularly relevant with regard to e-commerce.[12]

2 Scope of applicability

2.1 Processing of personal data

The Privacy Directive applies to processing of personal data wholly or partly by automatic means, and the processing otherwise than by automatic means of personal data which form part of a filing system or are intended

---

7 See documents of the Article 29 Working Party: *Processing of Personal Data on the Internet*, adopted on 3 February 1999, 5013/99/EN/final, WP 16. See also Opinion 1/2000 on certain data protection aspects of electronic commerce, adopted on 3 February 2000, 5007/00/EN/final, WP 28.

8 Article 5 of Directive 95/46/EC.

9 Article 8 of Directive 95/46/EC.

10 See on this topic: Van Eijk & Van Helden (2001).

11 Article 25 of Directive 95/46/EC. The transfer of data will not be further discussed in this work. On this topic: Aldhouse (1999). See also Working Document, *Transfers of personal data to third countries: Applying Articles 25 and 26 of the EU data protection directive*, document of the Article 29 Working Party, WP 12.

12 This discussion does not go into the rules with regard to sensitive data, ethnic origin, political opinions, religious beliefs and health related information. See on this topic Bainbridge 1996.

to form part of a filing system.[13] The recitals stress that the scope of the protection does not depend on the techniques used. With regard to manual processing the applicability of the directive is restricted to filing systems, *i.e.* a set of data that is structured according to specific criteria that allow easy access to the information. The concepts 'personal data' and 'processing' need to be discussed in more detail to obtain a better view of the scope of applicability of the directive.

Personal data are defined as:

'any information relating to an identified or identifiable natural person ('data subject'); an identifiable person is one who can be identified directly or indirectly, in particular by reference to an identifiable number or to one or more factors specific to his physical, physiological, mental, economic, cultural or social identity'.[14]

In other words, information related to persons can be considered personal data when it is possible to identify the person 'behind' the information. To determine if this is possible account should be taken of all the means that are likely to be used to identify the person.[15] Examples of personal data are: name, address, but also a telephone number, a licence plate number, a zip code or a customer number.

Not everyone has the possibility to link certain information to an individual. If someone does not have the reasonable means to recover the identity of the persons 'behind' the data he is handling, the data do not represent personal data to the person handling the data. This means the same information can be personal data in the hands of one organisation, but not necessarily in another. Information consisting of sound and image relating to natural persons is explicitly included in the scope of the directive.[16] The person to whom the data are related is referred to as the data subject. The Privacy Directive protects natural persons and is therefore only relevant for B2C e-commerce.

For some information it is not obvious whether or not it constitutes personal data: with regard to e-mail addresses, IP-numbers and cookies it can be debatable whether these constitute personal data.

An e-mail address constitutes personal data if the identity of the user of the address can be discovered without too much trouble. The individual can be easily identified if the address contains the name of the user and the organisation (or provider) that hosts the e-mail account, for example: 'm.y.schaub@utwente.nl'. But it is not always possible to uncover the identity of the person behind an e-mail address. A hotmail account allows the user to use

---

[13] Article 3(2) of Directive 95/46/EC.

[14] Article 2(a) of Directive 95/46/EC.

[15] Recital 26 of Directive 95/46/EC.

[16] Recital 14-17 of Directive 95/46/EC.

a nickname.[17] Hotmail users are required to enter personal data, but filling in false information does not hinder the use of the e-mail account. If the e-mail address is collected in combination with other personal data such as name and address, for example in the context of a sale, the e-mail address can be considered personal data even if there is no name in the address itself. A general address such as <info@company.com> generally does not constitute personal data.

The person connected to an IP-number (usually) cannot be identified directly. However, it is possible for an ISP to link the number to a certain computer and therewith to a person, rendering the number personal data in the meaning of the directive.[18]

Many websites make use of cookies. A cookie is a small amount of computer code installed on the PC during a website visit. The cookie is able to store information relating to the user of that PC and the website he visited. The use of cookies is regarded a privacy issue, but it is uncertain if the use of cookies can be considered processing of personal data in the meaning of the Privacy Directive.[19] The uncertainty on the legal position of cookies has been resolved as Directive 2002/58/EC (see Chapter 5) specifically deals with this issue.

Processing means:

'any operation or set of operations which is performed upon personal data, whether or not by automatic means, such as collection, recording, organisation, storage, adaptation or alteration, retrieval, consultation, use, disclosure by transmission, dissemination or otherwise making available, alignment or combination, blocking, erasure or destruction.[20]

Thus, virtually everything that is done with personal data is considered to be processing of that data. As soon as a customer visits the companies' website the processing can commence.[21] A common feature on e-commerce websites is the request to the visitor to type in personal information in order to create a personal account. Mentioning the names of employees and placing their photo's on the internet also falls within the ambit of the directive. The European Court of Justice confirmed that referring to persons by name or by other means on

---

17 Free e-mail accounts can be obtained at: <www.hotmail.com>.

18 *Privacy on the Internet, An integrated EU Approach to On-line Data Protection*, Working Document 37 of the Article 29 Data Protection Working Party, p. 21.

19 Gauthronet & Drouard (2001) state (at p. 81) that from a strictly legal point of view, cookies do not necessarily process personal data, see also Bergkamp & Dhont (2000), p. 75.

20 Article 2(b) of Directive 95/46/EC.

21 Consumers International (2001b) reports that over two thirds of the sites assessed in their study collected some sort of personal data.

internet websites constitutes processing of personal data wholly or partly by automatic means.[22]

Controller

The directive uses the term controller to indicate the user of the information. The controller is the person or organisation that determines the purpose and the means of the data processing. With regard to e-commerce this will normally be the business organisation providing the electronic service. The controller is primary responsible to ensure that the processing of the personal data within his company is in accordance with the rules of the privacy legislation.

In case of an electronically concluded contract, several parties can be involved with the handling of personal information. There is the company itself, but also intermediaries such as the ISPs that grant access and provide for the transportation of the information, possibly a bank is involved to arrange payment and a carrier to deliver the goods. In such situations, determining the controller of the personal data can be tricky, several controllers are involved with the handling of personal data in the completion of the whole process.[23] This work will only consider the obligations of the company that concludes the contract with the consumer. The position of the other parties is beyond the scope of this research.

Processor

The processor is the person or organisation that executes the processing on behalf of the controller. If the controller has outsourced the processing to another person or organisation, such as an application service provider, this ASP is the processor. The controller is responsible for the compliance with the privacy rules and should see to it that the processor installs the proper measures.

Geographical applicability

Article 4 of the Privacy Directive mentions three reference points for determining the applicable privacy legislation to the activities of a data controller: (1) country of establishment, (2) private international law, and (3) the location of the technical equipment.

Ad 1) The country of establishment

The controller has to comply with the privacy legislation installed pursuant to the Privacy Directive of the Member State of establishment. This rule is similar to the country of origin principle of the E-commerce Directive, but no

---

[22] Case C-101/01 *Bodil Lindqvist*, judgment of 6-11-2003, available on <http://curia.eu.int>.

[23] Bergkamp & Dhont (2000), p. 76-77, Berkvens & Prins (2002), p. 336-337.

principle of mutual recognition is formulated here. With regard to the term 'establishment' the recitals mention stable arrangements, referring to physical presence of the controller in the Member State. Furthermore, the recitals state that the legal form of the establishment is not the determining factor. Decisive is whether or not there are stable physical arrangements that imply the effective and real exercise of activities. The presence of a subsidiary office in a Member State can trigger the applicability of the privacy rules of that Member State.

Ad 2) Private international law

If the controller is not established in a Member State, it can still be subject to the laws of that state by virtue of private international law. Rules of private international law can amongst others be found in the Rome Convention (see Chapter 8).

Ad 3) Location of the technical equipment

If the controller is established outside the EU, but uses equipment situated on the territory of a Member State, the controller has to comply with the privacy laws of that Member State, except if the equipment is solely used for transit purposes. With regard to internet 'use of equipment' is not a very fortunate point of reference. It is not common to use the location of the internet servers as a criterion to determine the applicable law. The E-commerce Directive explicitly states that the location of the technology is not the place of establishment of a service provider (see the discussion of establishment in Section 3.5 of Chapter 2).[24] The Commission has admitted that the element 'use of equipment' is not easy to operate in this context and in need of further clarification.[25]

According to the recitals this rule should prevent that European individuals lack the protection of the directive because the controller is established outside the EU. It has been argued that placing cookies on the PC of an internet surfer within the EU could mean that European privacy laws apply. Placing a cookie involves using the hardware of the surfer, which can be considered equipment located within the EU and triggering the applicability of the European data protection laws.[26] However, whether the placing cookies can be considered to be processing of personal data within the meaning of the directive is debatable.

---

[24] See also Bergkamp & Dhont (2000), p. 99.

[25] First report on the implementation of the Data Protection Directive (95/46/EC), Brussels, 15-5-2003, COM (2003) 265 final, p. 17.

[26] Nouwt (2001), p. 422, Schreuders & Blok (2000), p. 417.

2.2 Exemptions

The Privacy Directive does not apply to:[27]

- activities that fall outside the scope of community law such as provided for by titles V (foreign and security policy) and VI (police and judicial cooperation) of the EU Treaty and in any case to processing operations concerning public security, defence, state security (including economic well-being of state when the processing operation relates to state security matters) and the activities of the state in areas of criminal law,
- processing of personal data by a natural person in the course of a purely personal or household activity. For example keeping a personal address list and corresponding with these persons.[28]

Furthermore, Member States are allowed to adopt measures that restrict the scope of some key articles[29] if this is necessary to safeguard:[30]

- national security,
- defence,
- public security,
- the prevention, investigation, detection and prosecution of criminal offences or of breaches of ethics for regulated professions,
- an important economic or financial interest of a Member State or of the EU, including monetary, budgetary and taxation matters,
- a monitoring, inspection or regulatory function connected with the exercise of official authority relating to the previous three indents,
- the protection of the data subject or the rights and freedoms of others.

3 Legitimate data processing

The Privacy Directive contains an exhaustive enumeration of grounds that allow the processing of personal data.[31] If the processing cannot be based on one of these grounds, the processing is not allowed. The directive sums up six grounds. Three of these can be considered relevant in relation to e-commerce:[32]

---

[27] Article 3(2) of Directive 95/46/EC.

[28] This can give rise to the question in how far keeping business related address lists and appointments in personal business agenda's fall within the scope of the directive.

[29] Article 6(1) relating to data quality, Articles 10 and 11(1) relating to information duties Article 12 relating to right of access of the data subject and Article 21 relating to the publicising of processing operations.

[30] Article 13 of Directive 95/46/EC.

[31] Article 7 of Directive 95/46/EC.

[32] The other three grounds mentioned in Article 7 of Directive 95/46/EC allow processing if it is needed to comply with a legal obligation, if it is needed to protect vital interest of the data subject or if it is necessary in the course of tasks carried out in the public interest or in the exercise of official authority.

a) the data subject has unambiguously given his consent; or
b) processing is necessary for the performance of a contract with the data subject or in order to take steps at the request of the data subject prior to entering into a contract; or
c) processing is necessary for the purposes of the legitimate interests pursued by the business organisation or by the third party or parties to whom the data are disclosed, except where such interests are overridden by the interests for fundamental rights and freedoms of the data subject.

Ad a) Consent

The data subjects' consent means freely given specific and informed indication of his wishes by which the data subject signifies his agreement to personal data relating to him being processed.[33]

Freely given means the organisation may not pressurise the consumer to give his consent.[34] Nor should the individual be penalised for not giving his consent, for example by being denied access to services that are not dependent on the provision of the personal information.

Informed means the individual should be made aware of what he is consenting to and what the possible consequences are. Communicating the purpose of the data collection is probably enough to achieve that the individual can give his informed consent. Clearly communicating the purpose can lead to the specific consent, *i.e.* concerning this purpose. As can be read in the following Section, informing the individual of the purpose of the data collection is compulsory.

What is meant by *unambiguously given consent* is not further specified. If the customer fills in an on-line form with his personal data, does this mean he unambiguously gives his consent to the processing of the data? If a data collection form is accompanied by information on the purpose of the data collection it can be assumed that if the client agrees to the processing with regard to the stated purpose by filling in the form. From that perspective, filling in the form can be seen as the freely given consent to the processing.

This is different when the information that is collected with the form is used for multiple purposes. In that case filling in the form cannot automatically be considered as consent with regard to all uses of the information. It is advisable to offer the consumer the opportunity to indicate to which uses of the information he wishes to consent and to which uses he objects.

Extra attention with regard to acquiring the consent of the data subject is needed if the collection of information is not visible to the client. Furthermore, the data subject cannot give his consent to operations that are a violation of his

[33] Article 2(h) of Directive 95/46/EC.

[34] *Cf.* Bergkamp & Dhont (2000), p. 77.

fundamental rights.[35] Obtaining the consent is not necessary if the processing can be based on one of the other grounds.

Ad b) Necessary for the performance of a contract

This ground justifies the collection and use of personal information needed to perform the electronic contract. In most cases related to e-commerce, the processing of personal data can be justified on this ground. For example, name and address are needed to ship ordered goods and arrange payment. Processing of personal information that is not needed for the performance of the contract cannot be based on this ground.

Ad c) Legitimate interests

If the processing cannot be based on one of the other grounds, but there is nonetheless a good reason to process the information, this ground can be used. This ground introduces a balance of interests between the legitimate interests of the company (or a different party that needs to use the information) and the interests of the data subject. This ground has room for a case-by-case approach.

The ground is somewhat vague, as it is not specified what is to be considered a 'legitimate interest'. In the recitals mention is made of *'legitimate ordinary business activities'*.[36] Marketing purposes can be considered legitimate business interest. Another application that can be justified on this ground is the use of personal data for on-line profiling. Profiles of customers can be used to improve the service provision and therewith the performance of the business, which can be considered a legitimate business interest.

It is up to the Member States do determine the details with regard to what is allowed and to what extent. In as far as the Member States have not specified the conditions relating to legitimate interests, the business organisations are left with a situation of uncertainty. Their own assessment of what is legitimate might be overruled in a later stage by the national privacy authority[37] or by a national judge.

If the data processing is based on this ground, the individual has the right to object to the use of data related to him if he has compelling grounds to do so.[38]

---

35 The Article 29 working party speaks of *'a minimum and non-negotiable level of privacy protection,'* Opinion 1/98, *Platform for privacy preferences (P3P) and the Open Profiling Standard (OPS)*, WP 11.

36 Recital 30 of Directive 95/46/EC.

37 According to Article 28 of Directive 95/46/EC, each Member State must install one or more public authorities responsible for the monitoring of the national privacy protection rules installed pursuant to the directive. An overview of the national data protection authorities and their contact information can be found on: <http://europa.eu.int/comm/internal_market/privacy/links_en.htm>.

38 If the objection is justified, the processing must cease. Article 14(a) of Directive 95/46/EC.

4 Requirements for proper data processing

Not only does the processing need to be based on one of the above grounds, the processing also has to be executed in accordance with several general principles relating to the data quality. The personal data must be:[39]

1) processed fairly and lawfully,
2) collected for specified, explicit and legitimate purposes and not further processed in a way incompatible with those purposes,
3) adequate, relevant and not excessive in relation to the purposes for which they are collected and/or further processed,
4) accurate and, where necessary, kept up to date; every reasonable step must be taken to ensure that data which are inaccurate or incomplete, having regard to the purposes for which they were collected or for which they are further processed, are erased or rectified, and
5) kept in a form which permits identification of data subjects for no longer than is necessary for the purposes for which the data were collected or for which they are further processed.

Purpose

The above criteria several times mention *the purpose* for which the data are collected and processed. Before the controller commences the processing of personal data, such a purpose must be formulated. This purpose must be specified, explicit and legitimate. The purpose should not be formulated too broad for then it risks not being specified and explicit. Nor should it be formulated too narrow, because all the envisaged uses should fall within the stated purpose. By formulating a (too) narrow purpose, the data controller might unnecessarily constrain himself. It is possible to formulate multiple purposes.

Legitimate means the purpose may not be in violation of fundamental rights of the individual. The purpose must be related to one of the grounds that allow processing of personal data.

The formulated purpose plays a central part in the assessment if the company has behaved properly with regard to personal information. Whether or not the processing is adequate, relevant, and not excessive will be determined in light of the formulated purpose(s). Equally, the question if the processing is accurate, up to date and not kept longer then necessary is answered with reference to the purpose.

Secure processing

Adding to these general principles, the Privacy Directive requires that the data processing is confidential and secure.[40] Confidential means that the

39 Article 6 of Directive 95/46/EC.

40 Articles 16 and 17 of Directive 95/46/EC.

data may only be processed upon instructions of the controller unless law requires otherwise. Secure means that appropriate technical and organisational measures must be implemented to protect the data against accidental or unlawful destruction, loss, alteration, unauthorised disclosure or access and any other forms of unlawful processing.

To determine what is 'appropriate' it is relevant to look at the state of the technique and the costs of the implementation of the measures in relation to the risks represented by the processing and the nature of the data. This means a balance must be struck between the seriousness of the consequences of security breaches and the costs involved to install security measures.[41]

In case of sensitive data more measures need to be taken to secure the data. National data protection authorities are responsible for further specification on how to comply with the relevant privacy regulations.

5 Information duties

When the data are collected from the data subject, the following information must be provided:[42]

1) the identity of the controller or his representative,
2) the purposes of the processing for which the data are intended,
3) any further information if this is necessary to guarantee fair processing in respect of the data subject, such as:
   - the recipients or categories of recipients of the data,
   - whether replies to the questions are obligatory or voluntary, as well as the possible consequences of the failure to reply,
   - the existence of the right of access to the data and the right to rectify the data concerning him.

The information is to be provided at the time that the data are recorded. If disclosure to a third party is envisaged, the information must be provided at the latest when the personal data will be disclosed.

The Working Party as installed according to Article 29 of the Privacy Directive recommends that besides its identity, the organisation should state its physical and electronic address.[43] If the general information requirements of the E-commerce Directive are provided properly the consumers will already have this information. In my view, it is superfluous to provide the information again.

41 *Cf.* Bainbridge (1996), p. 58.

42 Article 10 of Directive 95/46/EC.

43 Recommendation 2/2001 on certain minimum requirements for collecting personal data on-line in the European Union, adopted on 17 May 2001. Documents adopted by the Working Party can be found on <http://europa.eu.int/comm/internal_market/privacy/index_en.htm>.

However, it can be useful to indicate contact information for the consumer where he can make requests to exercise his rights.

The company has to indicate which of the requested information is obligatory, for example indispensable to be able to perform the contract. This can be indicated with an asterisk.[44] If a consumer does not wish to provide any of the optional information that is requested by the electronic vendor, this should not have any consequences such as the denial of access to the site or the services.

6 Rights of the data subject

Right of access

The data subject has the right to obtain from the controller:[45]

- confirmation as to whether or not data relating to him are being processed and information on the purposes of the processing, the categories of data concerned, and the recipients (or categories of recipients) to whom the data are disclosed,
- communication to him in an intelligible form of the data undergoing processing and of any available information as to their source,
- knowledge of the logic involved in any automatic processing of data concerning him at least in the case of automated individual decisions.

If the data subject requests this information, it should be given without constraint and without excessive delay or expense. The data subject has the right to make such a request at reasonable intervals.

Furthermore, the data subject should be able to obtain the rectification, erasure or blocking of data if the processing does not comply with the provisions of the directive, more in particular if the data are incomplete or inaccurate. Third parties should be notified of any rectifications, erasure or blocking carried out in compliance with these requirements, unless this proves to be impossible or means a disproportionate effort on the side of the controller.[46]

Right to object

Even if the data are collected and used according to the rules of the Privacy Directive and the national rules installed pursuant to the directive in some cases the data subject still has the right to object to this. This right exists:[47]

- if the processing is based on ground (c) discussed in Section 3 above (legitimate interests), the data subject has the right at any time to object

---

[44] The Article 29 Working Party indicates that this is sufficient; see their recommendation 2/2001, p. 4.

[45] Article 12 of Directive 95/46/EC.

[46] Article 12(b) and (c) of Directive 95/46/EC.

[47] Article 14 of Directive 95/46/EC.

to the processing of his personal data, on compelling legitimate grounds relating to his particular situation, except where otherwise provided by national legislation,
- if the personal data are intended for the use of direct marketing purposes, the data subject may object to this on request and free of charge. He must also be informed if his data are being disclosed to or used on behalf of third parties for direct marketing purposes. The data subject must then be offered the right to object, free of charge to such disclosure or uses.

What is meant by *compelling legitimate grounds* is not specified. The national data protection authorities are to determine this.

The Data Protection Working Party is of the opinion that a real opportunity to object to the disclosure of the personal information to a third party, such as subsidiaries or business partners, is offered by 'clicking a box' (a tick box).[48]

Invisible data processing

Internet related technologies allow that all sorts of processing and transferring of data are conducted without this being visible to the visitors of websites. If the collected information can be linked to an individual, the collection and use of the information is subject to the Privacy Directive. This is not always obvious, the targeted commercial messages can raise the impression that personal data are used, but this is not necessarily the case.

In any event, business organisations should strive to use software that is compliant with the data protection legislation. The visitor of a website should be informed about the information that is being collected and transmitted. It should also be possible to review the data that is being collected. Additionally, tools should be provided in the software so that the customers can manage the processing of their data such as refuse the storage or delete the information. This can be realised by presenting the customer with tick-boxes to indicate his wishes. The Article 29 Working Party is of the opinion that the software used for data processing should not be configured so that it by default allows collecting, storing and sending of personal information.[49]

The two most popular browsers[50] allow different levels of privacy settings so that the user can manage the data processing himself, but this does not free business organisations of their responsibilities under the European privacy legislation.

---

48 Recommendation 2/2001 of the Article 29 Working Party, p. 5.

49 Recommendation 1/99 *on Invisible and Automatic Processing of Personal Data on the Internet Performed by Software and Hardware*, adopted by the Article 29 Working Party on 23 February 1999, WP 17.

50 Microsoft's Internet Explorer and Netscape Navigator.

7 Privacy policy

The required information and options to object should be presented to the customer as much as possible before the data collection. To prevent that the screen becomes overloaded with information the business organisations can for example use a 'pop-up window'[51] that appears if the visitor clicks on a specified link.

Another solution is to place a hyperlink that directs the customer to the company's privacy policy. A privacy policy is a document stating all the relevant information relating to the processing of personal data by the company. The use of privacy policies on websites is widespread. As a result, many users will expect that the company will have a privacy policy.

In its recommendation on the subject the art 29 Working Party indicates that the privacy policy should be available directly on the homepage and anywhere where personal data are collected.[52] The policy should state the purpose(s) of the data processing, all the required information, the rights of the consumer and how these rights can be exercised. If use is made of automatic data processing or transfer of data to third parties the 'how and why' of these actions are to be included in the privacy policy. Preferably the policy should also include contact information in case the data subject has any further questions.[53]

---

[51] A pop-up window is a small window which appears over the window in which the webpage is displayed, the window can be opened by clicking on the indicated spot on the web page (for example labelled *'click here for information'*), by moving the cursor over the indicated spot or automatically once the user opens a certain web page.

[52] Recommendation 2/2001 of the Article 29 Data Protection Working Party, adopted on 17 May 2001, WP 43, at p. 7.

[53] *Cf.* recommendation 2/2001 of the Article 29 Data Protection Working Party, p. 7.

CHAPTER 5

The Directive on Privacy and Electronic Communications

1 General

Directive 2002/58/EC[1] (Directive on Privacy and Electronic Communications) is concerned with security of networks and the services provided via those networks. The directive replaces Directive 97/66/EC[2] (the Telecommunications Directive) in order to extent the applicability of the telecommunications directive to providers of electronic communication services.[3]

The directive is a *lex specialis* in relation to the Privacy Directive. The directive particularises and complements the general principles laid down in the Privacy Directive for the providers of communication services.[4]

The directive is part of the regulatory framework covering transmission networks and services. This regulatory framework consists of a general framework directive[5] and four specific directives.[6] These directives extent and adapt the applicability of the existing telecommunication legislation to include electronic communication services.

The Directive on Privacy and Electronic Communications addresses a variety of topics related to privacy and electronic communications: the security and confidentiality of the communications, the related traffic data, the location data,[7] calling line identification, itemised billing, automatic call forwarding, the directories of subscribers, but also unsolicited communications and the use of cookies.

---

1 Directive 2002/58/EC of the European Parliament and of the Council of 12 July 2002 concerning the processing of personal data and the protection of privacy in the electronic communications sector, OJ L 201, 31-7-2002, p. 37. For comments on the draft directive see Poullet, Louveaux & Pérez Asinari (2001).

2 Directive 97/66/EC of the European Parliament and of the Council of 15 December 1997 concerning the processing of personal data and the protection of privacy in the telecommunications sector, OJ L 24, 30-1-1998, p. 1.

3 'Communication services' means services offered by (for example) access providers and hosting providers.

4 Article 1(2) of Directive 2002/58/EC.

5 Directive 2002/21/EC of the European Parliament and of the Council of 7 March 2002 on a common regulatory framework for electronic communications networks and services (Framework Directive), OJ L 108, 24-4-2002, p. 33.

6 Directive 2002/20/EC on the authorisation of electronic communications networks and services, Directive 2002/19/EC on access to, and interconnection of, electronic communications networks and associated facilities, Directive 2002/22/EC on universal service and users' rights relating to electronic communications networks and services and Directive 2002/58/EC on privacy and electronic communications).

7 'Traffic data' are information needed for the transport of the message and the billing thereof, such as a telephone number, an IP-number, the duration of the communication and its volume. 'Location data' are information relating to the geographic position of terminal equipment used for the communication.

The provisions of this directive are in first instance relevant for the providers of publicly available communication services and networks such as ISPs and providers of communication networks and services. The reason that the directive is discussed in this work is that two provisions of this directive, namely Article 5 and Article 13, have consequences for e-commerce activities of other business organisations then those involved with offering communication services. These articles affect the instalment of information on PCs of users, such as cookies, and the sending of unsolicited commercial e-mail.

2 Scope of applicability

2.1 Electronic communication services

The directive is applicable to the processing of personal data in connection with the provision of publicly available electronic communication services in public communications networks in the Community.[8] Electronic communication service is defined as:[9]

'...a service normally provided for remuneration which consist wholly or mainly in the conveyance of signals on electronic communication networks, including telecommunications services and transmission services in networks used for broadcasting, but exclude services providing, or exercising editorial control over, content transmitted using electronic communications networks and services; it does not include information society services, as defined in Article 1 of Directive 98/34/EC. Which do not consist wholly or mainly in the conveyance of signals on electronic communications networks.'

In short this refers to services that consist in the conveyance of signals. It can be noted that information society services are explicitly excluded. This means the privacy and electronic communications directive contains obligations for transporters of the data and not for those using these networks to supply content.[10]

From that respect the inclusion of the articles concerning cookies and e-mail in this directive can be considered somewhat odd. The Articles 5(3) and 13 of the Directive on Privacy and Electronic Communications address the relationship between a company providing content and the recipient of that content.[11] What

[8] Article 3(1) of Directive 2002/58/EC.

[9] Article 2(c) of Directive 2002/21/EC.

[10] An ISP often offers both transmission services (*i.e.* access) as well as content services by hosting their own portal. The first services are covered by the electronic communications regulatory framework, the second (content related) are covered by Directive 2000/31/EC. *Cf.* recital 10 of Directive 2002/21/EC.

[11] *Cf.* Kabel (2003). See also recitals 25 and 40 of Directive 2002/58/EC.

is more, this sector specific directive was presented as Europe's answer to the spam problem.[12] It would have been better if the provisions were fitted in the E-commerce Directive, which is concerned with obligations of on-line service providers. Apparently, there was no consensus on these points at the time of the adoption of the E-commerce Directive.

2.2 Subscribers and users

The directive protects the interests of subscribers and users of publicly available electronic communication services and networks. A subscriber means:

'any natural person or legal entity who or which is party to a contract with the provider of publicly available electronic communications services for the supply of such services.'[13]

This definition can be found in Directive 2002/21/EC (the Framework Directive). The Directive on Privacy and Electronic Communications states that the definitions of this directive apply unless otherwise provided.[14] The definition includes both natural and legal persons, which means the protection has a wider range then the protection offered by the Privacy Directive, that only sees to natural persons.

User means:

'any natural person using a publicly available electronic communications service, for private or business purposes, without necessarily having subscribed to this service.'[15]

This is the definition as found in the Directive on Privacy and Electronic Communications. The term 'user' is also defined in Directive 2002/21/EC (the Framework Directive). However the definition in the Framework Directive is slightly different from the definition in the privacy and electronic communication directive. The definition in the Framework Directive includes legal entities: *'a legal entity or natural person using or requesting a publicly available electronic*

---

[12] See Commission press release with reference number IP/02/783 of 30 may 2002 and Commission press release with reference number IP/03/1015 of 15 July 2003. Press releases can be found in the virtual 'press room' at <http://europa.eu.int/comm/press_room/index.htm> a searchable database of press releases is available on the site.

[13] As defined in Article 2(k) of Directive 2002/21/EC.

[14] Article 2 of Directive 2002/58/EC.

[15] Article 2(a) of Directive 2002/58/EC.

communication service'.[16] It is unfortunate that the definitions of the same term are different in these directives. This can lead to confusion with regard to scope of the concept.

3 E-mail marketing

3.1 General rules

As can be read in Section 6 of Chapter 2, the E-commerce Directive states two general principles with regard to sending of unsolicited commercial communications by electronic mail. The Directive on Privacy and Electronic Communications adds several rules to these principles.

The Directive on Privacy and Electronic Communications defines electronic mail in a broad manner as:

'...any text, voice, sound or image message sent over a public communications network which can be stored in the network or in the recipients terminal equipment until it is collected by the recipient.'[17]

This includes all sorts of electronic messages, including 'traditional' e-mail messages containing text to PC, more advanced electronic messages containing sound and images, and SMS messages (texting) to mobile phones. The element 'until it is collected by the recipient' indicates that simultaneous participation of the sender and recipient is not required.[18]

Direct marketing

Article 13 affects the use of electronic mail for purposes of direct marketing. Direct marketing is not defined. For the notion of marketing, reference can be made to the definition of 'commercial communications' in the E-commerce Directive, *i.e. any form of communication designed to promote, directly or indirectly, the goods, services or image of a company, organisation or person pursuing a commercial, industrial, or craft activity or exercising a regulated profession.*[19]

The difference between 'marketing' and 'direct marketing' is that direct marketing is addressed and delivered to a specific (limited) group while marketing addresses a potentially unlimited number of recipients through a mass medium.[20]

---

[16] Article 2(h) of Directive 2002/21/EC.

[17] Article 2(h) of Directive 2002/58/EC.

[18] *Cf.* Opinion 5/2004 of the Article 29 Working Party, adopted on 27 February 2004, WP 90, at p. 4.

[19] Article 2(f) of Directive 2000/31/EC.

[20] See Asscher & Van Erve (2004), p. 29.

An indication with regard to the scope of this concept can also be found in the Privacy Directive. The recitals of this directive state that direct marketing activities carried out by political, charity or other organisations, for instance activities aimed at recruiting new members, fund raising or lobbying for votes are included in the concept of direct marketing in the meaning of the Privacy Directive. Expression of views, thoughts and ideas are not included.[21]

Two general principles with regard to the use of e-mail for direct marketing have to be taken into account:[22]

- it is not allowed to disguise or conceal the identity of the sender, and
- a valid return address where the recipient can send opt-out requests must be included.

These rules are relevant in both B2C as well as B2B e-mail marketing.

The wordings 'a valid return address' indicate that the address included in the message must be of actual use to the recipient to indicate that he no longer wishes to receive messages. This also implicates that the recipient can withdraw his consent to receiving commercial messages at any moment. The directive holds no obligation to install general opt-out registers.

3.2 Opt-in e-mail marketing

3.2.1 Prohibition for spam

According to the Directive on Privacy and Electronic Communications the use of electronic mail for the purposes of direct marketing is only allowed with regard to subscribers who have given their prior consent.[23] One of the main arguments for the introduction of this opt-in system is that the costs of the messages are borne by the conveyer and addressees of the messages. This provision has been declared the prohibition for spam in Europe.[24]

The provision protects subscribers. As can be read above, the definition of subscribers includes natural and legal persons, but the opt-in provision only sees to the protection of natural persons.[25] Member States are free to determine what regime they adopt with regard to messages to legal persons. The directive merely states that the interests of legal persons are to be sufficiently protected. Several Member States have chosen to install opt-in regime for legal persons.[26]

---

[21] See recital 44 and recital 30 of Directive 95/46/EC.

[22] Article 13(4) of Directive 2002/58/EC.

[23] Article 13 of Directive 2002/58/EC.

[24] *Cf.* the Commission press release of 15 July 2003, with reference number IP/03/1015, 'SPAM: European Commission goes on the offensive'.

[25] Article 13(5) of Directive 2002/58/EC excludes legal persons from the protection of the opt-in regime.

[26] See Thole (2004). See also the Commission communication on spam COM (2004) 28 final at p. 14 on the diversity in the Member States with regard to enforcement. The Commission recognises (at p. 9 of

In practice it might not always be easy to distinguish between addresses of legal persons and addresses of natural persons. The address of a legal person is for example 'company-name@provider.com'.[27] In any event, natural persons will normally read the messages sent to addresses of legal persons. These messages cause the same problems as messages to natural persons: they take up time, space and cause irritation. Messages send to a legal person do not change anything about the fact that the costs are largely borne by the recipient and the conveyor of the messages. From that perspective it would be more consistent if legal persons were also included in the scope of protection.

Also excluded from the protection of the opt-in regime are professional addresses such as 'employee@company.com'. With regard to such addresses it is the company that has the subscription and not the individual employee. The same situation can occur where one member of the family has a subscription, which supplies e-mail addresses for the whole family. Strictly speaking only the family member with the subscription is protected under the opt-in system of the directive. In practice it will be hard for the sender to make this distinction. Recipients that cannot rely on the opt-in regime can use the return address in the message to indicate that they wish to opt-out. If general opt-out registers are installed the e-commerce obligates companies to regularly consult and respect these registers.[28]

3.2.2 Prior consent

Consent refers to consent as meant in the Privacy Directive. This entails that a person should freely give a specific and informed indication of his wishes.[29] The recitals mention that consent may be given by any appropriate method enabling a freely given specific and informed indication of the users' wishes, including by ticking a box when visiting an internet website. The Article 29 Data Protection Working Party confirms that consent can be obtained by presenting a tick-box on-line at the time the information is collected.[30] The box

---

this communication) that applying a differentiated regime according to the nature of the subscriber may lead to specific difficulties for senders.

[27] The Article 29 Working Party points out that there can be problems for the sender to determine the capacity of the owner of the address and points out that it is the responsibility of the sender to make sure that the rules are respected (see p. 8 of opinion 5/2004).

[28] Article 7(2) regarding the opt-out registers applies to registers of natural persons, however recital 45 of Directive 2002/58/EC states that the provisions of Article 7 are fully applicable with regard to legal persons.

[29] Article 2(h) of Directive 95/46/EC, referred to by Article 2(f) of Directive 2002/58/EC, see Section 3 of Chapter 4 for a discussion of consent.

[30] Recommendation 2/2001, adopted on 17 May 2001, WP 43, p. 9.

should not by default be ticked to give permission, but should actively be clicked by the user to indicate the freely given consent.[31]

The consent needs to be obtained from the subscribers. As a result, using a 'tell a friend' method to spread commercial communications is problematic.[32] The 'tell a friend' method entails that the company facilitates the entering of the e-mail address of somebody else to send a commercial message to this person.

When a recipient has consented to the receipt of commercial messages, these messages cannot be labelled 'unsolicited commercial communications'. This affects the applicability of Article 7 of the E-commerce Directive. According to this article, unsolicited messages should be clearly identifiable as such upon receipt. It can be considered good business practice to effectuate this even if strictly taken this provision is not applicable. In any event, the messages are still subject to Article 6 of the E-commerce Directive, which states that commercial communications should be clearly identifiable as such.

When the entering of an e-mail address serves no other purpose then receiving commercial e-mails, the entering of the address can be seen as prior consent to the receiving of the messages. This is the case when companies have a field on their website where visitors can enter an e-mail address in order to sign up for a commercial newsletter. Controversially, if the e-mail address is requested for multiple purposes it can not be assumed that the entering of the address entails consent to the receiving of commercial messages. For example if a company uses an electronic promotional game on internet, where persons can play some sort of game and then are requested to type in their address to be informed if they won a price, this address can not be used to send commercial messages. Separate consent for this purpose has to be obtained.

The provisions do not allow the use of e-mail addresses that were collected from public spaces on internet, such as public e-mail directories, discussion forums, chat rooms and newsgroups (the so-called 'harvesting of e-mail addresses). In that case there is no prior consent of the owners of the addresses to receiving commercial messages.

In as far as e-mail addresses can be considered personal data in the meaning of the Privacy Directive, the collection of e-mail addresses from public spaces on the internet also falls foul under the provisions of this directive. The collection of addresses from public spaces can be considered unfair processing because the data are used for other purposes then the purpose for which the individuals have left their address in the public space.[33]

---

[31] The Article 29 Working Party is of the opinion that pre-ticked boxes are not compatible with the definition of consent. See opinion 5/2004, p. 5.

[32] Asscher & Van Velde (2004) conclude (at p. 31) that this is not a valid method.

[33] *Cf.* Working Document *Privacy on the Internet, An integrated Approach to On-line Data Protection,* adopted by the Article 29 Data Protection Working Party on 21st November 2000, WP 37, p. 37, as well as recommendation 2/2001 of the Article 29 Data Protection Working Party.

If use is made of address lists that are hired or purchased from third parties, the sender of commercial messages should verify that the addresses were properly collected, *i.e.* that prior consent was obtained from the owners and that the consent covers the intended use of the addresses. Address lists composed before the introduction of the opt-in regime that do not comply with the prior consent requirement can no longer be used.[34]

3.3 Soft opt-in e-mail marketing

3.3.1 An exception to the opt-in regime

The opt-in regime discussed in the previous Section constitutes a serious restriction on the use of e-mail for direct marketing purposes. The reason for this lies in the fact that such messages can impose an unequal burden on the recipient. However, the Directive on Privacy and Electronic Communications shows some lenience with regard to messages send to persons and organisations with whom a company has a customer relation. In case an e-mail address is collected during the sale of a product or a service, the address may be used for direct marketing of similar products or services, as long as the following conditions are met:[35]

- the address is collected in accordance with the stipulations of the Privacy Directive,
- the customer is given the opportunity to object free of charge and in an easy manner to such use when the address is collected,
- the opportunity to object is offered in each message that is send.

The soft opt-in regime protects subscribers, and legal persons are not exempted from the protection. Therefore, the soft-opt-in regime can be relevant for both B2B and B2C e-commerce.

The requirement that the customer must be given the opportunity to object can be implemented by presenting a tick box near the field where the e-mail address is collected. This requirement is less stringent then the prior consent discussed above. This is why it can be referred to as 'soft opt-in'. The difference with the more stringent prior consent is that there is no objection to have the box by default set to indicate consent. A clear statement should accompany the tick box indicating the consequences of (un-)ticking the box. This opportunity to object must be given clearly and distinctly.[36] A statement in the general terms of the company to this end does not suffice.

---

[34] *Cf.* Opinion 5/2004 of the Article 29 Working Party, adopted on 27 February 2004, WP 90, p. 6.

[35] Article 13(2) Directive 2002/58/EC.

[36] Recital 41 of Directive 2002/58/EC.

3.3.2 Similar products

The soft-opt-in regime only allows the sending of commercial messages concerning the companies' *own similar products and services.* This means the messages that are send under the soft opt-in regime must concern products or services that are similar to the products or services that were ordered during the collection of the e-mail address. If the company has a newsletter with information on a wide variety of products and services, this cannot be send. It also means that other companies cannot use the addresses collected during a transaction for direct marketing purposes.[37]

The extent of the notion 'similar products' is not further specified. If a customer buys a book on gardening from an on-line book-store, can he be send e-mails advertising all kinds of books or merely books related to gardening? The Article 29 Working Party indicates that 'similar' should be judged from the perspective of the recipient rather then the perspective of the sender. The reasonable expectations of the recipient are determinative.

As of yet it is not clear if a broad or restrictive approach will be adopted with regard to this question. The company can reduce the uncertainty by clearly indicating what the customer can expect, for example by stating the categories of products or services that it intents to use the address for. Possibly, the Member States will take a more precise stance when they implement the directive.

Differentiated marketing strategies

The two regimes (opt-in and soft opt-in) have as a consequence that the e-mail marketing activities of companies will have to be differentiated. The opt-in regime allows sending of all sorts of commercial messages, while the soft opt-in only allows messages of similar products. Especially if the concept 'similar products' is understood in a restrictive manner, this entails that a multitude of e-mail marketing messages need to be composed, depending on the ordered products.

The situation becomes more complicated if a customer buys different products in a single order or a variety of products over a course of time. Each time the customer buys a different product, the e-mail marketing to this customer possibly needs to be adapted. To prevent such differentiation, the company can choose not to use the soft opt-in option and always obtain prior consent, even if the e-mail address is collected during a transaction.

From the business point of view, the notion should not be interpreted in a strict manner, because this places unequal burdens upon companies with

[37] According to the Article 29 Working Party subsidiaries and mother companies are not the same company (and hence cannot use the addresses), see opinion 5/2004, p. 9.

regard to their e-mail campaigns. It is not clear if the business organisation can use the e-mail address that was collected during a sale if the consumer exercises his right of withdrawal.

3.3.3 Existing customer base

With the adoption of the new regime concerning e-mail marketing, the question comes up what is allowed with regard to addresses that were collected before the adoption of the new regime. In my view, the soft opt-in regime also means to cover addresses that were collected during sales that took place before the adoption of the new regime.[38] If the collection was in accordance with the rules of the Privacy Directive, there is no objection to use the addresses of the existing customer base, as long as the messages contain an opt-out opportunity.[39] Support for this view can be found in the recitals, which state that the soft-in exception is meant for the context of an existing customer relationship.[40] A significant restriction is that the addresses can only be used for messages of similar products. Addresses that were not collected in the context of a sale can no longer be used, unless at the time of collection the owners gave their prior consent to receiving commercial messages.

3.3.4 Concluding remarks

The discussed provisions related to e-mail will not be the answer to the spam problem. The regime does not protect legal persons, it will offer no relief against e-mails from outside the EU, and is not likely to be effective with regard to fraudulent senders of e-mail, who will not be inclined to obey legal rules.

It can be noted that most companies have already implemented a decent e-mail marketing system in order not to irritate their (potential) customers. The new regime places extra administrative burdens on such companies, while the effects on the actual problem remain to be seen.

Much will depend on the national enforcement mechanisms and the ability of the enforcers to trace the origin of electronic messages. The fact that various Member States have adopted different enforcement mechanisms can complicate matters.[41]

---

[38] *Cf.* Commission Communication on unsolicited commercial communications or 'spam', COM (2004) 28 final, at p. 9.

[39] In this manner: Thole (2004). Different: Asscher & Van Erve (2004), they argue (at p. 33) that it is unlikely that these addresses can be used to send unsolicited commercial messages.

[40] Recital 41 of Directive 2002/58/EC.

[41] See Thole (2004) for a discussion of several noteworthy differences between the national implementations of the directive.

The solution to the spam problem might not be in law but in other means such as filters. The Commission also recognised that establishing an opt-in regime is not enough to tackle the spam problem. In its communication on spam the Commission describes an integrated approach, including effective remedies and enforcement mechanisms, complaint mechanisms, international co-operation, technical and self-regulatory actions.[42]

4 Cookies and comparable programs

4.1 Introduction

Many websites make use of cookies.[43] A cookie is a small amount of computer code, which is placed on the visitors' computer. After a site has placed a cookie on the visitors' computer, the visitor is recognised each time the website is visited. There are also cookies that are used for the duration of a session and that are removed the moment the visitor leaves the site. The cookie can trace the visitors' behaviour on the site and can remember the personal settings.

Cookies can be used to personalise the services offered to the visitor, for example customise the advertisements presented or create a personal profile. Furthermore, cookies can be used to ease the log-in process to websites and simplify ordering procedures.

For example, an on-line bookstore using cookies can register that a client has visited the site and has ordered a gardening book. Upon a next visit to the site the customer can be presented with related (gardening) products. If the customer wishes to make another purchase, the order form need not be filled in again because the cookie has saved this data.

Cookies are celebrated for the enhancement of ease of use they represent and the possibilities to customise the services for the visitor. On the other hand cookies have been criticised because they make use of the visitors' equipment and they are considered a possible threat to privacy. The cookie involuntarily has the image of being some sort of spyware device, *i.e.* software that allows others to explore the information on the hard drive of your PC. Spyware (also: adware) can be connected to other (freely available) software. The spyware can monitor the activity of the user on the internet or the use of the (free) software product. This information is transmitted via the internet connection and can be used to

---

[42] Commission Communication on unsolicited commercial communications or 'spam', COM (2004) 28 final.

[43] Consumers International (2001b) reports on the amount of cookies used by US and EU sites, over a third of the visited sites tried to place at least one cookie.

present personalised banners on the user's screen. Cookies do not have the far-reaching effects of spyware.

Cookies are widely used and often people do not realise that cookies are placed on their computer while surfing. People who regularly surf on the web collect hundreds of them.[44]

4.2 The legal position of cookies and comparable programs

Before the adoption of the privacy and electronic communications directive, the general privacy directive was used to determine the legal position of cookies. Although it was generally acknowledged that cookies constituted a threat to privacy, cookies do not always constitute processing of personal data.[45] Therefore their legal position under the Privacy Directive is uncertain. This issue has been resolved as cookies and comparable programs are now specifically addressed in the Directive on Privacy and Electronic Communications.

Article 5(3) of this directive addresses the use of electronic communication networks to store information or to gain access to information stored in the terminal equipment of a subscriber or a user. This is generally seen as a provision affecting cookies. In the recitals it can be read that this also refers to the use of spyware, web bugs, hidden identifiers and other similar devices that can enter the users' terminal without their knowledge. The directive states that the use of such devices may seriously intrude on the privacy of the user.[46] At the same time the directive recognises that the use can serve legitimate purposes, and specifically mentions cookies in this respect.

The directive considers the use of cookies a legitimate and useful tool for analysing the effectiveness of a website, for advertising and for verifying the identity of users engaged in on-line transactions.[47] The directive thus allows the use of cookies or similar programs, as long as they are used for legitimate purposes.

When cookies or similar programs are used some stipulations must be taken into account:[48]

- the visitor should be given clear and comprehensive information in accordance with the Privacy Directive about the purpose of the program that is stored on his PC, and
- the visitor should be offered the right to refuse the storage.

---

[44] For additional reading on cookies: Siebecker (2003). He finds that under common law internet advertisers expose themselves to liability on trespass to chattels grounds by using cookie technology.

[45] Bergkamp & Dhont (2000), p. 75, Louveaux (1999), p. 3.

[46] Recital 24 of Directive 2002/58/EC.

[47] Recital 25 of Directive 2002/58/EC.

[48] Article 5(3) of Directive 2002/58/EC.

This should be done as user-friendly as possible. The right to refuse may be offered once for the use of various programs to be installed on the users' terminal equipment during the same session and may cover any use made of the programs in future sessions.[49] This means the right to refuse need not be offered each time a website is visited. From the recitals it can be learned that access to specific website content may be made conditional on the well-informed acceptance of a cookie or a similar device, if it is used for a legitimate purpose.[50]

The provision protects subscribers and users. This includes legal entities, therefore the provision is relevant in both B2C as well as B2B e-commerce. The rules do not apply if the cookie or the comparable program is needed for the sole purpose of carrying out or facilitating the transmission of a communication, or if this is strictly necessary in order to provide services explicitly requested by the user. What is understood to be 'strictly necessary' might be open to debate.

The two most popular browsers (Microsofts' Internet Explorer and Netscape Navigator) allow different settings with regard to cookies. It is possible to set these browsers in such a manner that they alert the user when a cookie is installed or even that they automatically deny the instalment of cookies.[51] The downside of activating the cookie-alert in the browser is that the user is then constantly interrupted by messages signalling that a cookie will be installed. A website that uses cookies can point the user to the possibilities in the browser, but also has its own responsibility to offer the visitor the possibility to refuse a cookie, for example with a tick box.

---

49 Recital 25 of Directive 2002/58/EC.

50 Recital 23 of Directive 2002/58/EC.

51 In Microsoft's Internet Explorer the desired settings can be made when clicking the 'tools' menu, choose 'Internet options' and then the security tab, the button labelled 'custom level' then allows the user to make personal settings. In Netscape, the 'tool' menu has the option 'cookie manager'.

CHAPTER 6

The Directive on Electronic Signatures

1 General

In the paper-based business environment wide use is made of signatures, that is *handwritten* signatures. Signatures are connected with law and legal consequences. Although legally a signature is not always required to conclude a contact, using a signature can have advantages. It means for example that evidence is available in case a conflict arises over the contract.[1]

The signature can have various functions. The most prominent function is the expression of the will to enter into a contract and provide the evidence of that will in case a dispute arises. Other functions of the signature are: identification of the signer, establishing the authenticity of a document, establishing capacity, confirmation of receipt, indicating originality and protecting the signer against rash decisions.[2] The signature has a solid position in the world of business relations.

The traditional handwritten signature cannot be used in the on-line environment. The increasing amount of business activities that is taking place in the on-line environment has triggered a search for equivalent mechanisms in that environment.[3] Technically, there are several solutions that are equal or even better than the handwritten signature.[4] Legally, the status of such techniques is uncertain as most rules and regulations referring to signatures stem from a period when electronic and digital techniques were non-existent.

Although all Member States to a certain extent accept and recognise electronic evidence and electronic signatures, the value attributed to such evidence is variable.[5] To harmonise the legal status of electronic signatures, the EU has adopted Directive 1999/93/EC[6] (Directive on Electronic Signatures).[7]

The directive aims to establish a legal framework, which facilitates the use of electronic signatures and contributes to their legal recognition.[8] The directive should also prevent that Member States adopt divergent rules with regard to this topic, as this might constitute a barrier to e-commerce.[9] The directive is a part of

1 *Cf.* Girot (2001), p. 308.

2 Van Esch (1999), p. 127-130, Kuner & Miedbrodt (1999), p. 144, Reed (2000).

3 *Cf.* Aalberts & Van der Hof (2000).

4 For an overview and detailed description of the technical possibilities see Ford & Baum (2001).

5 Dumortier & Van Eecke (1999), p. 109, see also Dumortier *et al.* (2003), p. 50.

6 Directive 1999/93/EC of the European Parliament and of the Council of 13 December 1999 on a Community framework for electronic signatures, OJ L 13, 19-1-2000, p. 12. For comments on the draft directive see Dumortier & van Eecke (1999), Julià-Barceló & Vinje (1998).

7 For comments on Directive 1999/93/EC: Morel & Jones (2002). Dumortier (2000) concludes that the directive is not the most handsome piece of legislation ever produced by the European legislator. See also: Siems (2002) who gives several arguments why the directive might be unnecessary or even harmful.

8 Article 1 of Directive 1999/93/EC.

9 Recital 4 of Directive 1999/93/EC.

the series of regulatory efforts of the EU in order to create a favourable regulatory framework.[10]

The general point of departure of the directive is that electronic signatures cannot be denied legal effect just because they are electronic. Furthermore, the directive prescribes that Member States are to recognise electronic signatures as equal to the handwritten signature when a certain set of requirements is met.[11]

Besides the legal recognition of electronic signatures, the directive establishes a legal framework for Certification Service Providers (CSPs), *i.e.* organisations that provide trusted services with regard to the use of electronic signatures. This legal framework is to ensure the proper functioning of the internal market with regard to the service provision related to electronic signatures. The service provision may not be made subject to prior authorisation schemes, but voluntary accreditation schemes to enhance the level of the service provision may be installed.[12] Additionally, several special liability rules for the certification service providers are introduced.

The directive also contains a country of origin principle: the home Member State of the certification service provider sees to it that the service complies with the national rules implemented pursuant to the directive. Member States may not restrict the provision of certification services originating in another Member State in fields covered by the directive.[13] It can be noted that, contrary to the country of origin principle as laid down in the E-commerce Directive, the country of origin principle in the Directive on Electronic Signatures concerns only the areas covered by the directive.

In 2003 an extensive report was published on the directive and its implementation, which concluded that the objective of the directive has not entirely been met, due to low uptake of the PKI technology and the manner in which the Member States implemented the directive.[14]

The following Sections will focus on the legal status of the electronic signature. The position of the certification service provider is not further considered in this work.[15]

---

10 See 'A European Initiative in Electronic Commerce', COM (1997) 157.

11 For an overview of the requirements that have to met by the electronic signature to be recognised as equal to the hand written signature see Annex A.

12 Article 3 of Directive 1999/93/EC.

13 Article 4 of Directive 1999/93/EC.

14 See Dumortier *et al.* (2003).

15 On the position of certification service providers: Hindelang (2002), Van Esch (2003), p. 42.

2 Scope of applicability

With a view to the rapid technological developments, the directive explicitly aims to be open to the use various technologies that allow authentication of data electronically.[16] Indeed, the directive does not mention any particular technology, but several provisions have a strong relation to the digital signatures techniques, supported by a Public Key Infrastructure (PKI).[17]

An important restriction of the scope of the directive is that it only addresses the status of the electronic signature. The directive explicitly does not address the legal validity of contracts nor does it see to the legal status of any other documents with regard to which Member States pose requirements of form.[18]

In other words, the directive sees to the legal status of the signature and not to the status of the document it is attached to. This is a considerable gap in the harmonisation that is reached by the directive. A signature will commonly be attached to a document, just as a handwritten signature is (generally) signed on a paper document. What is more, the intention of the signature is often to grant the document a certain (legal) status.

The legal status of the signed document must be assessed according to the (non-harmonised) rules of national law. Where a Member State does not allow the use of electronic documents instead of paper documents, the electronic signature cannot be used. Furthermore, the directive does not affect the national rules regarding the judicial consideration of evidence; it merely states that the electronic signatures should be admissible as evidence.[19] Lastly, the directive does not affect the freedom of parties to determine the terms and conditions under which they will accept electronic signatures in their relations.[20]

Before discussing the legal status of the electronic signature according to the directive, the next Section will provide some further explanation on electronic signatures.

---

16 Recital 8 of Directive 1999/93/EC.

17 See Section 3.3 below for an explanation of PKI.

18 Recital 17 and Article 1 of Directive 1999/93/EC. *Cf.* Aalberts & Van der Hof (2000), they note (at p. 21) that this is a major and unfortunate limitation.

19 Recital 21 and Article 5 of Directive 1999/93/EC.

20 *Cf.* recital 16 of Directive 1999/93/EC.

3 Electronic signatures

3.1 General

Legal texts rarely define the term 'signature'.[21] The dictionary states that a signature is a name written by hand, always in the same way, usually indicating that the signer has agreed to the signed document or that he has written the document himself.[22]

Some courts have accepted various variants to the handwritten signature on paper as legally acceptable, for example initials, use of rubber stamps, marks or copied signatures on faxes.[23]

In the electronic business environment, the handwritten signature cannot be used, for the obvious reason that paper and pen are lacking there. However, in e-commerce there is a special need for authentication not only of the identity of the contracting partner but also of the integrity of the document, as there is no direct contact with the other party and electronic documents can easily be altered.

There are various techniques available that can perform the functions of the handwritten signature.[24] Several of the available techniques even have further reaching possibilities then the handwritten signature. For example certain electronic signatures can protect documents to undesired disclosure or allow the determination of the exact time the document was created.

An electronic signature does not always look like a traditional signature, nor does it necessarily have the same functions. The term electronic signature refers to all sorts of technologies that can be used to replace one or more functions of the handwritten signature in an electronic environment. [25] The term electronic signature covers the use of passwords or personal identification numbers (PIN). For the purpose of signing use can be made of personal tokens. Tokens are (small) hardware devices held by an individual commonly used in combination with a password or a PIN. The device can look like a little calculator, a smart card or an apparatus that can be connected to a Universal Serial Bus (USB) port, normally available on a PC.

At the moment a popular technology is the use of one-time password generators, mostly used by banks for e-banking purposes. Commonly a hardware device that looks like a calculator is used for this technology. The device that is

---

[21] Reed (2000), Van Esch (2000), p. 108.

[22] Cambridge Advanced Learner's Dictionary, available online at <http://dictionary.cambridge.org/>.

[23] Reed (2000) for an overview of English case law, Dutch legal authors are reluctant to accept other forms then the classic handwritten name, Van Esch (1999), p. 125-126.

[24] For reading on technical details: Ford & Baum (2001).

[25] Aalberts & Van der Hof (2000), p. 2.

used to create the one-time passwords can only be used in relation to the institute that provided the user with the device.

There are also devices available that allow the signer to sign with a pen on a pad that digitises the handwritten signature.[26] This technology mimics the look and feel of the classic signature. The signature pad captures the biometric characteristics of the signature (*i.e.* the distinguishing traits of the signature), which allows identification of the signer by comparing the traits to previously recorded data on the signature. Biometric technologies use certain biological characteristics of the individual to verify their identity. Such technologies can for example use fingerprints, voice, hand geometry, iris and handwriting.[27]

Electronic signatures can be combined with time stamping techniques allowing the verification of the date and time of documents. In relation to electronic signatures Trusted Third Parties (TTPs) can play an important part. The TTP can offer higher security by guaranteeing that the user of the signature is who he claims to be.

3.2 Digital signatures

To secure electronic messages from being read or changed, use can be made of encryption techniques. Using cryptography techniques in relation to electronic messages is referred to as 'digital signing'. Digital signatures rely on cryptographic-based mechanism and are generally considered a subset of electronic signatures.[28] Cryptography can be used to secure electronic communications by transforming (encrypting) the message using an encryption key into incomprehensible data.[29] The decryption key can transform the data back into the original message. Examples of the use of cryptography are the Secure Sockets Layer application (SSL) and the Pretty Good Privacy application (PGP).

There are two basic types of cryptography: symmetric systems and asymmetric systems. In the symmetric cryptosystem,[30] the same key is used to encrypt and decrypt the message. In the asymmetric cryptosystem a pair of two different but related keys is used: a private key which is kept secret and a public key that is publicly available. Usually (but not necessarily) the private key is used to encrypt the message and the public key to decrypt it. This is also known as the public-key system. Encryption techniques can be combined with other techniques or with the services of TTPs resulting in more advanced types of digital signatures.

26 For example: <www.epadlink.com>.

27 On biometric technologies in relation to law: Prins (1998), Grijpink (2001).

28 Ford & Baum (2001), p. 49, Dumortier & Van Eecke (1999), p. 106, Aalberts & Van der Hof (2000).

29 Cryptography: the art of protecting information by transforming it into unreadable format. *Cf.* <www.webopedia.com>.

30 Also referred to as private-key or secret-key systems.

The more advanced the technology, the more functions can be performed by it. Simple encryption techniques can secure that the message is unread and unchanged. More advanced techniques such as the asymmetric system can also link the message with a particular key and thus with the user of that key because the public key will only work with the private key. As long as the user of the private key has managed to keep the key to his personal use, this will link the message to that particular user of the private key.

Use of digital signatures requires 'key management' commonly provided by TTPs or Certification Authorities (see below). The keys used to encrypt and decrypt the data must be generated, distributed, kept up to date possibly revoked or destroyed and archived. The technical details will not be further discussed;[31] it suffices to know that digital signatures have a wide range of possibilities. The technique allows the authentication of the identity of the sender (who is it from?), and can also ensure the integrity of the message (has the message been altered in the transition?). Because people who do not have the key to decrypt the message cannot read the message, the communication is confidential.

The use of digital signatures has broader possibilities then the use of handwritten signatures. Also, the function of the digital signature is mostly to secure the integrity of the document and to verify the identity of the signer rather then the expression of the will to enter into contract (which is a prominent function of the handwritten signature). In that respect, the digital signature technique can be seen as a security tool for electronic communication rather then a substitute of the handwritten signature.[32]

3.3 Certificates and PKI

The above-mentioned public-key system and key management is commonly provided by Certification Service Providers (CSPs) also referred to as Certification Authorities (CAs). A CSP is a TTP organisation that issues digital certificates used to create digital signatures and public-private key pairs. The role of the CSP is to guarantee that the individual granted the unique certificate is, in fact, who he or she claims to be.

How does this work? The CSP provides a person with a private key that can be used to encrypt his messages. The CSP also issues a certificate to this user of the signature that confirms his identity and contains the public key needed to decrypt his messages. The certificate is send together with the encrypted message. The recipient can use the public key to decrypt the message and verify if the message has not been altered and if it was indeed send by the owner of

---

31 For an elaborate explanation see Ford & Baum (2001), Chapter 4.

32 It has been argued that the word 'signature' does not do justice to the possibilities that the technique encompasses; see Aalberts & Van der Hof (2000), p. 3, Dumortier & Van Eecke (1999), p. 106.

the private key (the public key will not work with any other key). Of course the owner of the private key should keep this key secret and to his personal use.

To verify the identity of the user, the CSP can for example have an arrangement with a financial institution, such as a credit card company. Or the CSP can require the individual to come physically to its office and identify himself before issuing any keys and certificates for this person.

CSPs are a critical component in data security and e-commerce because they guarantee that the two parties exchanging information are really who they claim to be.[33] The reliability of the keys – and therewith the digital signature – is ensured by the CSP. A system of CSPs issuing digital certificates (also to each other) is called a Public Key Infrastructure (PKI).[34] As of yet, the PKI is in a developing stage. There is neither a single PKI, nor one particular technical standard that supports such an infrastructure.

4 Relevant definitions

4.1 The legal definition of electronic signatures

In the Directive on Electronic Signatures, several 'levels' can be distinguished with regard to the legal status of electronic signatures, depending on the type of signature used. The directive distinguishes between 'electronic signatures' and 'advanced electronic signatures'. Provided that several requirements are met, the advanced electronic signature is attributed a higher legal status then the 'normal' electronic signature. Before going into these different levels of legal status, the definitions for electronic signature used the directive are discussed.

Electronic signature

According to the directive, an electronic signature is:

'...data in electronic form which are attached to or logically associated with other electronic data and which serve as a method of authentication'.

This covers all sorts of technologies and services capable of authenticating data electronically.[35] The definition is kept open so as not to exclude any (future) technologies of the applicability of the Directive on Electronic Signatures. It can be

[33] See <www.webopedia.com>, an on-line dictionary and search engine specialised in computer and internet technology. On the use of digital signatures in e-business: Shiralkar & Vijayaraman (2003), Gupta, Tung & Marsden (2004).

[34] Also: a trust hierarchy.

[35] Recital 8 of Directive 1999/93/EC.

assumed that 'logically associated' relates to the technical manner in which the electronic signature is linked to other data. For example a PIN code is logically associated to the information that can be accessed by typing in the code. Authentication means verifying certain information, for example the origin of the document, the identity of the sender of the information.[36] It is not stated whether the 'authentication' should relate to the identity of the sender or the integrity of the message. All the above discussed electronic signatures potentially fall within the scope of this definition.[37]

Advanced electronic signature

An advanced electronic signature is an electronic signature that meets the following requirements:[38]

a) it is uniquely linked to the signatory,
b) it is capable of identifying the signatory,
c) it is created using means that the signatory can maintain under its sole control,
d) it is linked to the data to which it relates in such a manner that any subsequent change of the data is detectable.

In this definition, the authentication explicitly bears reference to both the signatory as well as to the document. The directive does not state in specific wordings that this refers to a digital signature based on a PKI. However, at the moment, this is the technique that comes to mind when reading these requirements.[39] *'Means that the signatory can maintain under its control'* as mentioned in requirement (c) then refers to the private key. This key is uniquely linked to the signatory as long as the signatory manages to keep the key secret, fulfilling requirement (a). A CSP can conform the identity of the signer, fulfilling requirement (b). The encryption technology used for digital signatures is capable of fulfilling requirement (d): any changes made to the document can be detected.

Standards for the use of electronic signatures are developed within the European Electronic Signatures Standardisation Initiative (EESSI).[40] Within this initiative a format for the use of advanced electronic signatures has been formulated.[41]

---

36 *Cf.* Gupta, Tung & Marsden (2004), p. 562.

37 Dumortier *et al.* (2003) at p. 29 note that the electronic signature does not cover methods and technologies for 'entity authentication' (for example access control), such as gaining access to a bank account with a PIN code. However, if the same code is used to confirm a transaction, this can be seen as data authentication in the meaning of the directive.

38 Article 1(2) of Directive 1999/93/EC.

39 In this manner: Aalberts & Van der Hof (2000), p. 22.

40 The EESSI is a working group within the Information & Communications Technologies Standardisation Board, for more information see <www.ict.etsi.org>. See also Dumortier *et al.* (2003), Chapter 3.

41 See formats developed by ETSI TC ESI available on the website <www.ict.etsi.org>.

4.2 Other relevant definitions

The directive meticulously defines the various terms involved in the placing of electronic signatures.

The *signatory* is the person who holds a signature creation device and acts either on his own behalf or on behalf of the natural or legal person or entity he represents.[42] A *signature creation device* is configured software or hardware used to implement the signature creation data, for example a chip card or some other device used to store the signature creation data (a hard disk) and used to create the electronic signature.[43] *Signature creation data* mean unique data, such as codes or private cryptographic keys, which are used by the signatory to create an electronic signature.[44] *Signature verification data* are data, such as codes or public cryptographic keys, which are used to verify an electronic signature.[45] These are stored on a *signature verification device* meaning configured software or hardware used to implement the signature verification data. The signature creation and verification devices are *electronic-signature products*: hardware or software or relevant components thereof, which are intended to be used by a certification service provider for the provision of electronic-signature services or intended to be sued for the creation or verification of electronic signatures.[46] A *certification service provider*[47] is defined as an entity or a legal or natural person who issues certificates or provides other services related to electronic signatures.[48] A *certificate* is an electronic attestation that links signature-verification data (for example the decryption key) to a person and confirms the identity of that person.[49] Such a certificate is issued by a CSP.

Noteworthy is the reference in some of the definitions to the use of private and public cryptographic keys, be it as an example, this is a strong indication that the directive was largely written with the use of digital signatures in mind.

---

42 Article 2(3) of Directive 1999/93/EC.

43 Article 2(5) of Directive 1999/93/EC.

44 Article 2(4) of Directive 1999/93/EC.

45 Article 2(7) and (8) of Directive 1999/93/EC.

46 Article 2(12) of Directive 1999/93/EC.

47 Also: a Certification Authority (CA).

48 Article 2(11) of Directive 1999/93/EC. The term 'certification service provider' in the directive is misleading as it also covers services that do not entail issuing of certificates.

49 Article 2(9) of Directive 1999/93/EC.

5 The legal status of electronic signatures

5.1 Level 1: The signature is to be treated equally to the handwritten signature

The previous paragraph mentioned that several 'levels' can be distinguished when it comes to the legal status of electronic signature according to the Directive on Electronic Signatures. Basically, two levels can be distinguished: (1) the electronic signature is considered equal to the handwritten signature and (2) the electronic signature is not to be denied legal effect. This Section will first discuss the higher level 1-status. Section 5.2 below discusses the lesser level 2-status.

An electronic signature is to be treated legally equal to an handwritten signature when it concerns an:[50]

1) advanced electronic signature based on
2) a qualified certificate created with
3) a secure-signature-creation device.

Ad 1) Advanced electronic signature
The definition of 'advanced electronic signature' was discussed above. If the 'normal' electronic signature lives up to the requirements summed up under (a) to (d) it qualifies as an advanced electronic signature. It was already noted that momentarily the use of the digital signature techniques comes to mind to attain this.

Ad 2) a qualified certificate
A qualified certificate is a certificate that meets the requirements laid down in Annex I of the Directive on Electronic Signatures and is issued by a CSP who fulfils the requirements summed up in Annex II of the directive. Annex I contains 10 requirements regarding the information that should be included in the certificate. Annex II contains a total of 16 requirements[51] relating to the quality of the service provider. In short it entails that the certification service provider must be secure, use proper methods (such as proper hardware, software and personnel) and have sufficient financial resources available.

The previously mentioned EESSI has developed standards that can be used for the implementation of the requirements of the directive and its annexes. Member States have to install an appropriate system that allows for supervision of the certification service providers that issue qualified certificates.[52]

---

[50] Article 5(1) of Directive 1999/93/EC.

[51] In fact there are 12 from (a) to (l) but the twelfth is split up in 4 sub-requirements.

[52] Article 3(3) of Directive 1999/93/EC. Member States may not make the provision of the services subject to prior authorisation, however they may introduce voluntary accreditation schemes see Article 3(1)

Ad 3) a secure-signature-creation device

The definition of signature-creation device was already stated above. It refers to software or hardware used to place the electronic signature or as the directive puts it eloquently: 'implement the signature-creation data'. To qualify as a *secure-signature-creation device*, the device must meet the requirements laid down in Annex III of the Directive on Electronic Signatures. This Annex contains 4 requirements relating to the quality of the device. Within the EESSI more specific security requirements are defined.[53] Conformity of the secure-signature-creation device with the requirements is to be supervised by appropriate public or private bodies, designated by Member States.[54]

Qualified electronic signatures

Signatures that fulfil all these requirements are also referred to as 'qualified electronic signatures'. An overview of the requirements can be found in Annex A of this book. Member States must ensure that these signatures can satisfy the legal requirements of a signature in relation to data in electronic form in the same manner as a handwritten signature satisfies these requirements in relation to paper based data.[55] This means that where in relation to paper documents a handwritten signature is required according to the law, equivalent status must be given to the qualified electronic signature in relation to electronic documents.[56]

However, it remains up to national law to determine the legal spheres in which electronic documents may be used.[57] As a consequence, where national law does not allow the use of electronic documents the electronic signature cannot be used. It can be noted here that the E-commerce Directive requires Member States to ensure that electronic contracting is possible.

---

and 3(2) of Directive 1999/93/EC. On this topic Dumortier *et al.* (2003), in particular Sections 1.3, 1.4, 1.6 and 1.7. This report emphasises (on. 145) that it is incorrect to consider the voluntary accreditation scheme as a means to control compliance of the CSP with the directive.

53 See the CEN Workshop Agreements, available on the EESSI website <www.ict.etsi.org/EESSI_home.htm>.

54 Article 3(4) of Directive 1999/93/EC. Commissioin Decision 2000/709/EC of 6 November 2000 on the minimum criteria to be taken into account by Member States when designating bodies in accordance with Article 3.4 of Directive 1999/93/EC, OJ L 289 of 16-11-2000, p. 42 contains the criteria Member States must take into account when designating such bodies.

55 Article 5(1) (a) of Directive 1999/93/EC, Dumortier *et al.* (2003), at p. 70 state that this establishes the refutable assumption a signature fulfilling these requirements is considered as satisfying the legal requirements of a handwritten signature in relation to the data it is attached to.

56 See Dumortier *et al.* (2003), p. 50.

57 Recital 21 of Directive 1999/93/EC.

Furthermore, the Directive on Electronic Signatures states that the qualified electronic signature should be admissible as evidence.[58] However it is up to national law to determine the value of the electronic evidence.[59]

Dumortier *et al.* (2003) state[60] that the directive also encompasses a non-discrimination rule: it prohibits the requirement by law of the use of the qualified electronic signature where there was no requirement for a handwritten signature in the first place.

5.2 Level 2: The electronic signature cannot be denied legal effectiveness

It is not always necessary to use a qualified signature as discussed above. If an electronic signature does not meet all the requirements summed up above, it can still have legal effect. The electronic signature then falls within the second level as provided for by the Directive on Electronic Signatures. This level does in fact, not grant any actual status. It provides that the electronic signature cannot be denied legal effectiveness nor may it be denied admissibility in legal proceedings, solely on the grounds that it is:[61]

- in electronic form,
- not based upon a qualified certificate,
- not based upon a qualified certificate issued by an accredited certification-service-provider, or
- not created by a secure signature-creation device.

As a result of this rule, all forms of electronic signatures have potential legal effectiveness. However, the status of the electronic signatures that fall within this level remains uncertain. A judge can refuse to accept the validity of electronic signatures, as long as the bases of the rejection is not one of these grounds. For example a judge can reject the electronic signature because he may find that the electronic signature does not fulfil the function it is intended for or if the used technology is unreliable or he might find there is reason to believe the encryption key has been compromised. The recitals underline that the legal recognition should be based upon objective criteria.[62]

---

58 Article 5(1) (b) of Directive 1999/93/EC, Dumortier *et al.* (2003) note at p. 50 that this rule is superfluous as all Member States accept electronic evidence.

59 Recital 21 of Directive 1999/93/EC.

60 At p. 156.

61 Article 5(2) of Directive 1999/93/EC.

62 Recital 21 of Directive 1999/93/EC.

This rule has as a consequence that the legal value of electronic signatures will have to be determined on a case-by-case bases, with reference to the technology used and the circumstances they were used in.[63]

The freedom of parties to contract on the use of electronic signatures remains intact. This means that parties can agree amongst them if and under what conditions they accept electronic signatures in their dealings.[64]

5.3 Critical remarks

It can be questioned if the Directive on Electronic Signatures makes a significant contribution with regard to the legal appreciation of electronic signatures. To begin with, except for the 'level 1-signatures', the directive does not establish what value the Member States and their courts of law should attribute to electronic signatures. Furthermore, the directive explicitly does not intent to regulate anything with regard to the conclusion or the validity of contracts. The directive does not affect the requirements of form such as the obligatory use of paper documents combined with signatures.[65]

Although potentially all electronic signatures have legal effect the directive does not give any clues as to which kind of signatures are to be used in different types of situations or transactions. It is up to the users of the signatures to determine which type they wish to use. If the signature is then questioned, appreciation (by a judge) on a case-by-case basis will have to determine if the used technique is sufficient or not. As a result, the legal consequences of the use of an electronic signature are still uncertain and can vary considerably from one Member State to another. Adding to this the manner in which the directive is implemented in the Member States can vary.[66]

For the legal value of the electronic signature, the handwritten signature is the reference point.[67] This is a strong indication that the directive only sees to situations where the electronic signature is used as a substitute for handwritten signatures. However, special needs of the information society (no face to face

---

[63] *Cf.* Dumortier *et al.* (2003), they state at p. 51 that a denial of legal effect must be fully supported by a sufficiently reasoned and rationally based evaluation, one that is individual in nature, rather then being general in design.

[64] Recital 16 of Directive 1999/93/EC.

[65] Article 1 and recital 17 of Directive 1999/93/EC.

[66] See Dumortier *et al.* (2003), they conclude that the objective of the directive has not been entirely met, partly due to the manner in which it has been implemented by Member States (p. 139). Van Esch (2003) reports on the differences in the manner in which the directive has been implemented in the Netherlands and in the United Kingdom.

[67] Article 5(1) of Directive 1999/93/EC reads: '*...in the same manner as a handwritten signature satisfies those requirements in relation to paper based data...*'.

contact, use of documents that are easily manipulated) might call for a need of electronic signatures in situations where a handwritten signature is not necessary or would normally not be used. The directive does not seem to take such needs into account, nor the fact that the electronic signature can have further reaching possibilities or different functions then the handwritten signature.

CHAPTER 7

The Brussels Regulation

1 General

Internet presence inevitably means an international presence. The cross border character of internet entails an increased risk for business organisations on internet of becoming involved in international disputes.[1] One of the most well-known examples of an international internet related dispute is the *Yahoo!* case.[2]

Yahoo! Inc. v. La Ligue Contre Le Racisme et L'Antisemitisme

On a website of the Californian based company Yahoo! nazi memorabilia were offered for sale. The display of such material is forbidden in France and Yahoo! was sued before a French court. The French Court decided that the material must be made inaccessible in France (experts stated that available technical solutions to restrict access can have up to 80 percent success rate). On request of Yahoo! a US District Court declared that the French judgment was unenforceable in The United States (*Yahoo! Inc.* v. *la Ligue contre le Racisme et L'antisemitisme*, 169 F. Supp. 2d 1181. N.D. Cal. 2001). Enforcing the judgment would violate the (highly valued) American First Amendment. Nonetheless, Yahoo!-France has complied with the judgment and the case instigated other companies to do the same. For example, the research conducted by Zittrain & Edelman (2002) showed that search results on google.de (Germany) and google.fr (France) are different from the search result on google.com, the former two do not show information that might infringe German or French laws.

The court that is competent to hear an international dispute is not necessarily a court in the country which law is applicable.[3]

With regard to jurisdictional questions in civil and commercial matters within Europe Council Regulation (EC) No. 44/2001 (the Brussels Regulation) is relevant. This regulation replaces the Convention on Jurisdiction and the Enforcement of Judgments in Civil and Commercial Matters[4] (the Brussels Convention).

---

1 See also: Steyn (2000).

2 *La Ligue Contre le Racisme et L'Antisemitisme* v. *Yahoo! Inc*, Interim Court Order No. 00/05309, T.G.I. Paris, 22 May 2000. *La Ligue Contre le Racisme et l'Antisemitisme* v. *Yahoo! Inc*, Final Order, T.G.I. Paris, 20 November 2000.

3 As opposed to American courts, which often apply the *lex forum* principle, meaning that if a court has jurisdiction it will apply the law of the state where it is situated.

4 Signed at Brussels, 27 September 1986, OJ L 299, 1968, p. 32, OJ C 189, 28-7-1990. For a consolidated version of the Convention: OJ C 27, 26-1-1998.

The Brussels Regulation is to update the rules of the Brussels Convention to meet the needs of the information society and the therewith-related e-commerce.[5] Additionally, using the regulation as the legal instrument for this subject simplifies the integration of the rules within new Member States of the EU. The regulation will be directly applicable in the new Member States, while the integration of a convention means that all the new countries have to become a party to the convention.[6]

For the most part, the Brussels Regulation is similar to the Brussels Convention, but several rules – notably in relation to consumer contracts – have been adjusted.[7] Just as the convention, the regulation contains a general ground establishing jurisdiction and several specific grounds deviating from the general rule. Furthermore, the regulation aims to simplify the formalities for recognition and swift enforcement of judgments delivered by a court in another Member State by a uniform procedure.

The following Sections will address the main principles of the Brussels Regulation.[8] The rules with regard to jurisdiction are far more complex then presented in this work, but discussing the rules *in extenso* would go beyond the aims of this book. The awareness of (at least) these main principles can be a reason for business organisations to implement measures that reduce the risk of being sued before foreign courts. It can also be a reason for organisations to seek further advise on this topic.

2 Scope of applicability

2.1 General

The Brussels Regulation applies to civil and commercial matters excluding revenue, customs or administrative matters.[9] Although it is not stated in the regulation that it applies to *international* jurisdictional issues, the regulation does not come into play when the conflict does not have an international aspect casting doubts on the state where the proceedings should be instituted.[10] The Brussels Regulation is applicable in all Member States except for

---

5 For a concise description of the realisation of Regulation (EC) No. 44/2001: Berliri (2003). For critical remarks on the transformation of the Convention to a regulation: Beaumont (2002).

6 See Vlas (2000).

7 On the Brussels Regulation and some important differences compared to the Convention see Van Haersolte-Van Hof (2001), Beaumont (2002).

8 For an extensive discussion of this topic: Van der Hof (2002), Foss and Bygrave (2000).

9 Article 1 of Regulation (EC) No. 44/2001.

10 Van der Hof (2002), p. 43.

11 Recital 21 of Regulation (EC) No. 44/2001, also: OJ C 340/101, 10-11-1997. In relation with Denmark the Brussels Convention remains applicable.

Denmark.[11] This is because the legal base of the regulation is found in Title IV of the EC Treaty.[12] Denmark has an opt-out Protocol from this title and cannot selectively opt-in.[13]

Prima facie the regulation affects EU Member States and the business organisations therein, however it can also have implications for non-EU based companies.[14] It is not unlikely that European courts will assume jurisdiction over non-EU companies based on the principles as stated in the regulation. This is supported by the European Court of Justice, which held that Title II of the Brussels Convention is in principle applicable where the defendant has its domicile or seat in a contracting state, even if the plaintiff is domiciled in a non-member country.[15] This case was decided under the Brussels Convention. The cases decided under the convention remain relevant insofar as the provisions of the Brussels Regulation are the same as those of the convention.

2.2 Exemptions

The Brussels Regulation does not apply to:[16]

- the status or legal capacity of natural persons, rights in property arising out of a matrimonial relationship, will and succession,
- bankruptcy, proceedings relating to the winding-up of insolvent companies or other legal persons, judicial arrangements, compositions and analogous proceedings,
- social security,
- arbitration.

3 General rule

The general principle of the Brussels Regulation states that jurisdiction lies in the Member State of domicile of the defendant, irrespective of his nationality.[17] The place of domicile of a company is the place where it has:[18]

---

[12] Namely Article 65 of the EC Treaty, for critical remarks on the choice of this legal bases see Beaumont (2002).

[13] See also Beaumont (2002), p. 13.

[14] Berliri (2003), p. 11.

[15] Case C-412/98, *Group Josi Reinsurance SA* v. *Universal General insurance Company (UGIC)* [2000] ECR I-5925. Discussed in: Vlas, Zilinsky & Ibili (2002) at p. 106.

[16] Article 1(2) of Regulation (EC) No. 44/2001.

[17] Article 2(1) of Regulation (EC) No. 44/2001. When the defendant is not domiciled in one of the Member States, the regulation is not applicable.

[18] Article 60 of Regulation (EC) No. 44/2001.

· its statutory seat, or
· its central administration, or
· its principal place of business.

If the statutory seat, the central administration and the principal place of business are in different countries, the plaintiff can choose where to sue the company.[19]

It is not indicated how the place of domicile as meant in this regulation relates to the country of establishment as meant in the E-commerce Directive (see Section 3.5 of Chapter 2). It would be practical if both rules have the same result and point to the same Member State.

The general rule that jurisdiction lies in the Member State of the defendant can be seen as a point of departure. The regulation contains some specifications and allows several derogations to this general rule. An important derogation is the freedom of parties to enter into an agreement on the competent court (prorogation).[20] In B2B relations, the business partners will generally include such a choice of court in their contracts. Furthermore there are special provisions that allow alternative courts in addition to the court that is competent according to the general rule (alternative jurisdiction) and special provisions that grant a court exclusive jurisdiction deviant from the basic rule (exclusive jurisdiction).

4 Alternative rules of jurisdiction

4.1 General

There are several disputes where the regulation allows the plaintiff a choice between a court in the Member State of the defendant and an alternative court. The ratio of offering the possibility of an alternative court is that the matter at hand might have a close connection to a certain court. In that case it can be more opportune to have the case decided at the court that has a close link with the matter instead of the court of the defendants' domicile. This derogation from the general rule should be applied restrictively, namely only when this is in the interest of due administration of justice.[21] Choosing an alternative court is allowed with regard to disputes in relation to:[22]

---

[19] Beaumont (2002), p. 15.

[20] Article 23 of Regulation (EC) No. 44/2001.

[21] See Case 33/78, *Somafer SA* v. *Saar ferngas AG* [1978] ECR 2183, paragraph 7. This judgment was passed under the Brussels Convention, the wordings of this article have not changed in the Brussels Regulation and therefore the case law remains relevant.

[22] Article 5 of Regulation (EC) No. 44/2001.

1) contracts,
2) maintenance,
3) tort, delict or quasi delict,
4) a civil claim for damages based on an act giving rise to criminal proceedings,
5) operations of a branch, agency or other establishment,
6) payment of remuneration claimed in respect of the salvage of a cargo or freight.

In the light of e-commerce ad. 1 (contracts), ad. 3 (tort) and ad. 5 (operations of localised establishments) are particularly relevant and will be further discussed.

4.2 Contracts

Defendants may be sued in a different Member State than their home state in matters relating to contract. Besides the court in the home state of the defendant the court in the country of performance of the obligation in question is competent to decide the case.[23] This is the same rule as was already known in the Brussels Convention. It means that jurisdiction is linked to the obligation relied on by the plaintiff (*i.e.* the obligation in question). If he relies on the payment then a court in the Member State of payment is competent. If the performance of the seller is brought into question, then a court in the Member State where the contract was performed (or should have been performed) is competent.

The Brussels Regulation adds an important specification to this rule. The regulation states that, unless otherwise agreed, the place of performance of the obligation in question is:[24]

- with regard to the sale of goods: the place in a Member State where, under the contract, the goods were delivered or should have been delivered,
- with regard to the provision of services: the place in a Member State where, under the contract, the services were provided or should have been provided.

This means that in contracts for sale of goods or delivery of services, a judge in the Member State where the goods or services are delivered (or should have been delivered) has jurisdiction over a conflict relating to that contract.

For other types of contracts, such as more complex types of contracts (not concerning the straightforward sale of goods or services) or contracts where the place of performance is not a Member State, jurisdiction is determined by the

---

[23] Article 5(1) a of Regulation (EC) No. 44/2001.

[24] Article 5(1) b of Regulation (EC) No. 44/2001.

place of performance of the obligation in question (*i.e.* relied on by the plaintiff in the dispute).[25]

The distinction between goods and services can be problematic when electronic delivery is possible.[26] Should such a delivery be considered the delivery of a good or the provision of a service? Nevertheless, in both cases the jurisdiction is situated at the receiving end of the object of the contract. This means that qualification of electronically delivered goods as either goods or services is not absolutely necessary. With regard to the emerging mobile commerce and wireless applications, electronic delivery could lead to problems regardless of how the electronically delivered good (or service) is qualified. In that case, the receiving end of the soft product could be anywhere.

4.3 Tort

In matters related to tort, delict or quasi delict, the court where the harmful event occurred or may occur is competent.[27] The place where the harmful event occurred can be either the place where the harmful event, giving rise to the damage took place or the place where the damage was suffered. If the two are not located in the same place, the complainant may choose where to sue.[28]

4.4 Operations of a branch, agency or other establishment

If the dispute arises as a result of the doings of a branch, agency or other establishment of a company, the courts where such a localised office is situated are competent in addition to the court of the main establishment of the company.[29]

For this rule to apply, the localised office must be of some permanency. This is the case when the office has its own management and is materially equipped to negotiate business.[30] An independent agent merely transmitting orders is not considered a branch, agency or establishment of the parent undertaking.[31] The

---

[25] Article 5(1) c of Regulation (EC) No. 44/2001, see Beaumont (2002) for an explanation of the consequences of this article.

[26] In case of digitised goods or soft products.

[27] Article 5(3) of Regulation (EC) No. 44/2001.

[28] Case 21-76 of 30 November 1976 *Handelskwekerij G. J. Bier BV v Mines de potasse d'Alsace SA* [1976] ECR 1735.

[29] Article 5(5) of Regulation (EC) No. 44/2001. The provision is equal to its predecessor; Article 5(5) of the Brussels Convention, therefore the case law related to the Brussels Convention retains its relevance.

[30] Case 33/78, *Somafer SA* v. *Saar-Ferngas AG.* [1978] ECR 2183.

[31] Case 139/80, *Blanckaert & Willems PVBA* v. *Luise Trost* [1981] ECR 819.

European Court of Justice has determined there should be material signs[32] and an easy discernible extension of the parent body.[33]

It is unlikely that this will include virtual offices such as websites and electronic agents. These electronic offices and agents lack the required material signs and can be seen as means of transmitting information and orders to the main location of the company. Literature generally supports that the accessibility of a website does not mean that there is a local establishment in the sense of the Brussels Regulation.[34] The same is valid for the enabling technology, such as a web server. Within the meaning of the Brussels Regulation, the technology does not constitute a branch, agency or other establishment that triggers the jurisdiction of the country in which it is located.[35]

The place of establishment of the company is then determinative for the place of jurisdiction and not the place where the website is hosted or accessible or where the electronic agent is used. This approach can also be found in the E-commerce Directive, which states that '*...the presence and use of technical means and technologies in themselves do not constitute and establishment...*'.[36]

5 Special rules of jurisdiction

5.1 Introduction

Besides the rules that appoint alternative courts that are competent in addition to the court appointed by the general rule, the Brussels Regulation contains rules that appoint exclusive jurisdiction in deviation from the general rule. This concerns the following topics:

1) insurance,[37]
2) consumer contracts,[38]
3) contracts of employment,[39]
4) immovable property,
5) validity, constitution and nullity of legal persons,
6) validity of entries in public registers,
7) patents and trademarks.

---

32 Paragraph 11 *Somafer SA* v. *Saar-Ferngas AG*.

33 Paragraph 12 *Blanckaert & Willems PVBA* v. *Luise Trost*.

34 Van der Hof (2002), p. 60, Foss & Bygrave (2000), p. 133, both authors argue that a different conclusion is possible with regard to the same wordings in relation to consumer contracts.

35 *Cf.* Gillies (2001), Van der Hof (2002), Foss & Bygrave (2000).

36 Article 2(c) of Directive 2000/31/EC.

37 Addressed by Articles 8-14 of Regulation (EC) No. 44/2001.

38 Addressed by Articles 15-17 of Regulation (EC) No. 44/2001.

39 Addressed by Articles 18-21 of Regulation (EC) No. 44/2001.

Additionally, an important deviation from the general rule is allowed by prorogation: parties are allowed to agree which court shall be competent to settle the disputes that arise between them with regard to a certain issue. In the following, consumer contracts and prorogation will be further discussed, these topics are considered to be particularly relevant in relation to e-commerce.

5.2 Consumer contracts

5.2.1 General

A consumer contract is a contract concluded between a company and a person that acts for purposes that lie outside his trade or profession (a consumer).[40] Consumers are generally considered being the weaker party vis-à-vis professional contracting partners. That is why law often contains protective rules to strengthen the position of the consumer.

The Brussels Regulation also contains several rules that grant the consumer such a protected status. The consumer has the right to bring proceedings either in a court in the Member State of the company or in a court of the country where the consumer himself is domiciled.[41] The company, on the other hand, can only bring proceedings before a court in the home state of the consumer.[42] These protective rules apply with regard to the following consumers contracts:

a) contracts for the sale of goods on instalment credit terms;
b) contracts for a loan repayable by instalments, or for any other form of credit, made to finance the sale of goods
c) in all other cases, if:
   · the contract has been concluded with a person who pursues commercial or professional activities in the Member State of the consumer's domicile or
   · by any means, directs such activities to that Member State or to several Member States including that Member State and the contract falls within the scope of such activities.[43]

The first two categories mention 'the sale of goods', however in the explanatory memorandum accompanying the proposal for a Council Regulation of 14 July 1999, the Commission states that the rules under (a) to (c) relate to both

40 Article 15(1) of Regulation (EC) No. 44/2001. A strict interpretation of the concept 'consumer' seems to be intended, Van der Hof (2002) p. 28.

41 Article 16(1) Regulation (EC) No. 44/2001.

42 Article 16(2) Regulation (EC) No. 44/2001.

43 Article 15(1) Regulation (EC) No. 44/2001. 'Pursuing commercial activities' in the meaning of this article should not be confused with 'pursuing an economic activity' in the meaning of the E-commerce Directive, which serves to determine the country of establishment of the business.

goods and services.[44] This resolves the issue whether or not digitised goods (or soft products) can fall within the scope of categories (a) and (b).[45] Indeed, it can be considered unfair to deprive the consumer of the protection offered by the regulation on the bases of the medium by which the product is delivered to the consumer.[46]

Category (c), the widest and the most important category, simply refers to 'the contract' avoiding the question whether it covers either goods or services. All sorts of contracts fall within this category. Expressly excluded from the applicability of the special rules are contracts of transport other than a contract that, for an inclusive price, provides for a combination of travel and accommodation.[47] This is a noteworthy exemption in relation to internet e-commerce; it covers for example airplane seat bookings made via internet.

5.2.2 Pursuing or directing commercial activities

The point of reference for category (c) is whether the company pursues commercial or professional activities in the Member State of the consumer's domicile or if it directs such activities to that Member State. Unfortunately the meaning of this in more practical terms is not explained. There is no definition for 'pursuing commercial activities' included in the regulation and it is not specified what is meant by 'directing such activities'. The difference between 'pursuing' and 'directing' is not clear, nor how the difference can be expressed in a practical setting. It can be assumed the two are closely related. The terms will not be considered separately. In any event the two words mean to refer to the same issue that is relevant here: where are the potential customers of the on-line company?

As a website is accessible worldwide this can lead to the conclusion that the website is 'directed at' consumers worldwide. The wordings 'by any means' contribute to such a broad interpretation.[48] On the other hand the explanatory memorandum of 14 July 1999 states that:

'The concept of activities pursued in or directed towards a Member State is designed for consumer contracts concluded via interactive websites. The fact that the consumer simply had knowledge of a service or possibility of buying goods via a passive website accessible in his country of domicile will not trigger the protective jurisdiction.'[49]

---

[44] Brussels, 14-7-1999, COM (1999) 348 final, p. 16.

[45] Foss & Bygrave (2000), p. 108.

[46] Foss & Bygrave (2000), p. 112.

[47] See Article 15(3) of Regulation (EC) No. 44/2001.

[48] *Cf.* Gillies (2001).

[49] Brussels, 14-7-1999, COM (1999) 348 final, p. 16.

This raises the impression that the decisive criterion is whether the website is interactive or not.[50]

This is comparable to the American approach where judges are reluctant to assume jurisdiction over defendants from other states with regard to passive websites.[51] According to US case law, some level of interactivity is required to be able to accept jurisdiction over websites of foreign companies.[52] American case law shows that websites can be arranged on a sliding scale ranging from the passive website that merely presents information to the highly interactive website.[53] It can be noted that if the website is passive it is not very likely that an electronic consumer contract will be concluded via the website.[54]

During the legislative procedure, the European Parliament had proposed a paragraph defining the concept 'activities directed towards one or more Member States'. The Parliaments suggested to define this as *'any attempt by an operator to confine its business to transactions with consumers domiciled in certain Member States'*.[55] The Commission rejected such a paragraph, arguing that this would lead to new fragmentation of the market within the community. Suppliers would then be able to expressly limit their activities to certain Member States to minimise the risk of being sued in other jurisdictions.

Furthermore, the Commission stated that the very existence of a consumer contract would be a clear indication that the supplier has directed his activities towards the state of that consumer's domicile.[56] The Commission thus links the question whether or not an activity is directed towards a Member State to the existence of a contract with a consumer in that Member State. This would mean all conflicts risen over consumer contracts fall within the scope of the protective jurisdiction. This approach disregards the fact that the purpose of the criterion is to determine whether or not an international consumer contract falls within the ambit of the protective jurisdiction in the first place.[57] Following the viewpoint of the Commission entails that the criterion would not be needed at all.

---

50 Joustra (2001), p. 81.

51 Biukovic (2002), p. 150.

52 See August (2002), p. 550 and the there discussed American case law.

53 Van der Hof (2002), p. 99, August (2002), p. 550 and cited cases.

54 A contract can then be concluded for example by telephone or if the consumer visits the company abroad. A contract concluded over the telephone is a distant contract but not an electronic contract and is not considered in this work.

55 Amended proposal for a Council Regulation on jurisdiction and the recognition and enforcement of judgments in civil and commercial matters of 26 October 2000, COM (2000) 689 final, p. 5.

56 Amended proposal for a Council Regulation on jurisdiction and the recognition and enforcement of judgments in civil and commercial matters, p. 6.

57 Schaub (2001) at p. 100.

5.2.3 Localising the e-commerce activities

The wordings of the regulation and the various clues produced during the legislative procedure do not make it irrefutably clear whether or not companies can limit their risk of being sued by consumers in other Member States by localising their on-line activities. Compared to the Rome Convention it appears that the Brussels Regulation has fewer possibilities to localise activities and thereby limit the risk of being sued before foreign courts.

Localising on-line activities means that a company can make efforts to expressly limit its activities to a certain geographical area. This can be expressed by using a localised domain name and a corresponding language. A more direct way to avoid contracts with consumers localised in 'undesired' jurisdictions, is to state that orders from those areas are not handled. This can be backed with technological measures such as IP-recognition.

It can be argued that consumers that deliberately ignore the statements made by the electronic vendor or even deliberately circumvent the efforts of the company to limit its activities to certain areas will not be able to rely on the protective jurisdiction.[58] Various authors argue that the electronic vendor should be able to limit the risk of being sued in a foreign Member State by localising its activities.[59] There are considerably less authors that argue that offers of goods and services on a website constitute the pursuit of commercial activities in all states where the website can be downloaded.[60]

Controversially, if a company translates its website into various languages this is a clear indication that the economic activities are directed at the countries where those languages are spoken, even if the site is not interactive. For example, if a French company translates its website in Dutch, this is an indication that the French company wishes to direct its activities at the Dutch market, thus triggering the protective jurisdictional rules for the consumers in the Netherlands.[61]

As an overall conclusion it can be stated that interactive websites will have to take into consideration that courts in the consumers' home state may have jurisdiction with regard to contracts concluded via the website. If a company wishes to limit the risk of being subject to foreign jurisdictions he should take

58 Prior to the adoption of Regulation (EC) No. 44/2001, a similar argument for this point of view was made by Drion (1998).

59 Van der Hof (2002), p. 100, Joustra (2001), p. 81, Van der Velden (2001), p. 99.

60 Reich (2001), p. 173.

61 Languages such as English and Spanish are spoken in various jurisdictions, but within Europe these languages can still be an indication that this implies that the activities are directed to Spain and the United Kingdom. What is more, the language options are often represented by an icon representing the flag of certain countries, this can be seen as an indication of the geographical area the website is aiming at.

measures to localise his on-line activities, preferably supported by technical measures.

5.2.4 Branch, agency or other establishment

Business organisations with their main office established outside the EU are affected by the rules of the Brussels Regulation if they maintain a branch, agency or other establishment in one of the Member States.[62] It is unlikely that a website, an electronic agent or a server constitutes a branch, agency or other establishment. The same arguments as mentioned above in Section 4.4 with regard to branch, agency or other establishment can be used here. The notion branch, agency and other establishment is given the same interpretation in the context of the consumer contracts as in the context of the above-discussed alternative jurisdiction.[63]

Nonetheless seen the different purposes of the articles related to consumer contracts and those related to alternative jurisdiction different interpretations might be possible.[64] Case law with regard to this issue is as of yet scarce and it is not unthinkable that in the future a highly localised website might be considered a branch, agency or other establishment in the meaning of the regulation. Especially if the company uses localised telephone numbers and returning addresses, such as for example the localised website of the American based company Amazon at <www.amazon.de>. This website states a localised address for the return of goods.[65]

5.3 Prorogation

The Brussels Regulation allows that parties agree which will be the competent court to decide on disputes between them with regard to a certain legal relationship.[66] The chosen court will have exclusive jurisdiction, unless parties agree otherwise.

Business partners are well advised to include a choice of court (a forum selection clause) in their international contracts to prevent that any misunderstanding arise over the competent court in case of a dispute. Case law of the European Court of Justice under the Brussels Convention determined that the contracting partner should explicitly accept the forum selection clause. It

[62] Article 15(2) of Regulation (EC) 44/2001.

[63] Case C-318/93 *Brenner & Noller* v. *Dean Witter Reynolds* ECR [1994] I-4275.

[64] Van der Hof (2002) argues that a broader interpretation of the concept in relation to consumer contracts might be possible (p. 102).

[65] Foss & Bygrave (2000).

[66] Article 23 of Regulation (EC) No. 44/2001.

is therefore advisable to mention the clause during the ordering procedure. Furthermore, the agreement on the competent court has to be:[67]

- in writing or evidenced in writing, or
- in a form that accords with practices which the parties have established between themselves, or
- in a form which accords with a usage of which the parties are or ought to be aware and which are widely known and regularly observed by parties involved in the particular commerce concerned.

Durable record

For the purpose of the first indent, electronic communications that provide a durable record of the agreement shall be equivalent to 'writing'.[68] It is not specified what is meant by a 'durable record'. Possibly, the same explanation as given to 'durable medium' (see Section 4 of Chapter 3) can be used here.

The durable record is meant to enable parties to verify the agreement in a later stage. To determine if the agreement was provided on a durable record this can be used as the decisive criterion. For example, if the agreement is stored on a server which both parties may access, the agreement can be considered stored on a durable record.

In accordance with practices

The second indent includes situations where parties have negotiated the terms of contracts that will be concluded between them in the future. Such negotiations will not be likely in case of B2C contracts, therefore it can be assumed that this provision is meant for B2B contracting.[69] However this is not explicitly stated in the wordings of the regulations.

A form which accords with the usage

The third indent refers to international accepted business practice. It is also stated that the usage must be regularly observed. This means the form must be self evident and widely used. This option is only allowed in 'international trade or commerce' indicating that this form is meant for B2B contracting. With regard to on-line contracting it can be noted that the use of hyperlinks is widespread. At least with regard to B2B contracting it can be acceptable to have the forum selection clause available during the ordering procedure with a clearly labelled hyperlink.

In relation to consumer contracts that fall within the protective jurisdictional rules discussed above, forum selection clauses can only be included in the contract if they do not interfere with the special jurisdictional rules for

---

67 Article 23(1) of Regulation (EC) No. 44/2001.

68 Article 23(2) of Regulation (EC) No. 44/2001.

69 *Cf.* Van der Hof (2002), p. 40.

consumer contracts. This is the case when a forum selection clause offers the consumer additional possibilities, or if the choice of court was made after the dispute has arisen.[70]

As a result of these rules, forum selection clauses in international electronic consumer contracts that appoint the court in the home state of the company as the only competent court will not be valid. Finally, it should be noted that a choice of court agreement cannot be concluded if the contract does not have an international character.[71]

[70] The same is valid for insurance and individual employment contracts, Article 23(5) of Regulation (EC) 44/2001.

[71] There is no reference in Regulation (EC) No. 44/2001 that the dispute or contract should be international, but problems of jurisdiction will normally not arise if the contract is not of an international nature, compare Van der Hof (2002), p. 42.

CHAPTER 8

The Rome Convention

1 General

For the same reasons as mentioned in the previous Chapter with respect to jurisdiction, rules that govern applicable law in international relations are considered to be particularly relevant in e-commerce. Not all electronic business relations are international, but the borderless nature of electronic communication devices increases the chance of international contacts.

Despite the efforts of the European Union to harmonise various aspects of Member States' law, there are still many differences.[1]

The 1980 Rome Convention on the Law Applicable to Contractual Obligations (the Rome Convention)[2] determines which law is applicable to contractual obligations in case of international contracts. In the wake of the conversion of the Brussels Convention on jurisdiction, the Commission is reviewing the need to modernise the Rome Convention and possibly convert it to a community instrument. The Commission issued a green paper with a number of legal questions with the intent to provoke reactions on the issue.[3] For the time being, the Rome Convention remains in place.

The point of departure in the Rome Convention is the freedom of choice of the contracting parties to determine the law applicable to the contract concluded between them. If no choice is made, the convention prescribes how the applicable law is determined and there are several special rules prescribing applicable law in deviation to the general rule, *i.a.* with regard to consumer contracts.

The following Sections will highlight some of the general principles relevant for international electronic contracting, as laid down in the Rome Convention.[4] The convention does not cover tortuous behaviour; nevertheless a few words are dedicated to the situation regarding applicable law in non-contractual matters in Section 5.

2 Scope of applicability

2.1 General

The Rome Convention applies to contractual obligations in any situation involving a choice between the laws of different countries.[5] Geographi-

1 Jessurun d'Oliveira (2002), at p. 127 characterises the existence of private international law in Europe as a manifestation of the shallowness of the European harmonisation.

2 OJ L 266, 9-10-1980.

3 Green Paper on the conversion of the Rome Convention of 1980 on the law applicable to contractual obligations into a Community instrument and its modernisation, presented by the Commission. Brussels, 14-1-2003 COM (2002) 654 final.

4 For a more elaborate discussion of the body of rules: Van der Hof (2002), Kronke (1998).

5 Article 1(1) of the Rome Convention.

cally, the convention applies to the territory of the contracting states.[6] This does not preclude that the application of the rules can have as a result that the law of a non-contracting state applies to the international contract.[7] The convention does not affect the application of choice of law rules laid down in Community law or in national laws that implement the Community laws.[8] Such a choice of law rule can for example be found in Article 12(2) of the Distant Selling Directive, which states that consumers cannot lose the protection granted by that directive by virtue of a choice of law of a non-Member State as long as the distant contract has a close relation with the territory of the EU. Nor does it affect the application of other international conventions to which the contracting states are (or will become) a party.[9] Finally, the convention does not restrict the application of the mandatory rules of the law of the court that has jurisdiction.[10]

2.2 Exemptions

Several topics are explicitly exempted from the scope of applicability of the Rome Convention:[11]

- questions involving the status or legal capacity of natural persons,
- contractual obligations relating to wills and succession,
- contractual obligations relating to rights in property arising out of a matrimonial relationship,
- contractual obligations relating to rights and duties arising out of a family relationship, parentage, marriage or affinity, including maintenance obligations in respect of children who are not legitimate,
- obligations arising under bills of exchange, cheques and promissory notes and other negotiable instruments to the extent that the obligations under such other negotiable instruments arise out of their negotiable character,
- arbitration agreements and agreements on the choice of court,
- questions governed by the law of companies and other bodies corporate or unincorporate such as the creation, by registration or otherwise, legal capacity, internal organisation or winding up of companies and other bodies corporate or unincorporate and the personal liability of officers and members as such for the obligations of the company or body,
- the question whether an agent is able to bind a principal, or an organ to

6 See Article 27 of the Rome Convention for a specification of the geographical applicability with regard to the Faroe Islands, the Netherlands Antilles and territory under the responsibility of the United Kingdom situated outside Europe.

7 Article 2 of the Rome Convention.

8 Article 20 of the Rome Convention.

9 Article 21 of the Rome Convention.

10 Article 7(2) of the Rome Convention.

11 Article 1(2)-(4) of the Rome Convention.

bind a company or body corporate or unincorporate to a third party,
- the constitution of trusts and the relationship between settlers, trustees and beneficiaries,
- evidence and procedure, without prejudice to Article 14 of the Rome Convention (burden of proof),
- contracts of insurance (unless it is a contract of re-insurance) which cover risks situated in the territories of the Member States of the European Economic Community.

3 Law applicable to international contracts

3.1 Freedom of choice

The general principle in the Rome Convention is the freedom of choice: the law chosen by the parties shall govern the contract.[12] Parties can also decide that the chosen law only governs part of the contract. The country of origin principle of the E-commerce Directive does not affect this rule as this is explicitly exempted from the scope of this principle.[13] There are several restrictions to the freedom of choice that have to be taken into account:
- the choice for a foreign law cannot exclude the application of the mandatory rules of the (one) country that the contract is connected with,[14]
- the Rome Convention does not affect the application of provisions from community acts that lay down choice of law rules relating to contractual obligations,[15]
- the choice of law does not affect the application of the rules of the mandatory law of the court that decides on a dispute relating to the contract,
- there are special rules with regard to the law applicable to contracts concluded with consumers (see below).[16]

The choice of law must be expressed or demonstrated with reasonable certainty.[17] The existence and validity of the choice are determined by the law the parties have chosen (the law that would govern the contract if the choice was valid).[18]

---

12 Article 3(1) of the Rome Convention.

13 Article 3(3) of Directive 2000/31/EC. The (problematic) relation between the country of origin principle and the rules of private international rule was discussed above in Section 3.9 of Chapter 2.

14 Article 3(3) and Article 7 of the Rome Convention.

15 Article 20 of the Rome Convention.

16 Article 5 of the Rome Convention.

17 Article 3(1) of the Rome Convention.

18 Article 3(4) and Articles 8, 9 and 10 of the Rome Convention.

It should be noted that the rules of the Rome Convention are relevant insofar the Vienna Convention on the sale of goods is not applicable.[19]

3.2 Absence of a choice

3.2.1 Most closely connected

If no choice is made, the law of the country with which the contract is most closely connected shall govern the contract.[20] To determine the country with which the contract is most closely connected the convention indicates several presumptions:[21]

1) The contract is presumed to be most closely connected with the country where the party who is to effect the performance which is characteristic of the contract has his habitual residence.
2) With regard to contracts concerning immovable property, the contract is presumed to be most closely connected with the country where the property is situated.
3) With regard to contracts concerning the carriage of goods, the contract is presumed to be most closely connected to the country in which the carrier has his principal place of business if this country is also the place of loading or the place of discharge or the principal place of business of the consignor.

3.2.2 The characteristic performance

The characteristic performance mentioned in the first presumption is generally not the payment of a sum of money, but the performance that the money is paid for. For example, in contracts of sale the characteristic performance will normally be the delivery of the sold goods.[22] The delivery is to be performed by the seller and therefore the law of the country of the seller is then applicable to the contract of sale. Generally this should not lead to any problems; usually the seller or the service provider delivers the characteristic performance.

If, in spite of this, the characteristic performance cannot be determined, for example if both parties have to deliver a characteristic performance, the presumption does not apply. In that case, other characteristics of the contract

[19] United Nations Convention on Contracts for the International Sale of Goods (1980), available at < http://www.uncitral.org/english/texts/sales/CISG.htm>.

[20] Article 4 of the Rome Convention.

[21] Article 4 of the Rome Convention.

[22] For the sale of goods this is valid insofar as the Vienna Convention on the International sale of goods does not apply.

have to be used to determine which country is most closely connected to the contract. Furthermore, the presumptions should be disregarded if circumstances point to another country with which the contract is more closely connected. For some issues it can remain debatable which country is most closely connected. To prevent misunderstandings it is advisable to include a choice of law clause in the contract.

3.2.3 Habitual residence

The first presumption points to the country where the seller has its habitual residence. In determining the habitual residence of a company, the physical location of the business is determinative. If the party that has to perform the characteristic performance is a body corporate or unincorporated, the country where it has its central administration is the country where the company has its habitual residence. In case of multinationals, the main establishment can be appointed as the place of residence, but the impression raised by the company is also relevant here. For example which address is stated on the website?[23]

4 Consumer contracts

4.1 Introduction

The Rome Convention contains special rules with regard to consumer contracts[24] that can interfere with the choice of law in a contract. These special rules apply in case of a contract of which the object is the supply of goods or services (or for the provision of credit for such contracts) to a person for a purpose outside his trade or profession.[25] As the rules see to both goods and services there should be no problem to include contracts relating to digitised goods within the ambit.

In case of on-line contracting it can be problematic to know whether or not the other party is acting as a consumer. Circumstances such as the type of goods sold or the address used by the other party can be relevant to deter-

---

23 See Van der Hof (2002), p. 150, she discusses possible problems related to this topic.

24 Except for contracts of carriage and contracts for the supply of services where the services are to be supplied to the consumer exclusively in a country other than that in which he has his habitual residence. Package tours are explicitly included, see Article 5(4) and (5) of the Rome Convention.

25 Article 5 of the Rome Convention. The wordings are comparable to the wordings in Regulation (EC) No. 44/2001, the Guiliano & Lagarde 1980 Rapport on the Rome Convention indicates that if the object of the contract is only partly for trade or professional reasons, the contract can be considered a consumer contract. *Cf.* Van der Hof (2002), p. 28.

mine this. To achieve more certainty on this point the company can ask (for example during the ordering procedure) if the customer is buying for business purposes or for private purposes. The company can also explicitly indicate on the website whether or not it is intended for consumers. To prevent that consumers place orders, the company can design the ordering procedure as such that the customer is obliged to fill in a trade registration number. If the consumer deliberately disguises his identity or ignores clear statements that the site is not meant for consumers, he risks losing the protection offered to consumers by the convention.

4.2 Protected status of the consumer

The special rules with regard to consumer contracts entail that the consumer can rely on the mandatory consumer protection rules of his home state.[26] A choice of law in the contract is then only valid insofar that it does not have the result of depriving the consumer of this protection. The consumer has this protected status if:

- the conclusion of the contract was preceded by a specific invitation addressed to him or by advertising and all the necessary steps to conclude the contract on the consumers part are taken in his country, or
- the consumers' order was received in the country of the consumer, or
- the contract concerns the sale of goods and the seller arranged for the consumer to travel abroad to induce him to buy.

These criteria protect the so-called passive consumer: the consumer did not seek to conclude a contract of an international nature but was approached in his own country by a foreign company. The last criterion concerns situations where the company has arranged that the consumer travels to him, in the second the company travels to the consumer to take his order. In the context of internet the first criterion is the most interesting and will be further discussed. The question that needs to be answered is: does a website (which is by its nature accessible world-wide) constitute a specific invitation addressed to consumers worldwide? Or does the surfing consumer willingly accept that he enters the international area forfeiting the protection of the laws of his home state?

4.3 Specific invitation

A specific invitation addressed to the consumer refers to advertisements or invitations to treat in the country of the consumer, for example on national television, in the national or local papers, magazines, etc.[27] In literature

[26] Mandatory rules are rules that cannot be deviated from by making other arrangements.

[27] See van der Hof (2002), p. 196.

different approaches with regard to the issue if internet websites constitute a specific invitation can be distinguished.[28]

The restrictive approach adheres to the proposition that although the website is accessible worldwide this does not mean that it is directed at the whole world. In other words, a website does not constitute a specific invitation in all countries, but only in those countries at which it is specifically or expressly directed. Expressly directing a website at a certain state can be done by using a national domain-name and language, for example using a .nl domain name and the Dutch language means that the website constitutes a specific invitation to Dutch consumers.

The broad approach adheres to the view that the use of internet brings about a foreseeable worldwide accessibility and therefore the express or at least foreseeable effect that the company invites consumers world-wide to purchase its goods or services.

Despite these different views, there seems to be some consensus in literature that the company can limit the risk of being exposed to foreign mandatory consumer protection laws by localising the on-line activities. [29] Besides the use of a certain language or domain name, other possibilities to limiting the geographical scope of the website are: using a specific type of currency, stating expressly that the website is meant for inhabitants of certain states or asking the consumer for his home state and not accepting orders from unwanted states.[30] The more measures taken to limit the geographical scope of the offer, the smaller the risk of being subject to foreign laws.

Compared to the group of consumers that is granted a protective status under the Brussels regulation by using the phrase 'directing economic activities at' (see Section 5.2 of Chapter 7), the 'specific invitation'-criterion of the Rome Convention grants the protection to a smaller group.[31]

The criterion also requires that all the necessary steps to conclude the contract on the part of the consumer need to be taken in the consumers own country. With regard to internet accessed on a PC at the home of the consumer this does not create any problems. This is different when the consumer uses a computer in another country (for example in an internet cafe when he is on a holiday) or a mobile terminal such as a mobile phone or a PDA. In that case the consumer can be anywhere.

The same requirement was included in the Brussels convention on jurisdiction, but it was abandoned in the Brussels regulation. It is likely that with the

---

[28] See van der Hof (2002), p. 195-202 and the there mentioned literature.

[29] See Van der Hof (2002), p. 200. Van der Hof (2003) at p. 172 finds there is a need for rules to clarify this issue.

[30] If a consumer lies about his place of residence this should not be held against the vendor, compare Van der Hof (2003), p. 172.

[31] *Cf.* van der Hof (2002), p. 200.

revision of the Rome Convention the criteria will be adapted to match the criteria in the Brussels regulation.

Conclusion

A choice of law clause will be ineffective if the consumer can rely on the protective status under the Rome Convention. If no choice is made the law of the country in which the passive (and thus protected) consumer is applicable to the contract. If the consumer cannot rely on the protective rules, the applicable law is determined according to the general rules discussed above.

4.4 Other concerns

Besides the special protective rules of the Rome Convention, there are several European directives that can interfere with the choice of law in consumer contracts: Directive 93/13/EEC on unfair terms in consumer contracts, Directive 1999/44/EC on the sale of consumer goods and associated guarantees and Directive 97/7/EC on distant contracting. If the contract has a close connection with the territory of one or more Member States, a choice for the law of a non-Member State cannot deprive the consumer of the rights granted to him by these directives. [32] The rules of the European directives and the national rules implementing them have privilege over the rules of the Rome Convention.[33] Adding to this, national legislation can contain provisions stating that inhabitants cannot alienate certain rights.[34]

5 Tortuous behaviour

The Rome Convention does not cover tortuous behaviour. If there is an international conflict related to non-contractual matters most countries use a traditional conflict of law rule to determine the applicable law: the *lex loci delicti commissi* (the law of the country where the harmful event occurred and where the harm was inflicted).[35] Member States have different manners in which they apply this rule and different factors can be important when determining the applicable law. To harmonise these rules, European legislation is forthcoming in the form of a regulation. The Commission presented a proposal for a regulation on the law applicable to non-contractual obligations in July

---

32 Article 7 of Directive 1999/44/EC, Article 6 of Directive 93/13/EC and Article 12 of Directive 97/7/EC. Comparable provisions can be found in Directive 2002/65/EC on the distant marketing of consumer financial services and Directive 94/47/EC on the use of immovable property on a timeshare basis.

33 Article 20 of the Rome Convention.

34 For example Article 6:147(4) of the Dutch Civil Code determines that the rules with regard to standard terms are always applicable if a consumer has its habitual residence in the Netherlands.

35 See Kronke (1998), p. 67-73, several internet related examples are discussed.

2003.[36] This proposal is also known as the 'Rome II' proposal. The proposal is related to the Rome Convention with regard to applicable law to contractual relations.

The general rule laid down in the proposal is that the law of the place where the damage arises (or is likely to arise) is applicable.[37] This comes down to a country of destination rule. Only when the obligation is manifestly more closely related to another country the law of that other country applies. Furthermore, several specific rules are laid down for damage caused by product liability,[38] unfair competition, violations of privacy and personality rights, violation of the environment, infringement of intellectual property rights and obligations arising out of an act other then a tort or delict.

The country of destination rule of the proposal does not coincide with the country of origin principle laid down in the E-commerce Directive. However, Article 23(2) of the proposal states that the regulation shall not prejudice the application of Community instruments, which subject the supply of services or goods to the laws of Member States where the service provider is established. The explanatory memorandum accompanying the proposal states that this refers to specific principles of the internal market relating to the free movement of goods and services, known as the mutual recognition and home country control principles.[39]

---

36 Brussels, 22-7-2003 COM (2003) 247.

37 Article 3(1) of the Rome II proposal.

38 This is governed by Directive 85/374/EC of 25-7-1985 on the approximation of the laws, regulations and administrative provisions of the Member States concerning liability for defective products, OJ L 210, 7-8-1985, p. 29. As amended by Directive 1999/34/EC of 10-5-1999, OJ L 141, 4-6-1999, p. 20.

39 Rowe (2004) states (at p. 95) that the scope and effect of this carve-out of the Rome II Regulation remain unclear.

CHAPTER 9

Conclusions

1 Introduction

In the previous Chapters the main legal texts of the European legislative framework regarding e-commerce were discussed.

The point of departure of this book is the E-commerce Directive (Directive 2000/31/EC). This directive lies at the heart of the European legislative framework intended to regulate and facilitate e-commerce. The E-commerce Directive is closely related to several other legal texts issued by the EU. The directive therefore cannot be considered in isolation. Six other European legal texts that are considered to be particularly relevant for e-commerce were discussed: the Distant Selling Directive (Directive 97/7/EC), the Privacy Directive (Directive 95/46/EC), the Directive on Privacy and Electronic Communications (Directive 2002/58/EC), the Directive on Electronic Signatures (Directive 1999/93/EC), the Brussels Regulation on Jurisdiction (Regulation (EC) No. 44/2001) and the Rome Convention (1980 Rome Convention on law applicable to contractual obligations).

This relatively new European legal framework cannot be ignored by business organisations involved with e-commerce, if they wish to attain optimal performance. First, it is relevant in order to avoid legal risks that might lead to fines or costly procedures. Second, the legal framework contains protective and facilitative elements that could work in the business organisations' favour.

The subsequent Sections present several general findings and conclusions of the analyses of the legal framework.

2 Technology neutral

The European legislator has strived to formulate technology neutral legal texts in order to prevent that the rules become outdated due to the rapid technological developments. It can be concluded that the legal texts cannot be considered veritably technology neutral. The state of the art of the technology at the time of drawing up the legislation has placed its distinctive mark on the legal texts. Reading the E-commerce Directive one gets the strong impression that the articles were composed with internet websites in mind. Especially the large amount of information duties and the manner of electronic contracting that is prescribed by the directive contribute to this impression.

The same occurs with the Directive on Electronic Signatures: it aims to be technology neutral, but there is a strong indication that the directive builds upon the possibilities offered by cryptography supported by a Public Key Infrastructure (PKI). In fact it contains explicit references to the use of digital signatures based on PKI. What is more, concerning the legal value of signatures, the digital signature is given a higher status then other techniques. In other words, the directive privileges this technique over other existing and future technologies.

In the effort of creating technology neutral rules, the legislator has included open and inconclusive wordings. For example, the E-commerce Directive does not indicate how the information duties it prescribes should be fulfilled, it indicates that these should be provided 'clearly an unambiguously'. The Distant Selling Directive does not prescribe which technology should be used to comply with the post-contractual information duties; it states that these must be provided on a 'durable medium'. These open wordings allow the use of different technologies, but on the other hand this leads to a certain amount of legal uncertainty. Compliance will have to be evaluated on a case-by-case bases.

In relation to this it can be noted that the legal framework is still in its infancy. Many points need clarification with regard to how organisations might conform. For example does an e-mail suffice as a 'durable medium'? What can be considered 'clearly, comprehensibly and unambiguously'? What kind of electronic signatures are acceptable under which circumstances?

In answering these questions lawyers and judges will need some minimum insight in technological (im)possibilities. For example, knowledge on how an IP-number works is needed in order to be able to establish if such a number constitutes personal data. To be able to assess the acceptability of a particular type of electronic signature, one must have some knowledge on the level of trustworthiness that can be attained with it.

3 Contract law neutral

The E-commerce Directive does not state how and when electronic contracts are concluded. From that respect, the directive can be labelled 'contract law neutral'. With regard to electronic contracting, Article 9 of the E-commerce Directive (merely) states that the Member States are to ensure that electronic contracting is possible.

In essence, the article assigns the Member States with the task to scrutinise their laws and, if necessary, eliminate any barriers to electronic trade. This can have far reaching consequences in the sense that adaptation of all national laws that refer to the use of paper, handwritten signatures or other elements that relate to the physical world might be required. It is up to the Member States to determine how they can best resolve this issue within their national legal systems.

Despite this 'contract law neutrality' several rules are formulated that have to be taken into account in relation to electronic contracting. The E-commerce Directive states that the electronic vendor is obliged to send an acknowledgement of electronic orders, but the directive does not state how the (not) sending of the acknowledgement will affect the conclusion of the electronic contract. Additionally, it states when the electronic order and the acknowledgement are deemed to be received, but it does not state what the legal consequences of the receipt are.

The lack of harmonisation on this point can lead to confusion where the various Member States have different rules concerning the conclusion of contracts. This is to some extend resolved by transparency requirements. The electronic vendor is to state clearly how the electronic contract is concluded, and more in particular, what steps need to be taken by the customer to conclude the electronic contract.

The same 'neutrality' can be found in the Directive on Electronic Signatures, this directive states that electronic signatures should be valid but it does not harmonise the legal consequences of electronic signatures as such. The Directive on Electronic Signatures explicitly does not regulate anything with regard to the conclusion or the validity of contracts.

4 Country of origin principle

Despite the many efforts to harmonise laws in order to favour the development of the internal market, there are still many differences between the various Member State laws. In order to prevent that companies involved in cross border e-commerce have to take into account the laws of all Member States, the E-commerce Directive contains the country of origin principle. In short this principle entails that the electronic business activities are subject only to the laws of the Member State in which the company is established. The principle looks very promising upon first sight, but a closer look reveals that it only offers partial relief.

The principle affects laws that fall within the coordinated field. The scope of the concept 'coordinated field' is essential to be able to determine the scope of the country of origin principle. Unfortunately, the concept has given rise to some debate. The EU seems to have intended that the concept should be given a wide interpretation (in favour of the business organisation). All laws that affect on-line commercial activities fall within its scope. However a number of rules explicitly do not fall within the coordinated field: rules applicable to goods as such, rules applicable to the delivery of goods and rules concerning off-line service provision. With regard to these topics, country of destination rules will have to be taken into account.

Besides the rules that do not fall within the coordinated field, the topics exempted from the scope of the E-commerce Directive in general do not fall within the reach of the home state control principle. Adding to this, the Annex to the directive sums up several topics that are specifically excluded from the country of origin principle. This list includes important issues such as the freedom to choose the law applicable to the contract and the obligations concerning consumer contracts. Finally, if there are sufficient grounds Member States may derogate from the principle on an incidental bases. It can be concluded that a substantial amount of rules do not fall within the ambit of the country of origin principle.

Finally, it should be noted that the country of origin principle has an odd relation with rules of private international law concerning applicable law. It was concluded that although the E-commerce Directive explicitly states that the principle does not constitute an additional rule of private international law, the principle can nonetheless have the effect of a special rule of private international law.

5 B2C e-commerce

To compensate for the weaker bargaining powers of the consumer, there are considerably more as well as more stringent rules that need to be taken into account with regard to B2C e-commerce compared to B2B e-commerce. In a B2B relation the contracting partners are in most instances allowed to deviate from the rules of the E-commerce Directive, but with regard to B2C e-commerce the rules are mandatory. Adding to this, the Distant Selling Directive contains a substantive amount of protective rules, under which the right of withdrawal, allowing the consumer to withdraw from the electronic contract without giving any reason. Furthermore, the Privacy Directive contains strict requirements that need to be taken into account if any personal information of the consumer is handled. Moreover, in case of a dispute, the consumer can in most instances rely on the protective rules of his home state and the dispute should be referred to a judge in the home state of the consumer.

It can be concluded that companies involved in B2C trading run into a tightly woven legal web that is in favour of the consumer. The protective rules are meant to raise consumer trust and therewith advance the development of B2C e-commerce. One can only assume that the raised level of trust will offer enough counterweight to compensate for the burdens placed on the business organisation by the legal framework.

6 E-mail marketing

The Directive on Privacy and Electronic Communications installs an opt-in regime with regard to commercial e-mail messages. This entails that commercial messages can only be send if the recipient has given his prior consent. A serious restriction to this regime is that it does not protect legal persons. Another problem is the scope of protection of this opt-in regime, which only protects 'subscribers'.

The directive also forbids the sender to conceal his identity and a valid return address must be included in each message so that recipients can opt-out. This obligation protects both natural and legal persons.

In how far this regime will produce any effect with regard to the growing amount of spam messages remains to be seen. The bulk part of these messages seems to originate from outside the EU, which makes enforcement of these rules problematic. Moreover, it can be expected that rogue traders are not likely to comply with the new regime. Nonetheless, the regime can be seen as an important achievement in the fight against spam.

As an exception to the opt-in rule companies are allowed to send commercial messages to their customers (both natural and legal persons), as long as they offer the customers the opportunity to opt-out. This exception only concerns commercial messages with regard to products and services similar to those that were ordered by the customer during the collection of the e-mail address.

As of yet there is some uncertainty as to how the concept 'similar' should be understood in this context. In any event, as a result of this exemption companies have to differentiate their e-mail marketing campaigns: a different e-mail campaign is needed depending on the products or services that were ordered by the customer and another separate campaign is needed for recipients who are not (yet) a customer.

7 Electronic signatures

An electronic signature has to meet a long list of requirements in order to be considered equal to the handwritten signature. It also requires the use of the service of a certification service provider (CSP) that lives up to the criteria stated in the Directive on Electronic Signatures. In other words, it takes some doing to replace the easily placed handwritten signature with an electronic equivalent.

If the electronic signature does not meet all the requirements, this does not mean that it cannot have legal value. However, the value has to be determined on Member State level. The Directive on Electronic Signatures (merely) states that an electronic signature cannot be denied legal value solely because it is electronic.

To achieve more certainty as to the legal value of electronic signatures, parties using such signatures in their relations can conclude a contract on the use of electronic signatures.

8 Patchwork

The legal framework concerning e-commerce can be characterised as a 'legal patchwork'. Not only because the legal aspects relevant for e-commerce are laid down in various European legal texts, but also because many rules relevant for e-commerce can be found in non-harmonised national laws.

The different European legal texts are not always synchronised: the directives are partly overlapping and inconsistent legal terminology is used. For example, the information duties of the E-commerce Directive overlap some of the information duties of the Distant Selling Directive. And, the E-commerce Directive contains rules affecting 'unsolicited commercial communications by electronic mail', while the Directive on Privacy and Electronic Communications affects 'electronic mail for the purpose of direct marketing'.

It can also be noted that different wordings are used to indicate how information duties must be fulfilled: some of the information must be available so that it can be 'stored and reproduced', other information must be available on a 'durable medium'. Yet other information must be available 'easily directly and permanently' or 'in a clear and comprehensible manner'. It is unclear why one legal text uses the concept 'durable medium' and another uses 'durable record'. It is not always obvious how these differences can be expressed in practical situations. An additional complicating factor is the different scope of applicability of the various legal texts.

Besides the rules prescribed by the European legislator, many rules relevant for European e-commerce can be found in Member State law. The European legal framework leaves various issues to the discretion of national law. An example of this is the legal consequences of the electronic signature. These consequences remain a national matter. Additionally, on various points Member States are allowed to maintain more stringent rules, for example the Distant Selling Directive is a minimum directive. The privacy directive is a framework directive; Member States are to determine more specifically the conditions for the processing of personal data.

A company that operates internationally should take into account that different legal systems might apply to its on-line activities. It was already concluded above that the country of origin principle as formulated in the E-commerce Directive only offers partial relief with regard to this issue.

In other words: the business organisation is faced with a fragmented and inconsistent legal framework that is laid down in a variety of European laws and in the laws of various Member States.

It can be concluded that the European legislator has not (yet) fully succeeded to create a clear legal framework for e-commerce. Besides the 'patchwork'-character discussed above, there is a multitude of open norms that sustain a certain amount of legal uncertainty and there is a considerable amount of issues that need further specification.

Bibliography[1]

AALBERTS & VAN DER HOF (2000)

B.P. Aalberts, S. van der Hof, 'Digital signature Blindness Analysis of Legislative Approaches to Electronic Authentication' (2000/7) *The EDI Law Review*, p. 1-55

ALDHOUSE (1999)

F. Aldhouse, 'The transfer of personal data to third countries under EU Directive 95/46/EC (1999/1) *International Review of Law, Computers & Technology*, p. 75-79

ALLEN & WIDDISON (1996)

T. Allen, R. Widdison, 'Can Computers Make Contracts?' (1996/1) *Harvard Journal of Law & Technology*, p. 25-52

APEL & GRAPPERHAUS (1999)

J. Apel, T. Grapperhaus, 'Das Offline-Online-Chaos oder wie die Europäische Kommission den grenzüberschreitenden Werbemarkt zu harmonisieren droht' (1999/12) *Wettbewerb in Recht und Praxis*, p. 1247-1259

ASSCHER & VAN ERVE (2004)

F. Asscher, J. van Erve, *Regulating Spam, Directive 2002/58 and* beyond, Research report of the Institute for Information Law, IViR 2004, available at < http://www.solidground.nl/IViR-sybari/ivir-sybari-final.PDF> last visited in May 2004.

AUGUST (2002)

R. August, 'International Cyber-Jurisdiction: A Comparative Analysis' (2002/4) *American Business Law Journal*, p. 531-573

BA (2001)

S. Ba, 'Establishing online trust through a community responsibility system' (2001/3) *Decision Support Systems*, p. 323-336

BAINBRIDGE (1996)

D. Bainbridge, *EC Data Protection Directive* (London 1996)

BARNES (2002)

S.J. Barnes, 'The mobile commerce value chain: analysis and future developments' (2002/22) *International Journal of Information management*, p. 91-108

BEAUMONT (2002)

P.R. Beaumont, 'The Brussels Convention becomes a regulation: implications for legal basis, external competence, and contract jurisdiction', in: Fawcett (2002.), p. 9-30

BERGKAMP & DHONT (2000)

L. Bergkamp, J. Dhont, 'Data protection in Europe and the internet: an analysis for the European Communicty's privacy legislation in the context of the world wide web' (2000/7) *The EDI Law Review*, p. 71-114

1 References of articles without indication of page numbers refer to electronic sources.

BERKVENS A.O. (2000)
Berkvens a.o. (eds.), *Onderneming en ICT* (Deventer 2000)
BERKVENS & PRINS (2002)
J.M.A. Berkvens, J.E.J. Prins, 'Privacy en elektronische handel', in: Van Esch & J.E.J. Prins (2002), p. 319-351
BERLIRI (2003)
M. Berliri, 'Jurisdiction and the Internet, and European regulation 44 of 2001', in: D. Campbell & S. Woodley (eds.), *E-commerce Law and Jurisdiction* (The Hague 2003), p. 1-12
BOELE WOELKI & KESSEDJIAN (1998)
K. Boele Woelki and C. Kessedjian (eds.), *Internet, Which Court Decides? Which Law Applies, Proceedings of the international colloquium in honour of Michel Pelichet organised by the Molengraaff Institute of Private Law, University of Utrecht and the Hague Conference on Private International Law* (The Hague 1998)
BOUDESTIJN & NOTENBOOM (2000)
A. Boudestijn, A.J.P. Notenboom, 'De zeven regels voor vaart in e-business' (2000/1237) *TBA*, p. 421-425
BIUKOVIC (2002)
L. Biukovic, 'Unification of cyber-jurisdiction rules: just how close are the EU and the US?' (2002/19) *Telematics and Informatics*, p. 139-157
BRACK (1981)
A. Brack, *Consument, recht en koopkracht. Juridische en sociaal-economische verkenningen* (diss.) (Deventer 1981)
BRAMER (2000)
Chr.P.G. Bramer, 'E-commerce vanuit Europees perspectief en Nederlands perspectief' (2000/4) *Ondernemingsrecht*, p. 394-400
CHOI, STAHL AND WHINSTON (1997)
S.Y. Choi, D.O. Stahl, A.B. Whinston, *The economics of electronic commerce*, (Indianapolis 1997)
DE COCK BUNING A.O. (2001)
M. de Cock Buning, E. Hondius, C. Prins, M. de Vries, 'Consumer@Protection.EU. An Analysis of European Consumer Legislation in the Information Society' (2001/3-4) *Journal of Consumer Policy*, p. 287-338
CONSUMERS INTERNATIONAL (2001)
K. Scribbins, *Privacy@net, An international comparative study of consumer privacy on the internet*, Report produced by Consumers International's Office for Developed and Transition Economies, available at <www.consumersinternational.org>
DICKIE (1999)
J. Dickie, *Internet and Electronic Commerce in the European Union* (Oxford 1999)

DREXL (2002)

J. Drexl, 'Community legislation Continued: Complete Harmonisation, Framework Legislation or Non-Binding measures – Alternative Approaches to European Contract law, Consumer Protection and Unfair Trade Practices?' (2002/6) *European Busines Law Review*, p. 557-582

DRIJBER (2001)

B.J. Drijber, 'De richtlijn elektronische handel op de snijtafel' (2001/4) *SEW*, p. 122-138

DRION (1998)

C.E. Drion, 'Kanttekeningen bij het preadvies van Maurice V. Polak 'internationaal privaatrecht: een vangnet voor het Internet'' (1998/3) *Computerrecht*, p. 111-119

DUMORTIER (2000)

J. Dumortier, 'De omzetting van de Europese richtlijn elektronische handtekeningen: een stand van zaken' (2000/4) *Computerrecht*

DUMORTIER ET AL (2003)

J. Dumortier, S. Kelm, H. Nillson, G. Skouma, P. van Eecke, *The legal and market aspects of electronic signatures*, Study for the European Commision – DG Information Society, Service Contract nr. C 28.400, Available at <www.law.kuleuve.ac.be/icri> (under research publications 2003 of electronic business)

DUMORTIER & VAN EECKE (1999)

J. Dumortier, P. Van Eecke, 'Electronic Signatures, The European Draft Directive On A Common Framework for Electronic Signatures' (1999/2) *Computer Law & Security Report*, p. 106-112

EDWARDS & WAELDE 2000

L. Edwards, C. Waelde (eds.), *Law and the Internet, A framework for Electronic Commerce* (Oxford 2000)

ENDESHAW (1998)

A. Endeshaw, 'Regulating the Internet: clutching at a straw?' (1998/16) *Computer Communications*, p. 1519-1526

ENDESHAW (2001)

A. Endeshaw, 'The legal significance of trustmarks' (2001/2) *Information & Communications Technology Law*, p. 203-230

VAN EIJK & VAN HELDEN (2001)

M.M.M. van Eijk, W.J. van Helden, *Klant te Koop. Privacyregels voor adressenhandel*, Achtergrondstudies en Verkenningen 24 (studie in opdracht van het College Bescherming Persoonsgegevens 2001, available at <www.cbpweb.nl> (follow the link "Publications")

VAN ESCH & PRINS (1993)

R.E. van Esch and C. Prins e.a (eds.), *Recht en EDI* (Deventer 1993)

VAN ESCH (1999)
R.E. van Esch, *Electronic Data Interchange en het Vermogensrecht* (diss.) (Deventer 1999)
VAN ESCH (2000)
R.E. van Esch, 'De Digitale Handtekening', in: Berkvens, et al (2000)
VAN ESCH (2001A)
R.E. van Esch, 'Elektronische handel', in: Franken, Kaspersen & De Wild (2001), p. 133-165
VAN ESCH (2001B)
R.E. van Esch, 'Recente ontwikkelingen in het vermogensrecht op het terrein van de elektronische handel' (2001/6443) *WPNR*, p. 373-381
VAN ESCH (2003)
R.E. van Esch, 'Electronic signatures: a survey of the directive and the legislation in the United Kingdom and the Netherlands', in: Snijders & Weatherill (2003), p. 27-57
VAN ESCH & BRAMER (2000)
R.E. van Esch, Chr.P.G. Bramer, 'Algemene voorwaarden en informatieplicht in cyberspace' (2000/6) *Computerrecht*, p. 283-288
VAN ESCH & PRINS (2002)
R.E. van Esch & J.E.J. Prins (eds.), *Recht en Elektronische Handel* (Deventer 2002)
FAWCETT (2002)
J. Fawcett (ed.), *Reform and development of private international law*, (Oxford 2002)
FINOCCHIARO (2003)
G. Finocchiaro, 'Electronic contracts and software agents, the conclusion of the electronic contract through "software agents" A false legal problem? Brief considerations' (2003/1) *Computer law & Security Report*, p. 20-24
FORD & BAUM 2001
W. Ford, M.S. Baum, *Secure Electronic Commerce, Building the Infrastructure for Digital Signatures and Encryption* (New Jersey 2001)
FOSS & BYGRAVE 2000
M. Foss, L. A. Bygrave, 'International Consumer Purchases through the Internet: Jurisdictional issues pursuent to European Law' (2000/8) *International Journal of Law and Information Technology*
FRANKEN, KASPERSEN & DE WILD (2001)
H. Franken, H.W.K. Kaspersen, A.H. de Wild (eds.), *Recht en Computer* (Deventer 2001)
GATT (2002)
A. Gatt, 'The enforceability of click-wrap agreements' (2002/6) *Computer Law & Security Report*, p. 404-410

GAUTHRONET & DROUHARD (2001)

S. Gauthronet, E. Drouhard, 'Unsolicited Commercial Communication an Data Protection, Commission of the European Communities' (Internal Market DG-Contract no ETD/99/B5-30000/E/96) 2001, the Report can be found on <http://europa.eu.int/comm/internal_market/privacy/studies_en.htm>

GIJRATH & KOLTHEK (2002)

S.J.H. Gijrath, R.J. Kolthek, 'Wetsvoorstel elektronische Handel: Gemiste kansen bij elektronisch contracteren?' (2002/6) *Computerrecht*

GILLIES (2001)

L. Gillies, 'A Review of the New Jurisdiction Rules For Electronic Consumer Contracts within the European Union' (2001/1) *JILT*

GIROT (2000)

C. Girot, *User Protection in IT Contract, A Comparative Study of the Protection of the User Against Defective Performance in Information Technology* (diss.) (The Hague 2000)

GREWAL, IYER & LEVY (2004)

D. Grewal, G.R. Iyer, M. Levy, 'Internet retailing: enablers, limiters and market consequences' (2004/7) *Journal of Business Research*, p. 703-713

GRIJPINK (2001)

J. Grijpink, 'Privacy law. Biometrics and privacy' (2001/3) *Computer Law & Security Report*, p. 154-160

GROSHEIDE (2000)

F.W. Grosheide 'The legal mapping and tracking of electronic commerce – a view from the EU', in: F.W. Grosheide (eds.), *Molengrafica 1999/2000*, p. 1-24

GUPTA, TUNG & MARSDEN (2004)

A. Gupta, Y.A. Tung, J.R. Marsden, 'Digital signature: use and modification to achieve success in next generational e-business processes' (2004/5) *Information & Management*, p. 561-575

VAN HAERSOLTE-VAN HOF (2000)

J.J. van Haersolte-Van Hof, 'Richtlijn elektronische handel – internationaal privaatrechtelijke aspecten' (2000/12) *NTER*, p. 325-327

VAN HAERSOLTE-VAN HOF (2001)

J.J. van Haersolte-van Hof, 'EEX-verordening treedt in werking per 1 maart 2002' (2001/9) *NTER*, p. 244-248

HARTKAMP & TILLEMA (1995)

A.S. Hartkamp, M.M.M. Tillema, *Contract law in the Netherlands* (The Hague 1995)

HENNING-BODEWIG (2001)

F. Henninng-Bodewig, 'E-commerce und irreführende Werbung.

Auswirkungen des Herkunftslandprinzips auf das europäische und deutsche Irreführungsrecht' (2001/7) *Wettbewerb in Recht und Praxis*, p. 771-777

HINDELANG (2002)
S. Hindelang, 'No Remedy for disappointed Trust – The liability regime for certification authorities towards third parties outwith the EC directive in England and Germany compared' (2002/1) *JILT*

HOEREN (2002)
T. Hoeren, 'Yaba No Naka', in: Kono, Paulus & Rajak (2002), p. 1-12

HOEREN (2004)
T. Hoeren, *Skriptum Internet-Recht* (stand februar 2004), available online at <http://www.uni-muenster.de/jura.itm/hoeren> follow the link 'Materialen'

VAN DER HOF (2002)
S. van der Hof, *Internationale on-line overeenkomsten* (diss.) (Den Haag 2002)

VAN DER HOF (2003)
S. van der Hof, 'European conflict rules concerning international online consumer contracts' (2002/2) *Information & Communication technology law*, p. 165-178.

HARINK (2003)
J. Harink, *Internet-technologie in inkoop. De kinderschoenen ontgroeid* (diss.) (Enschede: 2003)

HONDIUS (2001)
E.H. Hondius, 'Kroniek van het consumentenrecht' (2001/10) *NJB*, p. 460-469

HOQUE (2000)
F. Hoque, *e-Enterprise, business models, architecture and components* (Cambridge: 2000)

JAVERNPAA, TRACTINSKY & VITALE (2000)
S.L. Jarvenpaa, N. Tractinsky and M. Vitale, 'Consumer trust in an Internet store' (2000/1) *Information Technology and Management*, p. 45-71

JESSURUN D'OLIVEIRA (2002)
H.U. Jessurun d'Oliveira, 'The EU and a metamorphosis of private international law', in: Fawcett (2002), p. 111-136

JOUSTRA 2001
C.A. Joustra, 'Internationale overeenkomsten met internetconsumenten' (2001/4) *Contracteren*, p. 80-85

JULIÀ-BARCELÓ & KOELMAN (2000)
R. Julià-Barceló, K.J. Koelman, 'Intermediairy liability in the E-commerce Directive: so far so good, but it's not enough' (2000/4) *Computer Law & Security Report*, p. 231-239

JULIÀ-BARCELÓ & VINJE (1998)
R. Julià-Barceló, T.C. Vinje, 'Electronic Signatures, Another step towards a European Framework for electronic signatures: the Commission's Directive proposal' (1998/5) *Computer Law & Security Report*, p. 303-313

KABEL (2002)
J.J.C. Kabel, 'Reclamerecht on-line: problemen in theorie en praktijk', in: Van Esch & Prins (2002), p. 89-126

KABEL (2003)
J. Kabel, 'Spam: A Terminal Threat to ISP's, The legal position of ISP's concerning their anti-spam policies in the EU after the Privacy and Telecom Directive' (2003/1) *Computer und Recht*, p. 6-10

KAUFMAN WINN & HAUBOLD (2002)
J. Kaufman Winn, J. Haubold, 'Electronic promises: contract law reform and e-commerce in a comparative perspective' (2002/5) *European Law Review*, p. 567-588

KERR (2001)
I. R. Kerr, 'Ensuring the success of contract formation in agent-mediated electronic commerce' (2001/1) *Electronic Commerce Research*, p. 183-202

KHONG (2001)
W.K. Khong, 'Spam law for the Internet' (2001/3) *JILT*

KIGHTLINGER (2003)
M.F. Kightlinger, 'A solution to the Yahoo! problem? The EC e-commerce directive as a model for international cooperation on internet choice of law' (2003/3) *Michigan journal of international law*, p. 719-766

KONO, PAULUS & RAJAK (2002)
T. Kono, C.G. Paulus, H. Rajak (eds.), *Selected Legal Issues of e-commerce* (The Hague 2002)

KRONKE (1998)
H. Kronke, 'Applicable Law in Torts and Contracts in Cyberspace' in: Boele Woelki & Kessedjian (1998), p. 65-87

KUHN (1991)
M. Kuhn, *Rechtshandlungen mittels EDV und Telekommunikation. Zurechenbarkeit und Haftung* (München 1991)

KUNER & MIEDBRODT (1999)
C. Kuner and A. Miedbrodt, 'Written signature requirements and electronic authentication: a comparative perspective' (1996) *The EDI Law Review*, p. 143-154

LEROUGE (2001)
J.-F. Lerouge, 'Internet effective rules: the role of self-regulation' (2001/8) *The EDI Law Review*, p. 197-207

LICHTENSTEIN (1998)
S. Lichtenstein, 'Internet Risks For companies' (1998/7) *Computers & Security*, p. 143-150
LINNEMANN & VOLGENANT (2000)
J.J. Linnemann, O.M.B.J. Volgenant, *Juridische aspecten e-commerce* (Alphen aan de Rijn 2000)
LLOYD (1996)
I. Lloyd, 'An outline of the European Data protection Directive' (1996/1) *JILT*
LODDER (2002)
A.R. Lodder, 'Directive 2000/31/EC on certain legal aspects of information society servoces, in particular electronic commerce, in the internal Market', in: Lodder & Kaspersen (2002)
LODDER & BERGFELD (2002)
A.R. Lodder, J.P.R. Bergfeld, 'De moeizame strijd tegen spam' (2002/22) *NJB*, p. 1050-1057
LODDER & KASPERSEN (2002)
A.R. Lodder, H.W.K. Kaspersen (eds.), *eDirectives: Guide to European Union Law on E-commerce* (The Hague 2002)
LODDER & VOULON (2002)
A.R. Lodder, M.B. Voulon, 'Intelligent Agents and the Information Requirements of the Directives on Distance selling and E-commerce' (2002/3) *International Review of Law, Computers and Technology*, p. 277-287
LOOS (2001)
M.B.M. Loos, 'Op afstand gesloten contracten met consumenten' (2001/3) *NTER*, p. 130-138
LOUVEAUX (1999)
S. Louveaux, 'Privacy Issues', Esprit Project 27028, Electronic Commerce Legal Issues Platform Deliverable 2.1.3, available on <www.eclip.org>, under the link 'research papers'
MANKOWSKI (2001)
P. Mankowski, 'Das Herkunftslandprinzip als Internationales Privatrecht der e-commerce-Richtlinie' (2001/100) *Zeitschrift fur vergleichende Rechtswissenschaft*, p. 137-181
MANKOWSKI (2002)
P. Mankowski, 'Herkunftslandprinzip und deutsches Umsetzungsgezetz zur e-commerce-Richtlinie (2002/4) *IPRax*, p. 257-266
MITRAKAS (1997)
A. Mitrakas, *Open EDI and Law in Europe, A Regulatory Framework* (diss.) (The Hague 1997)

MOEREL (2000)
E.M.L. Moerel, 'E-commerce vanuit Europees perspectief' (2000/8) *Ondernemingsrecht*, p. 202-209
MOEREL (2002)
E.M.L. Moerel, with contributions of C.W. Noorda and E.J. Morée, *Online reclame* (Deventer 2002)
MOREL & JONES (2002)
F. Morel, R. Jones, 'De-mystifying electronic signatures and electronic signatures law from a European Union perspective' (2002/7) *Tolley's Communications Law*, p. 174-178
MORTELMANS & WATSON (1995)
K. Mortelmans and S. Watson, 'The notion of consumer in community law: a lottery?' (1995/4) *TvC* , p. 229-246
MURRAY (2000)
A.D. Murray, 'Entering into Contracts Electronically: The Real W.W.W.', in: Edwards & Waelde (2000)
VAN DER NET (2003)
C. van der Net, 'Civil liability of Internet providers following the Directive on Electronic Commerce', in: Snijders & Weatherill (2003), p. 49-57
NOLL (2002)
J. Noll, 'European Community & e-commerce: fostering consumer confidence' (2002/3) *Electronic Communication Law Review*, p. 207-219
NOORDA (2000)
C.W. Noorda, 'Online contracteren', in: Berkvens a.o. (2000), p. 95-106
NÖTEBERG, CHRISTIAANSE EN WALLAGE (2000)
A. Nöteberg, E. Christiaansse, R.A. Wallage, 'De rol van vertrouwen en bezegelingsdiensten in elektronische verkoopkanalen' (2000/1237) *TBA*, p. 413-415
NOUWT (2001)
J. Nouwt, 'E-commerce en het verwerken van persoonsgegevens' *WPNR* 2001/6443, p. 421-429
OLSEN 2001
L. Olsen, 'The information duty in connection with consumer sales over the net', in: Wilhelmsson, Tuominen & Tuomola (2001), p. 147-161
VAN DEN OOSTERKAMP (1999)
J.S. van den Oosterkamp, 'Enkele kanttekeningen bij het richtlijnvoorstel elektronische handel' (1999/6) *NTER*, p. 145-153
OUWEHAND (2000)
J.F. Ouwehand, 'Enige Juridische aspecten van B2B marktplaatsen', in: Berkvens et al (2000), p. 127-148

PEARCE & PLATTEN (2000)
G. Pearce, N. Platten 'Promoting the Information Society: The EU Directive on Electronic Commerce' (2000/4) *European Law Journal*, p. 363-378
PEPPARD (2000)
J. Peppard, 'Customer Relation Management (CRM) in financial services' (2003/3) *European Management Journal*, p. 312-327
POULLET, LOUVEAUX & PÉREZ ASINARI (2001)
Y. Poullet, S. Louveaux & M.V. Pérez Asinari, 'Data protection and privacy in global networks: a European approach...' (2001/2-3) *The EDI Law Review*, p. 147-196
PRINS (1998)
J.E.J. Prins, 'Biometric technology law. Making our body identify for us: legal implications of biometric technologies' (1998/3) *Computer Law & Security Report*, p. 159-165
PRINS & GIJRATH (2000)
J.E.J. Prins, S.J.H. Gijrath, *Privaatrechtelijke aspecten van elektronische handel*, (Deventer 2000).
PRINS & SCHREUDERS (1998)
J.E.J. Prins, E. Schreuders, 'Ingrediënten voor een nieuw privacy arrangement'(1998/5) *TvC*, p. 431-443
REED (2000)
C. Reed, 'What is a signature?' (2000/3) *JILT*
REICH (2001)
N. Reich, 'Consumerism and citizenship in the information society', in: Wilhelmsson, Tuominen & Tuomola (2001), p. 163-178
REKAITI & VAN DEN BERGH (2000)
P. Rekaiti, R. Van den Bergh, 'Cooling-off periods in the consumer laws of EC member states. A comparative law and economics approach' (2000/4) *Journal of Consumer Policy*, p. 371-407
ROTT (2003)
P. Rott, 'Minimum Harmonisation for the completion of the internal market? The example of consumer sales law' (2003/5) *Common Market Law Review*, p. 1107-1135
ROWE (2004)
H. Rowe, 'E-commerce: jurisdiction over on-line contracts and non-contractual cross-border disputes, part 2' (2004/3) *Butterworks Journal of International Banking and Financial Law*, p. 93-95
SAANEN, VERBRAECK & SOL (1999)
Y. A. Saanen, A. Verbraeck, H.G. Sol, 'Snapshot of e-commerce's opportunities and threats' (1999/3) *Electronic Markets*, p. 181-189
SALAÜN (1999)
A. Salaün, 'E-commerce, Consumer protection – Proposals for

Improving the Protection of Online Consumers' (1999/3) *Computer Law & Security Report*, p. 159-167

SANDER (2001)

C.J. Sander, *Consumentenbescherming bij transacties op afstand* (Den Haag 2001)

SANDER & BARTELS (1998)

C.J. Sander and S.E. Bartels, 'Vraagpunten bij de implementatie van de Europese Richtlijn op afstand gesloten overeenkomsten' (1998/5) *TvC*, p. 407-415.

SAXBY (2000)

S. Saxby, 'E-commerce gets a dose of regulation' (2000/4) *Computer Law & Security Report*, p. 218

SCHAUB (2001)

M.Y.Schaub, 'On-line consument nu nog beter beschermd!' (2001/2) *TvC*, p. 91-102

SCHAUB (2002)

M.Y. Schaub, 'Unsolicited e-mail, Does Europe allow spam? The state of the art of the European legislation with regard to unsolicited commercial communications' (2002/2) *Computer Law & Security Report*, p. 99-105

SCHELLEKENS (2001)

M. Schellekens, *Aansprakelijkheid van internet aanbieders* (Den Haag 2001)

SCHELTEMA & TJONG TJIN TAI (2003)

M.W. Scheltema, T.F.E. Tjong Tjin Tai, 'Overeenkomsten sluiten door openen en klikken?' (2003/4) *Computerrecht*

SCHMIDT & FRANKEN (2003)

A. Schmidt, H. Franken, 'Law as code, code as law – general remarks on legal requirements engineering', in: Snijders & Weatherill (2003), p. 117-138

SCHREUDERS & BLOK (2000)

E. Schreuders, P. Blok, 'Privacyregels en de WBP op het Internet' in: J.E.J Prins and J.M.A. Berkvens (eds.) *Privacyregulering in theorie en praktijk* (Deventer 2000), p. 401-421

SHIRALKAR & VIJAYARAMAN (2003)

P. Shiralkar, B.S. Vijayaraman, 'Digital signature: application development trends in e-business' (2003/3) *Journal of Electronic Commerce Research*, p. 94-101

SIEBECKER (2003)

M.R. Siebecker 'Cookies and the common law: are internet advertisers trespassing on our computers?' (2003/4) *Southern California Law Review*, p. 893-952

SIEMERINK (2003A)
L.A.R. Siemerink, 'ISP-contracten en aansprakelijkheid, verslag symposium' (2003/1) *JAVI*, p. 41
SIEMERINK (2003B)
L.A.R Siemerink, 'Elektronische gedragscodes: een voorbeeld uit de praktijk' (2003/10) *Mediaforum*, p. 318-323
SIEMS (2002)
M.M. Siems, 'The EU Directive on Electronic Signatures – A Worldwide Model or a Fruitless Attempt to Regulate the Future?' (2002/1) *International Review of Law, Computers and Technology*, p. 7-22
SIMMONS & SIMMONS 2001
Simmons & Simmons Law Firm, *E-commerce law, doing business online* (Bembridge 2001)
SMITH (2002)
G.J.H. Smith, *Internet Law and Regulation* (London 2002)
SNIJDERS & WEATHERILL (2003)
H. Snijders, S. Weatherill (eds.), *E-commerce Law* (The Hague 2003)
SPINDLER (2002)
G. Spindler, 'Herkunftslandprinzip und Kollisionsrecht – Binnenmarktintegration ohne Harmonisiering?. Die Folgen der Richtlinie im elektronischen Geschäftsverkehr für das Kollisionsrecht' (2002/4) *RabelsZ*, p. 633-709
STEYN (2000)
M.P.Th. Steyn, 'Rechtskeuze en e-commerce', in: Berkvens a.o. (2000), p. 261-281
STRAETMANS (2000)
G. Straetmans, 'Europese regelgeving inzake verkoop op afstand: een stand van zaken' (2000/9) *SEW* , p. 314-328
STUURMAN & WIJNANDS (1998)
C. Stuurman, H. Wijnands, *Electronic Commerce. Een privaatrechtelijk kader voor multilaterale EDI* (Deventer 1998)
TEMMINK (1995)
H.A.G. Temmink, 'Minimumnormen in EG-richtlijnen' (1995/2) *SEW*, p. 79-106
TERRETT & MONAGHAN (2000)
A. Terret, I. Monaghan, 'The internet – An introduction for lawyers', in: Edwards & Waelde (2000)
TERRYN (2003)
E. Terryn, 'Gedragscodes en labels in de elektronische handel' (2003/5) *Computerrecht*
THOLE (2004)
E. Thole, 'e-Privacyrichtlijn maakt geen einde aan spam' (2004/4) *NJB*

TIMMERS (1998)
P. Timmers, 'Business Models for Electronic Markets' (1998/2) *Electronic Markets*

TIMMERS (1999)
P. Timmers, *Electronic commerce, strategies and models for business-to-business trading* (Chichester 1999)

TRUNK (2002)
A. Trunk, 'European Directives in the Field of Electronic commerce: Interplay with German law.' In : Kono, Paulus & Rajak (2002), p. 25-39

TSALGATIDOU & PITOURA (2001)
A. Tsalgatidou and E. Pitoura, 'Business models and transactions in mobile electronic commerce: requirements and properties' (2001/2) *Computer Networks*, p. 221-236

VAN DER VELDEN (2001)
F.J.A. van der Velden, 'Internationale contracten en de bevoegde rechter: nieuwe regels van Europees procesrecht' (2001/4) *Contracteren*, p. 97-101

VLAS (2000)
P. Vlas, 'Herziening EEX: van verdrag naar verordening' (2000/6421) *WPNR*, p. 745-753

VLAS, ZILINSKY & IBILI (2002)
P. Vlas, M. Zilinsky, F. Ibili, 'Civil jurisdiction and enforcement of judgements in Europe' (2002/XLIX) *Netherlands International Law Review*, p. 105-138

VOULON (2002)
M.B. Voulon, 'Elektronische vertegenwoordiging' (2002/6) *Computerrecht*

VOULON (2004)
M.B. Voulon, 'Intelligent agent: instrument in plaats van actor' (2004/1) *JAVI*

VOULON & LODDER (2002)
M.B. Voulon, A.R. Lodder, 'Duitse uitspraak inzake informatieplichten op website' (2002/6) *Computerrecht*

DE VREY (2004)
R.W. de Vrey, 'Eerlijk is eerlijk: de consument voorop? Het richtlijnvoorstel 'oneerlijke handelspraktijken' nader bezien' (2004/1) *TvC*, p. 2-11

WAGEMANS (2002)
A.W. Wagemans, 'Zelfreguleringsinitiatieven', in: R.E. van Esch, J.E.J. Prins (eds.), *Recht en elektronische handel*, (Deventer 2002), p. 61-85

WALDEN (1996)
I. Walden 'The application of Directive 95/46/EC' (1996/3) *The EDI Law Review*, p. 85-98

WEATHERILL & BEAUMONT (1999)
S. Weatherill, P. Beaumont, *EU Law. The essential guide to the legal workings of the European Union* (London 1999)
WEITZENBOECK (2001)
E. M. Weitzenboeck, *Electronic Agents and the formation of contracts,* ECLIP Research Paper (EP 27028) available on the ECLIP website <www.eclip.org> under the link *'Research Papers'*
WILHELMSSON, TUOMINEN & TUOMOLA (2001)
T. Wilhelmsson, S. Tuominen & H. Tuomola (ed.), *Consumer Law in the Information Society* (Den Haag 2001)
ZWEIGERT & KÖTZ (1998)
K. Zweigert, H. Kötz, *An Introduction to Comparative Law* (Oxford 1998)
ZITTRAIN & EDELMAN (2002)
J. Zittrain & B. Edelman, 'Localised Google search result exclusions', <http://cyber.law.harvard.edu/filtering/google/> last accessed 20 January 2004.

Abbreviations

ASP	Application Service Provider
B2B	Business to Business
B2C	Business to Consumer
CA	Certification Authority
C2C	Consumer to Consumer
EC	European Community
ECJ	European Court of Justice
EU	European Union
EDI	Electronic Data Interchange
EEC	European Economic Community
ERP	Enterprise Resource Planning
GATS	General Agreement on Trade in Services
GATT	General Agreement on Tariffs and Trade
TRIPS	Trade Related aspects of Intellectual Property Rights
HTML	Hyper Text Markup Language
ICT	Information and Communication Technology
ISP	Internet Service Provider
JAVI	Juridische Aspecten van Internet
NJB	Nederlands Juristenblad
NTER	Nederlands Tijdschrift voor Europees Recht
OJ	Official Journal
PDA	Personal Digital Assistant
PKI	Public Key Infrastructure
RabelsZ	Rabels Zeitschrift für ausländische und internationales Privatrecht
SEW	Sociaal-economische wetgeving Tijdschrift voor Europees en economisch recht
SSL	Secure Socket Layer
TBA	Tijdschrift voor Bedrijfsadministratie
TvC	Tijdschrift voor Consumentenrecht
TTP	Trusted Third Party
UN	United Nations
UNCITRAL	United Nations Commission on International Trade Law
URL	Uniform Resource Locator
WPNR	Weekblad voor Privaatrecht, Notariaat en Registratie
WTO	World Trade Organisation
WWW	World Wide Web

Glossary[1]

Adware

1) Adware is software that is able to gather information on the browsing patterns of a user of a computer through the computers' internet connection. The information is used to display advertisements. Adware is also referred to as spyware.

2) Software with advertisements embedded in it.

Application Service Provider (ASP)

An ASP is a third party entity that manages and distributes software-based services and solutions to customers across a wide area network from a central data centre. ASPs are a way for companies to outsource some or almost all aspects of their information technology needs.

Asymmetric cryptography

See public-key system.

Agent

An agent is a program (software tool) that gathers information or performs some other service without your immediate presence. An intelligent agent refers to an agent with the capacity to act autonomously.

Back-office

Of or relating to the inner workings of a business or an institution.

Business-to-Business (B2B)

The exchange of services, information and/or products from one business to another, as opposed to between a business and a consumer.

Business-to-Consumer (B2C)

The exchange of services, information and/or products from a business to a consumer, i.e. a person acting for reasons outside his trade or profession.

Banner

A typically rectangular advertisement placed on a website either above, below or on the sides of the *website*'s main content and is linked to the advertiser's own website.

Browser

Short for web browser, a software application used to locate and display web pages. The two most popular browsers are Netscape Navigator and Microsoft's Internet Explorer.

[1] Explanation of terms can be found on <www.webopedia.com>, <www.nolo.com>, <www.m-w.com> and <www.whatis.com>.

Button

An indicated spot or area on a web page that can be clicked in order to select an option or a command. Buttons can be used in electronic ordering procedures, clicking a button can indicate the customers acceptance of contract terms or indication that he wishes to proceed to the next stage of the ordering procedure.

Certificate

An attachment to an electronic message used for security purposes. The most common use of a (digital) certificate is to verify that a user sending a message is who he or she claims to be, and to provide the receiver with the means to encode a reply.

Certificate Authority (CA)

Also referred to as Certification Service Provider (CSP). A CA is a trusted third-party organization or company that issues digital certificates used to create digital signatures and public-private key pairs. The role of the CA in this process is to guarantee that the individual granted the unique certificate is, in fact, who he or she claims to be. Usually, this means that the CA has an arrangement with a financial institution, such as a credit card company, which provides it with information to confirm an individual's claimed identity. CAs are a critical component in data security and electronic commerce because they guarantee that the two parties exchanging information are really who they claim to be.

Checkmark

A mark that is used to check the tick box, this can be used on *websites* or in software programmes to indicate the users wishes.

Click

To tap on a mouse button, pressing it down and then immediately releasing it. To click on means to select (a screen object) by moving the mouse pointer to the object's position and clicking a mouse button.

Cookie

A piece of information that a website stores on a visitor's hard drive so that the website can retrieve the information when the visitor returns to the site. For example, a website may use a cookie to retrieve a visitor's name and address so the visitor doesn't have to enter that information again. A website can legally use cookies to personalize a visitor's experience, to track a visitor's movements on a site or to target a visitor for specific advertisements.

Cryptography

The art of protecting information by transforming it (encrypting it) into an unreadable format. Only those who possess a secret key can decipher (or decrypt it) the message into plain text. Encrypted messages can sometimes be broken by cryptanalysis, also called code breaking, although modern cryptography techniques are virtually unbreakable.

Deeplink

A link from one website to another that bypasses the second website's homepage and takes the user directly to an internal page on the site.

Decryption

Decryption transforms ciphertext (an encrypted message) back to the original text.

Digital signature

An electronic signature that makes use of cryptography techniques.

Digitised goods

Digitised goods are products that can be transformed to a digitised form allowing them to be stored in electronic form and transported over networks, for example music and software. To be transported in the physical world such products need a carrier, such as a CD. The physical carrier makes it possible to classify the products as 'goods' from a legal point of view. In the on-line environment this physical carrier to transport the product is lacking which makes the qualification as a 'good' problematic. This often concerns products that are associated with intellectual property rights. Also referred to as 'soft products'.

Domain name

A name that identifies one or more IP-addresses. Domain names are used in URLs to identify particular web pages. The domain name system overlays the IP-address system as the names are more user friendly then the long IP-numbers.

E-business

The use of ICT in one or more processes of the business organisation.

E-commerce

The use of ICT in how the business organisation interfaces with business partners and (potential) customers.

Electronic contract

A contract that is concluded solely with the help of electronic means without the contracting partners being in each others' presence.

Electronic Data Interchange (EDI)

Exchange of standardised messages such as orders and invoices, commonly over a closed and secure network.

Electronic signature

A technique used to perform one or more functions of the handwritten signature in the electronic environment.

Encryption

Encryption can transform a text message into unintelligible ciphertext.

Framing

The act of displaying another company's web page within a bordered area of a website. For example, when a user enters a search engine request, the search engine might display the contents of an online store within the search engine's website, framed by the search engine's text and logos. When a web page is framed within another website, the URL or domain name of the framed web page is not displayed and users are not able to bookmark that site.

Homepage

1) The main page of a website. Typically, the homepage serves as an index or table of contents to other documents stored at the site.

2) The first web page that is displayed after starting a web-browser like Netscape's Navigator or Microsoft's Internet Explorer.

Hotmail

A popular on-line e-mail service that can be obtained at <www.hotmail.com>. A hotmail account can be required free of charge and can be approached on-line. This means there is no need to install special software. A browser and an internet connection suffice to use the account.

Hyperlink

An element in an electronic document that links to another place in the same document or to an entirely different document. Typically, you click on the hyperlink to follow the link. Hyperlinks are the most essential ingredient of the WWW. Hyperlinks are often simply referred to as links.

IP-address

See IP-number.

IP-number

IP is the Abbreviation of Internet Protocol. An IP-number (or IP-address) is something like the postal system. It allows you to address a package and drop it in the system. The IP-number consist of a series of numbers (for example: 192.87.17.19) which is not very user friendly, the system is overlaid by the domain name system which allows the connection of the numbers to a alphanumereric identifier (such as: "www.utwente.nl").

Internet Service Provider (ISP)

A company that provides services related to internet. These services can consist of hosting websites, providing access, providing an e-mail account etc.

Intelligent agent

See agent.

Interchange agreement

An agreement that contains the arrangements for electronic data interchange.

Interface

(1) A boundary across which two independent systems meet and act on or communicate with each other. In computer technology, there are several types of interfaces, for example user interface, hardware interface, software interface.

(2) To communicate with, to connect with or interact with by means of an interface.

Interstitial

Meaning in between, an advertisement that appears in a separate browser window while you wait for a web page to load. Interstitials are more likely to contain large graphics, streaming presentations, and applets than conventional banner ads, and some studies have found that more users click on interstitials than on banner ads. Some users, however, have complained that interstitials slow access to destination pages.

Internet

A global network connecting millions of computers.

Key

In cryptography, a key is a variable value that is applied using an algorithm to a string or block of unencrypted text to produce encrypted text, or to decrypt encrypted text. The length of the key is a factor in considering how difficult it will be to decrypt the text in a given message.

Link

See Hyperlink.

Net
The term the net is commonly used as a synonym for internet or the WWW.

Off-line
Not connected, opposite of on-line.

On-line
1) People are considered on-line when they are connected to a computer service through a modem. That is, they are actually on the line.
2) Equipment are considered on-line when it is turned on and connected.

Opt-in
The terms opt-in and opt-out are used to characterise the regulatory approaches towards unwanted e-mail (see also spam). An opt-in regime means that it is not allowed to send messages without the recipients' previous consent.

Opt-out
The terms opt-in and opt-out are used to characterise the regulatory approaches towards unwanted e-mail (see also spam). An opt-out regime means that it is allowed to send messages until the recipient has indicated that he no longer wishes to receive messages.

Passive website
A website that presents information with no interactive possibilities.

Peer-to-Peer (P2P)
A type of network where information is exchanged between computers without the use of an intermediary server where the information is stored. A well known example of software that allows P2P sharing of information is Kazaa, available at <www.kazaa.com>.

Personal Digital Assistant (PDA)
A handheld device that combines computing, telephone/fax, internet and networking features. A typical PDA can function as a cellular phone, fax sender, web browser and personal organizer.

Pop-up window
A (small) window that appears over the window in which a web page is displayed. Pop-up windows can be used by on-line advertisers, such pop-ups can appear unasked for over the web page. They can also be used to provide additional information about items shown on the web page.

Pop-under window
A (small) window that appears under the window in which a web page is shown. The windows appear under the window of the web page and become visible after the user has closed the main window.

Portal
A portal site is a website or service that offers a broad array of resources and services. An example of a portal site is the homepage of an Internet Service Provider.

Pretty Good Privacy (PGP)
A technique for encrypting messages. PGP is available for free and can be used to protect messages on the internet. PGP is available at <www.pgpi.com> for personal use and at <www.pgp.com> for commercial use.

Public key system
A cryptographic system that uses two different but related keys: the public key and the private key. The public key is publicly available and the private key is kept secret. An example of a public key system is PGP. Also known as an asymmetric cryptosystem.

Public Key Infrastructure (PKI)
A system of digital certificates, certification authorities (or TTP'S), and other registration authorities that verify and authenticate the validity of each party involved in an internet transaction. PKIs are currently evolving and there is no single PKI nor even a single agreed-upon standard for setting up a PKI. A PKI is also called a 'trust hierarchy'.

Push technology
To send data to a receiver without the receiver requesting it. Broadcast media are push technologies because they send information out regardless of whether anyone is tuned in.

Pull technology
To request data from another program or computer. The WWW is based on a pull technology where the client browser must request a web page before it is sent.

Scroll
Viewing information on a screen when the displayed information does not fit on the screen, the viewer can scroll down then the information appears below on the screen while the information above disappears. It is also possible to scroll horizontally.

Secure Sockets Layer (SSL)
A protocol for transmitting private documents via internet. SSL works by using a private key to encrypt data that's transferred over the SSL connection. Many Web sites use the protocol to obtain confidential user information, such as credit card numbers. By convention, URLs that require an SSL connection start with https: instead of http:.

Search engine
A program that searches documents for specified keywords and returns a list of the documents where the keywords were found. Popular search engines are <www.google.com> and <www.alltheweb.com>.

Server
A computer or device on a network that manages network resources.

Shareware
Software distributed on the basis of an honour system. Most shareware is delivered free of charge, but the author usually requests that you pay a small fee if you like the program and use it regularly. By sending the small fee, you become registered with the producer so that you can receive service assistance and updates. You can copy shareware and pass it along to friends and colleagues, but they too are expected to pay a fee if they use the product.

Short Messaging Service (SMS)
Short text messages sent to and from mobile phones (see also texting).

Soft opt-in
See also opt-in. Soft opt-in means that sending of commercial e-mail is allowed if the company has a customer relation with the recipients.

Soft products
See digitised goods.

Spam
Electronic junk mail or junk newsgroup postings. Spam is generally e-mail advertising for some product sent in large amounts to a mailing list or a newsgroup.

Spyware
Also called adware, spyware is any software that covertly gathers user information through the user's Internet connection without his or her knowledge, usually for advertising purposes.

Streaming

A technique for transferring data such that it can be processed as a steady and continuous stream. Streaming allows to watch multimedia images and can start displaying before the whole file is transmitted.

Symmetric cryptography

A cryptographic system that uses a single key for both encryption and decription as opposed to the asymmetric system that uses two different (but related) keys.

Texting

Texting means sending a short written message to a mobile phone. It is also known as SMS, which is the abbreviation of Short Messaging Service.

Tick box

A tick box allows a user of software programs or on the WWW to indicate his preferences. A setting is indicated to the user and by clicking on the indicated spot the user can either set the preference 'on' or 'off', ticking or un-ticking the box commonly results in the (dis)appearance of a checkmark in the box.

Timestamp

A timestamp is the current time of an event that is recorded by a computer. To guarantee the time on a certain electronic document, a TTP can be used to 'timestamp' the document, i.e. the TTP can attach its digital signature to the document including the time it was placed.

Trusted Third Party (TTP)

An independent organisation that provides trust-related services, such as issuing certificates to guarantee the identity of signatories that use electronic signatures. See also certificate authority (CA).

Uniform Resource Locator (URL)

The global address of documents and other recourses on the WWW.

Virtual

The opposite of physical, internet is general referred to as the 'virtual environment' existing of non-tangible data stored on servers, as opposed to the physical environment with tangible things.

Web page

A document on the WWW. Every web page is identified by a unique URL (Uniform Resource Locator).

Website

A site (location) on the WWW or collection of related web pages. Each website contains a homepage, which is the first page users see when they enter the site.

World Wide Web (WWW)

A system of internet servers that support specially formatted documents. The documents are formatted in a script called HTML (Hyper Text Markup Language) that supports links to other documents, as well as graphics, audio, and video files. This means you can jump from one document to another simply by clicking on links. Not all internet servers are part of the World Wide Web.

Annex A

Overview of the requirements that have to be met by an electronic signature to be considered legally equal to handwritten signatures as provided for by Directive 1999/93/EC on electronic signatures

The electronic signature must be an advanced electronic signature, meaning it must meet the following requirements (article 2 (2) of Directive 1999/93/EC)

a) it is uniquely linked to the signatory;
b) it is capable of identifying the signatory;
c) it is created using means that the signatory can maintain under his sole control; and
d) it is linked to the data to which it relates in such a manner that any subsequent change of the data is detectable;

The advanced electronic signature must be based on a qualified certificate. This means the certificate must contain (annex I of Directive 1999/93/EC):

a) an indication that the certificate is issued as a qualified certificate;
b) the identification of the certification-service-provider and the Member State in which it is established;
c) the name of the signatory or a pseudonym, which shall be identified as such;
d) provision for a specific attribute of the signatory to be included (if relevant), depending on the purpose for which the certificate is intended;
e) signature-verification data which correspond to signature-creation data under the control of the signatory;
f) an indication of the beginning and end of the period of validity of the certificate;
g) the identity code of the certificate;
h) the advanced electronic signature of the certification-service-provider issuing the certificate;
i) limitations on the scope of use of the certificate, if applicable;
j) limits on the value of transactions for which the certificate can be used, if applicable.

The certificate must be issued by a certification-service-providers that meets the following requirements (annex II of Directive 1999/93/EC):

Certification-service-providers must:

a) demonstrate the reliability necessary for providing certification services;
b) ensure the operation of a prompt and secure directory and a secure and immediate revocation service;
c) ensure that the date and time when a certificate is issued or revoked can be determined precisely;
d) verify, by appropriate means in accordance with national law, the identity and, if applicable, any specific attributes of the person to whom a qualified certificate is issued;

e) employ personnel who possess the expert knowledge, experience, and qualifications necessary for the services provided, in particular competence at managerial level, expertise in electronic signature technology and familiarity with proper security procedures; they must also apply administrative and management procedures which are adequate and correspond to recognised standards;
f) use trustworthy systems and products which are protected against modification and ensure the technical and cryptographic security of the process supported by them;
g) take measures against forgery of certificates, and, in cases where the certification-service-provider generates signature-creation data, guarantee confidentiality during the process of generating such data;
h) maintain sufficient financial resources to operate in conformity with the requirements laid down in the Directive, in particular to bear the risk of liability for damages, for example, by obtaining appropriate insurance;
i) record all relevant information concerning a qualified certificate for an appropriate period of time, in particular for the purpose of providing evidence of certification for the purposes of legal proceedings. Such recording may be done electronically;
j) not store or copy signature-creation data of the person to whom the certification-service-provider provided key management services;
l) before entering into a contractual relationship with a person seeking a certificate to support his electronic signature inform that person by a durable means of communication of the precise terms and conditions regarding the use of the certificate, including any limitations on its use, the existence of a voluntary accreditation scheme and procedures for complaints and dispute settlement. Such information, which may be transmitted electronically, must be in writing and in readily understandable language. Relevant parts of this information must also be made available on request to third-parties relying on the certificate;
m) use trustworthy systems to store certificates in a verifiable form so that:
- only authorised persons can make entries and changes,
- information can be checked for authenticity,
- certificates are publicly available for retrieval in only those cases for which the certificate-holder's consent has been obtained, and
- any technical changes compromising these security requirements are apparent to the operator.

The electronic signature must be created by a secure-signature-creation device, this means the device should meet the following requirements (annex III of Directive 1999/93/EC):

1. Secure signature-creation devices must, by appropriate technical and procedural means, ensure at the least that:

a) the signature-creation-data used for signature generation can practically occur only once, and that their secrecy is reasonably assured;
b) the signature-creation-data used for signature generation cannot, with reasonable assurance, be derived and the signature is protected against forgery using currently available technology;
c) the signature-creation-data used for signature generation can be reliably protected by the legitimate signatory against the use of others.

2. Secure signature-creation devices must not alter the data to be signed or prevent such data from being presented to the signatory prior to the signature process.

Index